DECOLONIZING ROMAN IMPERIALISM

The framework of 'Romanization' developed by Haverfield in 1905 – that Romans 'civilized' their imperial subjects, particularly those in the 'barbarian' western provinces – remains hegemonic, notwithstanding multiple attempts at revisionism. It has been reasserted, rejected, or modified, but still frames the debate. *Decolonizing Roman Imperialism* investigates how the postcolonial challenge to decolonize the production of historical knowledge has motivated Roman scholars to question the paradigm of Romanization: to review its historiography, to seek fresh approaches, and to rewrite it. The book provides an intellectual genealogy of the debate that will be valuable for every student of the Roman Empire and of Roman Britain, and invites them to rethink the legacy of ancient Roman imperialism.

DANIELLE HYEONAH LAMBERT is a research associate in the Department of Classics at Royal Holloway, University of London. Having lived in Seoul, New York, and London, she has become conscious of different intellectual traditions across colonial centres and peripheries. Channelling her experience into critical perspectives, she has been exploring varied narratives of colonial imperialisms and in-between histories of Roman imperialism.

DECOLONIZING ROMAN IMPERIALISM

The Study of Rome, Romanization, and the Postcolonial Lens

DANIELLE HYEONAH LAMBERT

Shaftesbury Road, Cambridge CB2 8EA, United Kingdom

One Liberty Plaza, 20th Floor, New York, NY 10006, USA

477 Williamstown Road, Port Melbourne, VIC 3207, Australia

314–321, 3rd Floor, Plot 3, Splendor Forum, Jasola District Centre, New Delhi – 110025, India

103 Penang Road, #05–06/07, Visioncrest Commercial, Singapore 238467

Cambridge University Press is part of Cambridge University Press & Assessment, a department of the University of Cambridge.

We share the University's mission to contribute to society through the pursuit of education, learning and research at the highest international levels of excellence.

www.cambridge.org
Information on this title: www.cambridge.org/9781009491020
DOI: 10.1017/9781009491044

© Danielle Hyeonah Lambert 2024

This publication is in copyright. Subject to statutory exception and to the provisions of relevant collective licensing agreements, no reproduction of any part may take place without the written permission of Cambridge University Press & Assessment.

When citing this work, please include a reference to the DOI 10.1017/9781009491044

First published 2024

A catalogue record for this publication is available from the British Library

Library of Congress Cataloging-in-Publication Data
NAMES: Lambert, Danielle Hyeonah, 1988– author.
TITLE: Decolonizing Roman imperialism : the study of Rome, Romanization, and the postcolonial lens / Danielle Hyeonah Lambert, Royal Holloway, University of London.
DESCRIPTION: Cambridge ; New York, NY : Cambridge University Press, 2024. | Includes bibliographical references and index.
IDENTIFIERS: LCCN 2024000799 | ISBN 9781009491020 (hardback) | ISBN 9781009491051 (paperback) | ISBN 9781009491044 (ebook)
SUBJECTS: LCSH: Rome – Colonies – Historiography. | Roman provinces – Historiography. | Imperialism – Historiography. | Decolonization – Rome – Provinces. | Postcolonialism – Rome – Provinces.
CLASSIFICATION: LCC DG87 .L355 2024 | DDC 325/.337–dc23/eng/20240416
LC record available at https://lccn.loc.gov/2024000799

ISBN 978-1-009-49102-0 Hardback

Cambridge University Press & Assessment has no responsibility for the persistence or accuracy of URLs for external or third-party internet websites referred to in this publication and does not guarantee that any content on such websites is, or will remain, accurate or appropriate.

To my parents, Moon-Hee Joh and Eun-Suk We
To my husband, Kristian Lambert
To my brother, Seong-Eun Joh
And to my daughter, Arabelle Lambert
With all your unfailing support, this book is completed.

Contents

Acknowledgements		*page* viii
	Introduction	1
	The Commitment to History	3
	Travelling Theory, Paradigm Shift, and Tipping Point	8
1	The Discourse on Romanization in the Age of Empires	15
	The Gentlemanly Tradition	17
	The Rise of Professional Academics	25
	The Dawn of American Scholarship	40
	Appendix 1: The Continental Factors	46
2	Postcolonial Themes	51
	History as Knowledge and Power	56
	History of the Self and the Other	59
	History of the Interaction between the Self and the Other	65
	Appendix 2: Postcolonialism *à la française*	72
3	Postcolonial Questions in the Age of Decolonization	81
	Othering Romans: Destabilizing the Parallel Discourse	89
	Roman Imperialism: Defensive or Aggressive?	106
	Romanization: Negotiation, and a Tipping Point	116
	Becoming Roman: Power and Knowledge	133
	Appendix 3: History and Classics in Postwar France	146
4	Towards a Paradigm Shift in the Age of Globalization	151
	Creolization: Webster	158
	Globalization: Hingley	166
	Imperial Possession: Mattingly	180
	The Lexus and the Olive Tree, or the *Terra Sigillata* and the *Epona*	191
	Appendix 4: Separate or Franglais?	194
	Historical Intervention	197
References		206
Index		225

Acknowledgements

I am deeply indebted to my doctoral supervisor, Professor Henrik Mouritsen, who has overseen this project from its inception. Without his insight, this ambitious project would not have been possible. Thanks to his encouragement, I was able to muster confidence to turn my position as a non-native English speaker and a minority in Britain into my unique perspective for the research. I would like to express my sincere thanks to my doctoral examiner, Professor Phiroze Vasunia, for his invaluable feedback, advice, and support. I am grateful to Michael Sharp at Cambridge University Press for his enduring support during the long process and to Professor Martin Millett, who read the manuscript, provided me with helpful feedback, and allowed this project to be published. Lastly, this book is dedicated to my family, whose unfailing love has supported me.

Introduction

> For the past 100 years, Western colonialism has had a bad name. Colonialism has virtually disappeared from international affairs, and there is no easier way to discredit a political idea or opponent than to raise the cry of 'colonialism.' ...
> It is high time to reevaluate this pejorative meaning. The notion that colonialism is always and everywhere a bad thing that needs to be rethought in light of the grave human toll of a century of anti-colonial regimes and policies. The case for Western colonialism is about rethinking the past as well as improving the future. It involves reaffirming the primacy of human lives, universal values, and shared responsibilities – the civilizing mission without scare quotes – that led to improvements in living conditions for most Third World peoples during most episodes of Western colonialism.[1]

In September 2017, an essay entitled 'The Case for Colonialism' written by an American political scientist, Bruce Gilley, appeared in *Third World Quarterly*. It immediately provoked a controversy that spilled over to mainstream newspapers like wildfire and, unsurprisingly, set off a firestorm of responses. For instance, Portia Roelof and Max Gallien indict it as 'a travesty, the academic equivalent of a Trump tweet, clickbait with footnotes'.[2] Petitions soon followed, calling for apology and retraction. The controversy escalated when fifteen members of the editorial board resigned over its publication, which they saw as a violation of the journal's postcolonial legacy, whereas Noam Chomsky, also a member of the editorial board, defended the academic freedom of Gilley. Eventually, it came to an end when Gilley's provocative article was withdrawn just before Columbus Day, which is increasingly observed to remember European colonization of the Americas rather than as a celebratory national holiday. This incident, on the one hand, demonstrates that

---

[1] Gilley 2017: 1.   [2] Roelofs and Gallien 2017.

blatant praise of colonialism is no longer tolerated in the contemporary public sphere, but, on the other hand, reflects that doubts about postcolonialism are mounting at the same time. It has rekindled debates about the legacy of colonialism and postcolonialism in various forums. The current discourse has come a long way since the publication of Edward W. Said's foundational text of postcolonialism, *Orientalism*, more than four decades ago in 1978.[3] Yet, the recent event returns us to reflect from ground zero. After decolonization, what is the merit of postcolonialism today?

The same question resonates in the scholarship of Roman history. Although Roman scholarship tends to maintain a sceptical stance in relation to modern theories, the wave of postcolonialism broke into the scholarship – particularly into Romanization studies, which mainly argued that Rome expanded its culture and civilization to its provinces for them to adopt and assimilate into. Since Theodor Mommsen introduced the concept of *Romaniserung* ('Romanizing') in *Römische Geschichte* in 1885 and Francis J. Haverfield subsequently formulated the framework of Romanization in 1905, the model thrived throughout the twentieth century to attract many scholars' interest and to generate an ongoing discourse.[4] The following generations of Roman historians and archaeologists continued to update, modify, and/or revise the framework in accordance with the latest archaeological research and/or changing intellectual climate. In recent decades, postcolonialism in particular steered the course of development of Romanization studies. Postcolonial agendas to decolonize historical and cultural knowledge prompted some Roman historians and archaeologists to recognize that the framework of Romanization has been constructed through the double layers of imperialism – not only ancient Roman but also modern Western.[5] Thereafter, postcolonialism inspired them to re-examine the model of Romanization and nowadays has firmly entered the lexicon of discourse on Romanization. Nevertheless, the scholarship of Roman history, along with many other disciplines, expresses conflicting sentiments towards postcolonialism: innovative yet questionable, experimental yet ungrounded, and forward-thinking yet ahistorical.

---

[3] Said 1978.
[4] Mommsen 1909; Haverfield 1923. Mommsen developed this theory in his fifth volume of *Römische Geschichte*, published as *The Provinces of the Roman Empire* in English. Cf. French scholarship on Roman history, where Camille Jullian first formulated and introduced the framework of Romanization. See Jullian 1920.
[5] Among postcolonial thinkers, Amar Acheraïou argues that the Western colonialist/imperialist discourse has formed 'rhetorical and ideological palimpsest' tracing back to the Classical past. Acheraïou 2008.

It begs a series of questions in much the same spirit. These are the questions that I attempt to explore and answer here in this book. To put it more precisely, this book investigates how postcolonialism travelled to the scholarship of Roman history and reoriented the discourse on Romanization. It does not attempt to provide a comprehensive historiographical review of recent studies on Roman imperialism and Romanization, but rather ventures to understand the path and impact of the travelling ideas of postcolonialism between the point of departure and the point(s) of arrival. Ultimately, it aims to explore how revising the historical narrative of Romanization holds the wider significance and potential to shift the understanding of not just the ancient past but also the contemporary world.

The Commitment to History

> But when it comes to this beautiful, resilient, overlooked, traumatised community, I've got skin in the game. I've got 27 years of experience. So no matter what stories come up in the papers about our trigger-happy gang members or state-dependent single mums, I remember everything first hand. In fact we all do. So why is it that we as a community have no control over our narrative? Our main storytellers are rappers, but the rappers of today are facing the same struggles N.W.A did around the time I was born.[6] How? Housing, schools, crime, unemployment, is that it? We now provide a fuel for a multi-billion dollar storytelling industry, and all we have to show for it is new versions of the same story.
>
> And I've got an idea. We should revisit our story, and instead of retelling it, we should rewrite it. I'm not saying we should fabricate history. I'm saying let's learn to interpret what we are going through in a way that makes us stronger and leaves us with a better idea of how to manage it.[7]

This is how George Mpanga, known as George the Poet, a British spoken-word performer and poet with Ugandan heritage, opens his podcast *Have You Heard George's Podcast?*[8] Serenely narrating his evocative words, he articulates his commitment to weaving a new narrative of his community, replacing those narratives dominated by violence and deprivation which render the community incomprehensible to many. In the power of narrative,

---

[6] N.W.A was an American rap group active from 1987 to 1991.   [7] George the Poet 2019.
[8] Mead 2020.

he finds the best hope to break the chains of current dynamics and to picture a different future.

Homi K. Bhabha, a prominent postcolonial thinker, probably best unravels the 'right to narrate' and its potential, as explored by George the Poet. In fact, this phrase is the title of the Preface to Bhabha's *The Location of Culture*, from which he develops the subsequent chapters. He contends that when we revisit and revise the historical narrative of national and communal identities, this will necessitate rethinking 'our myths of belonging' and the place of ourselves and our neighbours around the world.[9] The historical narrative of a nation which often provides the foundation of a nation as an 'imagined community', as Benedict Anderson famously coined, assumes 'horizontal comradeship' amongst its members and 'homogeneous empty time' of modernity and progress.[10] Bhabha alerts us that this blanket narrative does not embrace 'alternative histories of the excluded' – those located outside the horizontal camaraderie and homogenous progress: for example, the narratives of migrants, refugees, minorities, and colonized. Narratives forgotten, erased, or denied for the sake of general and universal history do not dissipate eventually but evolve into 'unspoken, unrepresented pasts that haunt [the present]' in many forms and stages of social division that we witness from up close and from afar.[11] To translate and insert these repressed pasts in order to retell history is 'to [renew] the past ... that innovates and interrupts the performance of the present'.[12] To rewrite history is to enact '"past-present" [that] becomes part of the necessity, not the nostalgia, of living'.[13] In other words, it is to estrange ourselves from the current sense of the home and the world, to relocate the position of ourselves and our neighbours in the world, and to unsettle the current imagined community and reconstruct it.

However, this does not result in a pluralist anarchy of local histories, Bhabha asserts. It is not to collect various narratives to make rainbow history of diversity. Precisely, Bhabha rejects the idea that cultural diversity is the basis for the revision of history. He explains that cultural diversity presumes culture to be a knowable object, rather than a source of knowledge, and totalizes different cultures under the innocuous notion of multiculturalism. '[C]ultural diversity is the recognition of pregiven cultural "contents" and customs' as opposed to the appreciation of cultural significance, value system, and authority.[14] He argues that cultural diversity projects a false utopian vision where imagined communities form their

---

[9] Bhabha 2004d: xx.   [10] Anderson 1991.   [11] Bhabha 2004d: 18.   [12] Bhabha 2004d: 10.
[13] Bhabha 2004d: 10.   [14] Bhabha 2004a: 50.

own unique collective identities through their mythic narrative and exist side by side while separately enclosed and undisrupted by the entwined histories. Accumulating local histories to fill in the map of cultural diversity does not provide a breakthrough to reveal their interconnectedness through history, to question the imagined borders between communities, and to rethink our sense of belonging.

Instead, Bhabha advances *cultural difference* to become a cornerstone of how to rewrite history and, by extension, how to revise our myths of belonging. He argues that cultural difference, in contrast to the relativism of cultural diversity, brings 'the ambivalence of cultural authority' to the fore. Cultural difference is only noticed at the boundaries of cultural authority, where its authority as a stable system of reference, tradition, truth, and community is contested, (mis)read, or (mis)appropriated. At the very moment of pronouncing cultural difference, cultural authority exposes its inherent limit of applicability and introduces a split in cultural identifications. This split in cultural identifications hinges on how individuals and communities identify themselves with(in) historical narratives. One of the recent incidents surrounding the cultural symbol of the Black Lives Matter movement well captures the cultural difference that Bhabha conceptualizes. When Dominic Raab, Foreign Secretary in the British government between 2019 and 2021, was asked by Julia Hartley-Brewer, a broadcaster on talkRadio, if he would 'take the knee' to show support for the Black Lives Matter movement, he replied that he considered the action 'a symbol of subjugation and subordination, rather than one of liberation and emancipation', as shown on the HBO TV series *Game of Thrones*. Both cultural meanings of the same action of 'taking the knee' have historical origins, either a medieval gesture of subjection or a modern twist of nonviolent resistance, but the cultural difference in how one identifies with the cultural symbol reflects which historical narrative one associates oneself with or refuses to associate with. Simultaneously, the very moment of articulating cultural difference acknowledges that cultural authority to determine the referential significance is fluctuating.

Cultural difference brings us back to the right to narrate, more specifically the right to rewrite history as a strategy to challenge and destabilize cultural authority. Cultural difference highlights that cultural authority is based on and legitimized by historical memory – a selective processing of the pasts which reiterates, reproduces, and endorses some pasts, while it represses, obliterates, and excludes others. Unpacking the relationship between past and present enshrined in cultural authority, Bhabha divulges that national historical memory is not a linear progression of imagined community from primordial past to modern present, but a modern strategy to cast pasts in a homogenous narrative to establish cultural authority in the present:

> The enunciation of cultural difference problematizes the binary division of past and present, tradition and modernity, at the level of cultural representation and its authoritative address. It is the problem of how, in signifying the present, something comes to be repeated, relocated and translated in the name of tradition, in the guise of a pastness that is not necessarily a faithful sign of historical memory but a strategy of representing authority in terms of the artifice of the archaic. That iteration negates our sense of the origins of the struggle. It undermines our sense of the homogenizing effects of cultural symbols and icons, by questioning our sense of the authority of cultural synthesis in general.[15]

Therefore, according to Bhabha, writing or rewriting history is not simply an empirical study of the past but becomes an active performance to influence the cultural authority in place. In order to revise mythic memory, historical intervention is to be carried out. He argues that '[s]uch an intervention quite properly challenges our sense of the historical identity of culture as a homogenising unifying force, authenticated by the originary Past, kept alive in the national tradition of the People'.[16]

Bhabha also phrases this historical intervention as '"projective" past, a form of future anterior'.[17] It is projective because repressed pasts that haunt the present are yet to become an integral part of the collective historical narrative. These pasts do not merely add omitted details to the grand narrative of linear progress, but interrupt the narrative of homogenous modernity and attempt to negotiate a different future. In the words of Bhabha, '[t]he aim ... is to rearticulate the sum of knowledge from the perspective of ... the minority that resists totalization ... where adding *to* does not add up but serves to disturb the calculation of power and knowledge, producing other places of subtler signification'.[18] Instead of leading towards a pluralist anarchy of disconnected local histories, inscribing alternative histories of the excluded across the boundaries of imagined communities throws light on the transnational reality. '[T]he history of postcolonial migration, the narratives of cultural and political diaspora, the major social displacements of peasant and aboriginal communities, the poetics of exile, the grim prose of political and economic refugees' – which fluctuate between cultural identifications, translate cultural significances

---

[15] Bhabha 2004a: 51–2.   [16] Bhabha 2004a: 54.   [17] Bhabha 2004d: 361.
[18] Bhabha 2004b: 232–3.

The Commitment to History

and values, and challenge universality of any cultural authority – provide a key to better understand how communities are interconnected through margins unregistered in national histories. These histories, then, become a creative space to connect historical dots in an unprecedented way and to explore the dynamics underlying social conflicts and contradictions. Bhabha contends that this historical intervention of projective past could achieve even more. Postcolonial re-inscription of history holds the possibility of 'a radical revision in the concept of human community itself', as illustrated by Bhabha with an example from Salman Rushdie's *Satanic Verses*:

> The Western metropole must confront its postcolonial history, told by its influx of postwar migrants and refugees, as an indigenous or native narrative *internal to its national identity*; and the reason for this is made clear in the stammering, drunken words of Mr 'Whisky' Sisodia from *The Satanic Verses*: 'The trouble with the Engenglish is that their hiss hiss history happened overseas, so they dodo don't know what it means'.[19]

He concludes that when we revise history with the postcolonial right to narrate, this shall 'not merely change the *narratives* of our histories, but transform our sense of what it means to live, to be, in other times and different spaces, both human and historical'. While Bhabha made his commitment to theory to envisage the revision of human community through historical intervention, here I suggest that we adopt his theory and translate it to the commitment to history to make historical interventions.

Then, the question turns again to: what is the merit of postcolonialism in Roman history? What kind of role can the ancient history of Roman imperialism and Romanization play in historical intervention to revise our myths of belonging? At a cursory glance, postcolonial studies mainly explores the impact and legacy of modern European colonization, and postcolonial rewriting of history accordingly attempts to negotiate a different sense of community based on revising the relatively recent history of modern European imperialism, rather than ancient Roman imperialism. However, ancient Roman history, as a part of classical antiquity, has been an integral part of Western historical narrative, including the history of modern European imperialism, and, by extension, Western cultural authority.[20] For instance, when Bhabha illustrates how English text has established itself as the cultural authority of the West that

---

[19] Bhabha 2004d: 9.   [20] See Hingley 2000; Vasunia 2013.

can be universalized, 'the English book' in this sense becomes interchangeable with 'the Classics' in its claim to universal and timeless cultural authority: 'Still the idea of the English book (or the Classics) is presented as universally adequate: like the "metaphoric writing of the West", it communicates "'the immediate vision of the thing, freed from the discourse that accompanied it, or even encumbered it'".[21] Since ancient Roman history has served as the locus of Western civilization, intellectual tradition, and cultural authority, postcolonial rewriting of Roman imperialism and Romanization will open up a vital avenue to revise the Western sense of archaic originary Past rooted in classical antiquity and, accordingly, each of our myths of belonging.

Travelling Theory, Paradigm Shift, and Tipping Point

Nonetheless, it is an intellectual voyage of considerable distance that postcolonial theories have embarked on to enter Romanization studies. During their journey, postcolonial ideas on history and historiography have been reconfigured in their meaning and significance through various interpretations, applications, and evaluations. This process inevitably brought about a difference between postcolonial ideas in their primary sense and postcolonial perspectives applied to the scholarship on Romanization studies. In order to understand the process of how postcolonial perspectives have reoriented the discourse on Romanization, we need to explore not only primary texts of postcolonial ideas, but also secondary postcolonial interpretations and applications in the context of Roman scholarship, which will be discussed further in Chapters 3 and 4. Understanding how postcolonial ideas have travelled to Romanization studies and what new significances they have acquired will illuminate how they have reshaped the discourse on Romanization.

The concept of *travelling theory* put forward by Said is useful here.[22] In *The World, the Text, and the Critic*, published in 1983, Said explains that the passage of any travelling theory involves interaction with political realities, historical developments, and intellectual environments that are different from its original surroundings and, thereby, unfold divergent patterns of its circulation, consumption, and application. The travelling idea is not a simple misinterpretation or misrepresentation, but a new idea 'to some extent transformed by its new users, its new positions in a new time and place'.[23] Therefore, readers and users of the travelling idea should situate it

---

[21] Bhabha 2004g: 149, 2004b: 189–90.   [22] Said 1983: 226–47.   [23] Said 1983: 227.

in its specific social, political, and historical time and place and understand how it relates to its specific temporal and spatial surroundings:

> No reading is neutral or innocent, and by the same token every text and every reader is to some extent the product of a theoretical standpoint, however implicit or unconscious such a standpoint may be. I am arguing, however, that we distinguish theory from critical consciousness by saying that the latter is a sort of spatial sense, a sort of measuring faculty for locating or situating theory, and this means that theory has to be grasped in the place and the time out of which it emerges as a part of that time, working in and for it, responding to it; then, consequently, that first place can be measured against subsequent places where the theory turns up for use. The critical consciousness is awareness of the differences between situations, awareness too of the fact that no system or theory exhausts the situation out of which it emerges or to which it is transported.[24]

Here, Said neither encourages nor criticizes the phenomenon whereby ideas and theories travel to different contexts. Rather, he emphasizes that understanding a travelling idea requires a comparative study between the point of departure and that of arrival and/or between different points of arrival. Admittedly, different social, political, and historical realities do not solely determine or explain varying patterns of diffusion, consumption, and application. Nevertheless, social, political, and historical conditions in which ideas travel and diffuse unavoidably influence their respective significance in each context and, therefore, are critical in order to grasp the new idea transformed by its locality.

In fact, postcolonial studies is one of the best examples of a travelling theory, since it was established as a new branch of academic study, as the French poststructuralist thoughts of Michel Foucault, Jacques Derrida, Gilles Deleuze, and Jacques Lacan travelled into the Anglo-American intellectual world. Also, many other ideas on (post)colonial experiences cross-fertilized across disciplines and borders to form the basis of postcolonial theories, which, in turn, travelled again to have far-reaching impact on the current intellectual climate.[25] Thus, a comparative study between the point of departure and that of arrival will enhance our understanding of the travel of postcolonial thought. For our purpose, we will follow the route of the diffusion of postcolonial ideas into the scholarship of Roman history. In order to grasp the process, factors specific to the discipline of Roman

---

[24] Said 1983: 241–2.
[25] Postcolonial studies was influenced by literature, history, political studies to sociology and psychology. Selected key texts from wide-ranging disciplines include: Derrida 1976; Foucault 1972, 1977, 1979; Lyotard 1984.

history as well as those shared within wider Anglo-American scholarship will be considered. Although these factors will not be exhaustive, investigating the diffusion of postcolonial ideas in the context of surrounding factors will provide a broader picture of the environment in which postcolonial ideas came into contact with the scholarship of Roman history and influenced Romanization studies in particular. Accordingly, the point of arrival of postcolonialism determines the main scope of this book, that is, the discourse on Romanization in Anglo-American scholarship from the mid-twentieth to the twenty-first century. In addition, the French discourse on Romanization will be discussed in brief in Appendices at the end of each chapter as a comparative point of arrival. Following the passage of travelling ideas, this book ultimately aims to understand the paradigm shift that postcolonialism triggered in the discourse on Romanization.

The frequently quoted term *paradigm shift*, from Thomas S. Kuhn's epoch-making *The Structures of Scientific Revolutions*, which was first published in 1962, has now firmly entered popular vocabulary, requiring little further explanation.[26] The Kuhnian paradigm shift is an appropriate, as well as useful, concept to conceive how various alternative models of Romanization proposed from the second half of the twentieth century onwards have challenged the traditional worldview – views on the ancient Roman world, views on the relationship between the past and the present, and views on imperial history and colonialist historiography. Yet the emerging paradigm shift in Romanization studies did not occur independently. The shift, which originated from postcolonialism, travelled to the scholarship of Roman history and then, in turn, triggered a paradigm shift in the discourse on Romanization. In a sense, the wave of emerging paradigm shifts in the discourse on Romanization could be understood as a part of the wider intellectual epidemics initiated by the paradigm shift of postcolonialism.

In order to comprehend the process of how postcolonialism travelled to propel a similar paradigm shift in Romanization studies, I would like, at the risk of resorting to a less scholarly notion, to introduce another concept. A *tipping point* is a concept popularized by Malcolm Gladwell's eponymous bestseller from 2000, *The Tipping Point: How Little Things Can Make a Big Difference*, which examines social epidemics, ranging from Paul Revere's midnight ride to spread the news of impending British arrival and the popularity of *Sesame Street* to the outbreak of syphilis in Baltimore.[27] What is meaningful to our enquiry is that Gladwell sheds light on how an idea can travel across a given field and *infect* wider disciplines to tip

[26] Kuhn 1962.   [27] Gladwell 2000.

a worldview: in other words, to shift a paradigm beyond its immediate reach. As Jason Cowley in the *Guardian* notes, 'tipping point' could be another way of looking at the phenomenon of paradigm shift.[28] Gladwell also makes clear that he tackles more or less the same phenomenon – only from a different angle:

> Epidemics are, at their root, about this very process of transformation. When we are trying to make an idea or attitude or product tip, we're trying to change our audience in some small yet critical respect: we're trying to infect them, sweep them up in our epidemic, convert them from hostility to acceptance.[29]

For our purpose, postcolonialism would be one of the intellectual epidemics of transformation that tipped to provoke widespread paradigm shifts. If Kuhn's paradigm shift explains how postcolonial revision of history supplants colonialist historiography and – theoretically – revolutionizes the worldview, Gladwell's tipping point could offer valuable insights into how the paradigm shift of postcolonialism travels, diffuses, and – practically – revolutionizes the predominant worldview by inspiring further paradigm shifts in different corners. This includes the paradigm shift in Romanization studies.

Among many conceptual tools which Gladwell proposes in order to understand the phenomenon of social epidemics, the diffusion model could be particularly useful to our analysis of postcolonial ideas travelling to Romanization studies:

> what sociologists call the diffusion model, which is a detailed, academic way of looking at how a contagious idea or product or innovation moves through a population. ... If you plot that progression on a paragraph, it forms a perfect epidemic curve – starting slowly, tipping just as the Early Adopters start using the seed, then rising sharply as the Majority catches on, and falling away at the end when the Laggards come straggling in.[30]

Following his description, we can draw an epidemic curve to visualize the travel of postcolonial ideas to Romanization studies. It may be difficult to hold that postcolonialism was well received in the scholarship of Classics or ancient history in general during the mid-to-late twentieth century. Yet, during this early phase, various influences, such as Marxism, the Annales school, the cliometrics revolution, and poststructuralism, were instrumental in making the intellectual environment of Roman history scholarship relatively more hospitable to various intellectual currents, in which postcolonial

---

[28] Cowley 2008. [29] Gladwell 2000: 166. [30] Gladwell 2000: 196–7.

ideas later came to take hold. Then, slowly and gradually, postcolonial ideas travelled to the scholarship of Roman history and 'contaminated' Roman historians and archaeologists, prompting them to question the colonialist epistemology built into the discipline. The Early Adopters, who started to tinker with the seed of postcolonial ideas, published a few key works and circulated the seed across the discipline. Four chapters will guide us through the passage of how travelling ideas of postcolonialism diffused into the discourse on Romanization to prompt a paradigm shift.

The first chapter sets the scene. It sketches the broader landscape of the scholarship of Roman history when the framework of Romanization was first introduced and examines the original model of Romanization in the wider context of the intellectual climate in the early twentieth century. The second chapter ushers us into the travelling idea of postcolonialism. It concerns the point of departure, discussing postcolonial thought in its primary sense. Instead of providing a landscape overview of postcolonial theories that span from literature to sociology to economics, it delves into the key themes that Roman historians and archaeologists engaged with – that is, postcolonial questions on history and historiography. The third chapter moves on to explore the route of travelling ideas and the point of arrival. In order to understand the path of diffusion, it explores the political, historical, and intellectual environment surrounding the scholarship of Roman history and investigates the context into which postcolonialism travelled. It then investigates how Roman historians and archaeologists began to adopt postcolonial ideas and to pose postcolonial questions to the framework of Romanization from the mid-twentieth century. The fourth chapter probes alternative paradigms that scholars put forward from their respective postcolonial perspectives.

The concluding Historical Intervention tackles the question that remains. Looking back on the journey of the travelling ideas of postcolonialism thus far, it attempts to reflect on their impact on the discourse on Romanization as a heuristic tool to bring about a paradigm shift in the dominant historical narrative and to revise our myths of belonging. Some further thoughts on travelling theory by James Clifford and Edward W. Said lend a critical lens to better comprehend the theory of postcolonialism travelling into Romanization studies. In his article 'Notes on Travel and Theory' published in 1989, Clifford crucially points out that the path of travelling theory is not always linear but more complex:

> these stages read like an all-too-familiar story of immigration and acculturation. Such a linear path cannot do justice to the feedback loops, the

ambivalent appropriations and resistances that characterize the travels of theories, and theorists, between places in the 'First' and 'Third' worlds.

Theirs is not a condition of exile, of critical 'distance,' but rather a place of *betweenness*, a hybridity composed of distinct, historically-connected postcolonial spaces.

Theory is always written from some 'where,' and that 'where' is less a place than itineraries: different, concrete histories of dwelling, immigration, exile, migration. These include the migration of third world intellectuals into the metropolitan universities, to pass through or to remain, changed by their travel but marked by places of origin, by peculiar allegiances and alienations.[31]

The path of postcolonial ideas travelling to Romanization studies is far from a linear movement across one academic discipline to another. By contrast, its complex path could lay claim to one of the most daring intellectual aspirations of travelling ideas. It traverses the periphery and the centre of both ancient and modern times, brings the spaces connected through both ancient Roman and modern Western imperial history together, and thereby presents a possibility of decolonizing the colonialist history and historiography which is deep-rooted through multiple layers.

The journey of travelling postcolonial ideas has not come to an end to face its verdict. Yet, Said's optimism regarding the potential of travelling theories, expressed in his essay 'Traveling Theory Reconsidered' published in 2001, might well be extended here.[32] At one point he even entertains the notion of 'transgressive theory', which travels to challenge hasty totalization and dogmatic orthodoxy and to find ways to reconcile contradictions in the original travelling theory while rekindling its spirit:

> The work of theory, criticism, demystification, deconsecration, and decentralization they imply is never finished. The point of theory therefore is to travel, always to move beyond its confinements, to emigrate, to remain in a sense in exile.
>
> To speak here only of borrowing and adaptation is not adequate. There is in particular an intellectual, and perhaps moral, community of a remarkable kind, *affiliation* in the deepest and most interesting sense of the word. As a way of getting seriously past the weightlessness of one theory after another, the remorseless indignations of orthodoxy, and the expressions of tired advocacy to which we are often submitted, the exercise involved in figuring out where the theory went and how in getting there its fiery core was reignited is invigoration – and is also another voyage, one that is central to intellectual life in the late twentieth century.[33]

---

[31] Clifford 1989. [32] Said 2012. [33] Said 2012: 451–2.

His earlier suggestion that travelling theory is almost a necessary evil of modern intellectual life, new ideas morphed by their locality, is dispelled. Instead, Said concludes that travelling theories hold the potential to actualize their radical force in new environments without dwelling on totalization or orthodoxy. Reflection on the value of postcolonialism to the discourse on Romanization in light of the significance which Said came to attach to the potential of travelling ideas brings this work to a close. The Historical Intervention argues that the travel of postcolonial ideas to Romanization studies offers a key to decolonize the history and historiography not only of ancient Roman but also of modern Western imperialism and, furthermore, to destabilize the sense of archaic originary Past enforced through colonialist history and historiography. Now, let us visit the formation period of Romanization studies prior to the travelling ideas of postcolonialism.

CHAPTER I

The Discourse on Romanization in the Age of Empires

> St. Augustine looked at Roman history from the point of view of an early Christian; Tillemont from that of a seventeenth-century Frenchman; Gibbon, from that of an eighteenth-century Englishman; Mommsen, from that of a nineteenth-century German. There is no point in asking which was the right point of view. Each was the only one possible for the man who adopted it.[1]

Thus wrote Robin G. Collingwood in *The Idea of History* in 1946. It would be too bleak a view to read his comment as one of cynical resignation which suggests that it is futile to grasp historical truth (however it is defined). Rather, he provides a salutary reminder that what is handed down to us as 'history' is, fundamentally, less historical reality, more history of thought. He does not mean that the history of thought written hitherto is entirely unfounded on historical reality and, therefore, useless or invalid. Instead, it is neither dogmatic assertion nor rejection of historical truth, but constant awareness of the distance between historical reality and history of thought that offers critical perspectives and constructive steps towards a richer understanding of the past.

In this sense, the development of the discourse on Romanization shows the significance of Collingwood's insight. Romanization studies was conceived at the height of European imperialism and American optimism in the early twentieth century – before a turn of events, including the World Wars, the Great Depression, and decolonization – and thus displayed a perspective characteristic of the era, that of being sympathetic towards the great ancient power of the Roman Empire. In Britain in particular, Christopher Stray argues, not only the framework of Romanization but the discipline of Roman history itself owes its emergence to the rise of British imperial ideology in the era.[2] The changing attitude towards the flourishing British

---

[1] Collingwood 1946: xxii.   [2] Stray 1998, 2010.

Empire, signalled by Queen Victoria being named as the Empress of India in 1876, had gradually shifted the locus of authority from Greek democracy to Roman imperialism and increased interest in various aspects of the Roman Empire, including Romanization.[3] This sympathetic perspective does not wholly invalidate the Romanization studies of the period. On the contrary, the recognition that Romanization studies is a product not only of ancient historical realities but also of the contemporary social, economic, and political realities allows later historians and archaeologists to investigate the subject matter with sceptical historicism. Questioning the underlying assumptions born of the time – those of the past as well as of the present – enabled them to contextualize and re-evaluate ideas from the earlier studies and, furthermore, to utilize their own contemporary influences as their own intellectual assets. When, from the mid-twentieth- century onwards, decolonization and postcolonialism moulded historians of the following generation with new social, economic, and political configurations, they availed themselves of new intellectual currents of the time to reflect on the imperial legacy embedded in the earlier discourse and to propose alternative paradigms. Romanization throughout twentieth-and twenty-first-century scholarship was not a moribund ancient phenomenon, but a living and breathing past in constant conversation with the present. Following the history of thought on Romanization through the course of this book, here we will explore how the interplay between the ancient past and the contemporary lens has mediated the distance from various perspectives.

This chapter, first of all, traces the origin of the Romanization framework: that is, how the discourse on Romanization commenced and took root in early twentieth-century scholarship. Broadly speaking, the Roman Empire had been an unfailing reference point throughout modern Western intellectual dialogues. Since the eighteenth century, the long-standing elite tradition of classical education and the Grand Tour, as well as the subsequent neoclassical movement in art and architecture, have established ancient Greek and Roman civilization as a staple in modern Western intellectual discourse. Stray states that Greece and Rome represented 'unity as complementary elements – as male and female parents of Europe' in which Greece stood for individuality and freedom and Rome for discipline and order.[4] Yet, until the late nineteenth century, the Roman Empire was more often discussed as a cautionary tale of imperial despotism and decadence and did not command much respect or celebration. It was only after the late nineteenth century, particularly when the British Empire

---

[3] Hingley 2000: 19–27.   [4] Stray 1998.

The Gentlemanly Tradition

came to establish itself as 'the empire on which the sun never sets' with its power and influence, that Roman imperialism kindled fresh interest. Similarly, the ever-expanding powers of France and America made Roman imperialism more relevant to modern Western minds.[5] Whether in order to better comprehend their own British, French, and American powers by comparison or to ape or surpass one of the great ancient powers, intellectuals and scholars of the time looked to the Roman Empire, alongside many other great historical empires, for wisdom and insights.[6] Views on the Roman Empire were, nevertheless, far from uniform. Professionalization of the discipline from the early twentieth century mixed with the deep-rooted gentlemanly tradition instigated new dynamics in the discourse on Romanization. Standpoints ranged from that of British imperial civil servants to that of American professional academics; approaches varied from the old gentlemanly tradition of exemplary history to new professional academics' critical history, and evaluations diverged from admiration to disapproval. Despite wide-ranging differences, none escaped from their own social, economic, and political surroundings, shaped by European and American imperialism. The comparisons between the ancient Roman Empire and the contemporary British, French, and American empires, either overtly or covertly, underpinned the works of the time.

The Gentlemanly Tradition

In an age when academic historians seem to embody old traditions shelved in ivory towers and popular TV historians engage with the wider public of the twenty-first century, it is not easy to imagine professional academic historians as the one-time avant-garde. Against the well-established tradition of gentlemen scholars, they pioneered a new critical history which was to refashion history as a modern academic discipline of the early twentieth century. While this gradual shift within the discipline was unmistakable, the old conventions of gentlemen scholars still lived on during this period. In fact, the overarching climate that governed Roman history in transition is traceable to the Victorian and Edwardian tradition

---

[5] Hingley 2008.
[6] 'Among the factors responsible for the special place given to Rome over other empires in the nineteenth century was the central role of Latin in the educational curriculum; the legacy of eighteenth-century Augustanism; Victorian admiration for the administrative, legal, and judicial apparatus of ancient Rome; the complicated historical relationship between Christianity, Rome, and Britain; and British identification with the civilizing mission of the Romans.' Vasunia 2013: 130.

of Classics. Throughout the Victorian and Edwardian periods, Roman history had been subsumed under the mighty discipline of Classics. Situated as a sub-category of Classics, Roman history in general shared and inherited the gentlemanly tradition of Classics, which enjoyed its heyday during the Victorian and Edwardian ages.[7] It, in essence, describes an intellectual protocol of the time whereby Classics and the gentleman class symbiotically defined and sustained each other. Classical education, which started at public school and continued at either Oxford or Cambridge University, effectively formulated the taste of gentlemen, inculcated their morality, shaped their discourse, fostered solidarity among the elites, and ultimately signified a badge of status; in turn, amateur-gentlemen scholars educated in this manner dominated and directed the field of Classics.[8] In other words, this specific class represented the face of the Classics. With respect to Roman history, Edward Gibbon, who is immortalized by his monumental work *The History of the Decline and Fall of the Roman Empire* (despite his anti-Christian stance), proudly epitomized the tradition of gentlemen scholars and was succeeded by politician-gentlemen scholars such as Lord Cromer, Sir C. P. Lucas, and Lord Bryce in the early twentieth century.[9] Vance relates that within the gentlemanly tradition 'the writing of ancient history continued to be regarded mainly as a literary activity, philosophy teaching by examples, rather than a severe academic discipline aspiring to be the condition of science'.[10] The gentlemanly tradition approached Roman history not as an unknown world to be investigated and reconstructed with critical eyes, but as a mirror to reflect upon its universal lessons through politico-moral exemplars and warnings.

There had been many gentlemen scholars before, but what distinguishes the twentieth-century gentlemen scholars from their predecessors of the Victorian era is their direct involvement in the British imperial administration.[11] For example, Evelyn Baring, otherwise known as the Earl of Cromer, after his stellar colonial career in India and Egypt, served as the president of the Classical Association and published his presidential address, *Ancient and Modern Imperialism*, in 1910.[12] Also, Sir Charles

---

[7] See Jenkyns 1980; Vance 1997; Stray 1998.
[8] In the United Kingdom, the term 'public school' refers to a type of fee-paying school independent from government management, as opposed to state schools.
[9] Gibbon 1776; Cromer 1910; Lucas 1912; Bryce 1914.   [10] Vance 1997: 54.
[11] For the long-lived legacy of the Roman Empire in shaping British identity up to the twentieth century, see Hingley 2000.
[12] Cromer 1910.

The Gentlemanly Tradition 19

P. Lucas, after having served as a distinguished civil servant in the Colonial Office for decades, took an academic position at the Working Men's College in London and published *Greater Rome and Greater Britain* in 1912.[13] Having worked as colonial civil servants and politicians in the field, they formed unique perspectives different from those of both their predecessors and contemporary professional academics. However, it was not the case that gentlemen scholars stood on the opposite side to professional academics. Rather, they encouraged, influenced, and communicated with professional academics to develop the discourse on Romanization. Richard Hingley and Phiroze Vasunia respectively in *Roman Officers and English Gentlemen* and *The Classics in Colonial India* elucidate the profound legacy of the gentlemanly tradition in the scholarship of Classics and ancient history.[14] Although the gentlemanly tradition has already been discussed in detail, and with discernment, in these works, another closer look at the most frequently discussed works of Cromer and Lucas, with particular focus on Romanization, will help us to trace the intellectual genealogy of the Romanization debate at its nascent stage.[15] In contrast to professional academics, gentlemen scholars' principal credential and/or asset as historians was their field experience in British colonies. They did not attempt to assume scholarly objectivity, but rather drew heavily on their personal observations and experiences to offer hands-on insights in comparing and contrasting modern British imperialism with ancient Roman imperialism. For instance, Cromer explains the reality of ancient Roman provincial administration by personally identifying himself with Pliny the Younger and voices his sentimental attachment with pride: 'I have a strong fellow-feeling for that Bithynian praetor whose justice has been immortalized by Catullus, for I have had a somewhat personal experience of the race of company-mongers to which Catullus belonged, and of their angry vituperation – though in prose rather than in poetry'.[16] He derives his authority to understand Roman imperialism mainly from his experience as a British consul-general. Lucas also credits the opinion of Cromer regarding the comparison between Roman and British imperialism on account of his field experience: '[Cromer] gives as the result of his almost unrivalled experience, "the conclusion that the British generally, though

---

[13] Lucas 1912.
[14] Published in recent decades, both works consider one of the current strands of scholarship in investigating the relationship between the Classics and European, particularly British, colonial history. Also see Goff 2005.
[15] Other works include: Mills 1905; Curzon 1907; Balfour 1908; Sands 1908; Stobart 1912; Bryce 1914.
[16] Cromer 1910: 56.

they succeed less well when once the full tide of education has set in, possess in a very high degree the power of acquiring the sympathy and confidence of any primitive races with which they are brought into contact'".[17] The fact that they consider their field experience to be the primary resource for their historical understanding allows us a glimpse into the underlying assumptions that they had about the history of the Roman Empire.

Here, the often-overlooked premise of gentlemen scholars' history comes into sight – that Roman imperialism and British imperialism are comparable in nature. If British colonial officers had experience in governing colonies, it is assumed that they could vicariously understand what ancient Roman provincial governors underwent, since the two experiences of ruling a colonized population are not dissimilar in essence in spite of the temporal and spatial gap.[18] Based on this underlying belief, gentlemen scholars derived their authority to understand ancient Roman imperialism from comparing and contrasting it with modern British imperialism. Conversely, it was evident to them that the study of the ancient Roman Empire would further the understanding of how to govern, as well as improve the administration of the modern British Empire. Deeming ancient Roman and modern British imperialism to be analogous, they maintained that the study of their historical antecedent would give the British particular advantages in better grasping their own imperialism and in improving upon their ancient counterpart. This view sustained the significance and utility of the comparative study, which fundamentally served as a mirror study for gentlemen scholars. In other words, subscribing to the idea that the past reflects the present and vice versa, gentlemen scholars used the past as a mirror to reflect on their British position and to enhance their British imperial endeavours. In the preface to his presidential address to the Classical Association, Cromer recounts that his professional experiences framed such a viewpoint on history:

> As an additional plea in justification of the choice of my subject, I think I may say that long acquaintance with the government and administration of a country which was at different times under the sway of the Macedonian and the Roman does to some extent bridge over the centuries, and tends to bring forcibly to mind that, at all times in respect to certain incidents, the world has not so very much changed in 2,000 years.[19]

[17] Lucas 1912: 128.
[18] For instance, the colonial legacy of using Roman titles in British colonial office has endured in some instances. The British Foreign Office still uses the term 'pro consul' for diplomatic titles in embassies.
[19] Cromer 1910: 2–3.

The Gentlemanly Tradition 21

Although Lucas believes that Roman imperialism had more in common with French imperialism than with its British counterpart,[20] he still shares the same underlying assumption that history repeats itself. On the whole, within this gentlemanly tradition, history was not a linear progress, but a cyclical and/or spiral movement – the latter being repetition with progress – therefore, a philosophy teaching by example.

Despite their shared philosophy on history, Cromer and Lucas maintain opposite stances on Roman imperialism. At the risk of oversimplification, they conceive two contrasting notions of Roman imperialism: defensive imperialism and military despotism. Cromer argues that the principal driving force for both ancient Roman and modern British imperialism was 'the imperious and irresistible necessity of acquiring defensive frontiers'.[21] Though various factors, such as ambitious individuals and powerful institutions, played parts in shaping distinct courses for each imperial power, he insists that the desire to obtain defensive frontiers is natural. Hence, history repeatedly witnesses the ebb and flow of imperial powers. Of all the empires throughout history, Cromer gives the Roman and British empires more weight for in-depth analysis, since he considers each to represent a paragon of imperialism, from ancient and modern times respectively. According to Cromer, the temperament of the Romans and the British was better suited to thrive in imperial endeavours than that of their own contemporary rivals: '[t]here is, in fact, a good deal of similarity between the Roman and British character. Both nations appear to the best advantage in critical times'.[22] Soon it becomes not too difficult to trace in his work a patchwork of prominent ideas of the early twentieth century that range from racial theories and social anthropology to nationalism. To identify the Roman Empire with a nineteenth-century sovereign state and to presume that the Roman Empire formed a coherent national character demonstrates problems inherent in Cromer's hasty application of contemporary thoughts to the comparative study of the Roman and British Empires. It led him to conclude that the Romans and the British, as nations, accomplished the most out of the natural course of imperial evolution.

Cromer's contemporary, Lucas, was no less influenced by the same set of contemporary ideas. However, Lucas arrives at the opposite verdict and condemns the Roman Empire as a form of military despotism – that is, the antithesis of the British civilizing family-like Empire. He distinguishes benevolent British imperialism from abusive Roman imperialism on the grounds that the British as a race, as a society, and as a nation are *naturally*

---

[20] Lucas 1912: 14.   [21] Cromer 1910: 19–20.   [22] Cromer 1910: 34.

more inclined to give benefit to the world via Britain's civilizing imperialism: 'There is in fact no parallel to it in history of the world. The gradual growth of younger British peoples within and not without the Empire, the maintenance of the connexion between the younger and the old, coupled with the continuous development from terms of subordination to terms of practical independence, is peculiar to the British race'.[23]

In comparison, Lucas explains that the continental races – that is, modern France and ancient Rome – share the tendency to impose a form of tyrannical imperialism: 'The French colonization of Canada had in it a touch of Roman settlement. It was in its essence largely military colonization. It was despotically arranged, organized, and held together, in order to keep the land against notable Indian fighters with hostile British colonies behind them'.[24]

In addition to his prejudiced view on racial qualities, Lucas selects an arguably biased set of examples to support his argument. He often confines his discussion of British imperialism to self-governing colonies (i.e. settler colonies) and treats other colonies, including British India, which were de facto debarred from obtaining independence, as a separate category in need of an exceptional explanation. Confining his discussion to self-governing colonies to a large extent, he projects an overly optimistic – and arguably deceptive – view to portray colonies as siblings within a supportive family and to trust the purported goodwill of British explorers, traders, and missionaries. Eventually, as subtly suggested by the title of his book *Greater Rome and Greater Britain*, Lucas argues that Rome was great, but Britain was even greater.

And yet Cromer and Lucas agree that the Romans surpassed the British in one aspect: that is, in how they assimilated the colonized. Whilst approving of Roman success in this with the label of Romanization, they nonetheless hold back their full praise of Roman achievement by rather unconvincingly explaining that Romans were more successful at assimilation only because the task was much easier in ancient times. In so doing, they artfully rationalize the relative failure of the modern British. They provide a list of reasons to justify why Romanization was easier. Cromer points to ancient polytheism and so-called unorganized primitive tribes as factors that gave Romans an upper hand in assimilation, while insisting that modern monotheism and intricate stratification of societies and institutions proved to be major stumbling blocks for the British. In other words, modern complications that were unknown in ancient times

[23] Lucas 1912: 22. [24] Lucas 1912: 14.

naturally made assimilation much more challenging for the modern British. Furthermore, he argues that the pitfalls of spreading the imperial language fortunately escaped the Romans, whereas the British learned about them the hard way. Based on his experience, he asserts that the goodwill to promote integration by spreading the language often backfired; English language failed to encourage the colonized to feel sympathy towards the colonizers and instead empowered the colonized to more forcefully and tactically rise against the colonizers. He leaves this question – why the spread of language worked against British imperialism but not against Roman imperialism – hanging and moves on to conclude that the British faced more challenges than the Romans. However, after a lengthy defence of the British Empire, Cromer admits one British flaw – the apparent incongruity of their purpose in imperialist integration – that is, more precisely, the hypocritical discrepancy between their professed ideal and their ulterior desire.

> [A Roman imperialist] would have added that the last thing in the world he intended was to put into the heads of the provincials that, by copying Rome and Roman customs, they would acquire a right to sever their connection with the Empire and to govern themselves; in fact, that his central political conception was not to autonomize, but to Romanize, or at least Hellenize, the world.
> But what would be the reply of the leading imperialist of the world – of the Englishman? He would be puzzled to give any definite answer, for he is in turn always striving to attain two ideals, which are apt to be mutually destructive – the ideal of good government, which connotes the continuance of own supremacy, and the ideal of self-government, which connotes the whole or partial abdication of his supreme position.[25]

Cromer's acknowledgement that British imperialism contains an internal paradox is meaningful, if not revealing. Turning to the Roman Empire as a point of reference, he not only advocates that British accomplishments were on a par with those of the great ancient imperial power, but also criticizes the shortcoming of British imperialism. In other words, he uses the Roman Empire as a lens to more fully explore both the bright and dark sides of British imperialism.

Lucas, on the other hand, unequivocally upholds the British model of assimilation even though it might have appeared to be unsuccessful at times. He holds 'the race and colour problem' accountable for posing a modern challenge to the British. He then unapologetically minimizes the issue by glossing over it as collateral damage that is an unavoidable

---

[25] Cromer 1910: 117–18.

result in the course of achieving an evolved form of imperialism that promotes freedom and diversity. The Romans simply did not allow racial conflicts to arise, since Roman military despotism reduced their own imperialism to nothing more than subjection and uniformity:

> It may be summed up that in the Roman Empire there was a perpetual opening out of citizenship. The tendency was all towards fusion and uniformity, and race imposed few or no barriers. In the British Empire we have started with British citizenship of one kind or another as coterminous with British soil, in whatever part of the world the soil may be; but the tendency has been to greater diversity rather than to greater uniformity; and the lessening of distance accentuated, instead of obliterating, distinctions of race. But at the same time it must be borne in mind that the grant of universal citizenship in the Roman Empire was combined with the stereotyping of military despotism. It would be perhaps more accurate to say that all Roman citizens became lowered to the level of Roman subjects, than that all Roman subjects were raised to the level of Roman citizens. Equality came in the Roman Empire as the result of the loss of freedom. Diversity has developed in the British Empire as the result of the growth of freedom. The race and colour problem has increased in difficulty in our Empire in proportion as some of the Provinces of that Empire have become more and more self-governing.[26]

Lucas refers to Roman imperialism to expand on why racial problems hindered assimilation in the British Empire. Yet, what is even more striking in his comparative study is that he not only uses ancient Roman imperialism to make sense of modern British imperialism but also vice versa. He perceives ancient Roman and modern British imperialism as opposites that mirror each other, and places them in a dialectical framework.

Nowadays, the gentlemen scholars' understanding of the Roman Empire comes across as being poles apart from that of contemporary historians in the twenty-first century. So distant that one might wonder whether it is useful to trace back to the early twentieth-century gentleman-scholar tradition in order to comprehend the development of late twentieth- and early twenty-first-century historiography. The gentlemen scholars had different agendas, approaches, and philosophies in their studies of Roman history from those of their professional academic counterparts. As former British colonial civil servants, they believed that history repeats itself, with or without progress, viewed Roman imperialism as an example from the past, either good or bad, to learn lessons from, and aimed at

[26] Lucas 1912: 100–1.

improving their own imperialism in light of ancient Roman imperialism. Naturally, their expertise and their focus fell less on Roman imperialism and more on their own empire. Even though they did not fully concentrate on Roman history per se, their studies are nonetheless worth investigating. Vasunia unfolds the significance and legacy of their works: 'Classics is still embedded in national politics and national culture at this point, and to speak authoritatively about antiquity can also be a way to make an intervention in (the history of) the present'.[27] In other words, they established the enduring parallel discourse between ancient Roman and British imperialism, as the widespread use of the term *Pax Britannica*, modelled on *Pax Romana*, demonstrates. The understandings of both British and Roman imperialism have become so entangled and entrenched with one another that it becomes futile to disentangle them. Ancient imperialism was evaluated using the framework of modern imperialism, and the understanding of one imperialism was projected onto the other. Hingley points out the pitfalls of this parallel discourse, that is, the inherent circular argument: 'A circular process occurred, in which interpretations of the Roman past were used to inform the late Victorian and Edwardian present, although in this process the parallels that were drawn were selective and determined by the needs of that present. As a consequence, the present, at least in part, was used to recreate the past in its own image'.[28] The discourse of one imperialism sustained that of the other. As Vasunia declares, '[t]his is . . . an account of collusion between classics and empire'.[29] This parallel discourse continued to have lasting impact not only on Cromer and Lucas' contemporaries but also on succeeding generations.

The Rise of Professional Academics

Search for truth, scientific method, and scepticism of mind defined professional academic historians and ushered in the era of critical history; so goes the common understanding. The tide of change rolled in when positivism, which had been dominant since the nineteenth century across Europe and across various disciplines, rather belatedly crossed the threshold of the British scholarship of Roman history, or to be precise, the newly formed discipline of Roman history at the University of Oxford as a part of Literae

---

[27] Vasunia 2013: 120.   [28] Hingley 2000.
[29] Vasunia 2013. In this monograph, Vasunia delves further into how modern British imperialism was systematically built into the process of producing and circulating academic knowledge of the discipline.

Humaniores, also known as Greats.[30] By the time of the First World War, professionalization of Classics, including Roman history, had slowly settled in and led to the creation of academic positions as well as academic societies and journals.[31] On the other hand, on the Continent, the trend was well underway from the nineteenth century onwards, epitomized by German scholarship of *Altertumswissenschaft*. Entitling their discipline a *science* of antiquity, German professional academic classicists and historians adopted methods and approaches of natural scientists, such as collaborative research, critical analysis of evidence, and discovery of objective truth. Mommsen, the figurehead of Roman history in this age, in the spirit of positivism compiled a colossal corpus of Latin inscriptions and Roman law.[32] In recognition of Mommsen's contribution, Haverfield says, 'it is the age when Roman history was reborn ... The old looseness of pharaseology, the old indifference to many branches of evidence, the old inaccurate idea of what things mattered have now to disappear'.[33] It was, in fact, Haverfield, a disciple of Mommsen (along with a contemporary French historian, Camille Jullian[34]), who introduced the positivist history to the British scholarship which until then had been dominated by exemplary history of the gentlemanly tradition. Whilst Mommsen changed the landscape of the field with his methodical rigour in the study of epigraphy and law, Haverfield followed in Mommsen's steps to apply his own methodical rigour to archaeology.[35] Afterwards, Collingwood, a student of Haverfield in turn, further expanded the critical history beyond positivist history. A philosopher as much as a historian, he delved into the philosophy of history and approached Roman history with both methodological rigour and epistemological questioning.

However, as Stray argues, '[c]lassical scholarship did not become class-neutral when it became professionalized; it simply took a place in a reconstructed social order'.[36] Nor did it become value-free as it seemed or claimed. Professional academic historians attempted to search for

---

[30] Literae Humaniores is the name the University of Oxford gives to its undergraduate course in Classics. An 1830 statute included Roman history in the course. Stray 1998: 122.
[31] The Society for the Promotion of Roman Studies was founded in 1910, and the *Journal of Roman Studies* was first published in 1911.
[32] Mommsen's notable works include: Mommsen 1909, 1911.   [33] Haverfield 1911: xiv.
[34] Camille Jullian, roughly speaking, held an equivalent significance to Haverfield in French scholarship on Roman history. His importance and legacy will be discussed in more detail in the Appendix to this chapter.
[35] For Mommsen's influence on Haverfield, see Freeman 1997a; Hingley 2000: 113–14; Following in Mommsen's steps, Haverfield also made a considerable contribution to epigraphy by being in charge of RIB (Roman Inscriptions of Britain) along with Collingwood.
[36] Stray 1998: 118.

historical truth detached from religious or moral values, but this change of orientation itself took place within the surrounding social, political, and historical realities. In the face of pluralization of knowledge and curriculum, professional academics tried to assert the position of Roman history as an academic discipline that mattered; an increasing number of industrial bourgeoisies in the reconstructed social hierarchy still aspired to acquire a classical education to earn the badge of status and supplied the increasing demand for classical education; the expanding British Empire raised public interest in the history of the Roman Empire as a source of guidance and inspiration. The backdrop provided both internal and external incentives not only to maintain the privileged position of Roman history in the social hierarchy, but also to write the elite-driven Roman history for the elite, or the aspiring-to-be-elite, audience. For example, when considering the ordinary non-elites, Haverfield does not find many things of significance, because 'the rustic poor of a county seldom affect the trend of its history'.[37] Professionalization and critical history writing, therefore, resulted in prolonging the identification with the elite class handed down from the gentlemanly tradition by recasting exemplary history for the gentleman class into analytical political history for the imperial elites. Vance states that '[s]ceptical revisionism, in combination with – or in tension with – imaginative responsiveness to the romantic-poetic and legendary dimension of . . . Roman history, could permit the old exemplary history to be reinvented as more explicitly ideological and all the more easily appropriated for modern political . . . purposes'.[38]

The apparent parallel between the Roman elites and the British Imperial elites underpins Roman historiography of the time. The identification was far from an implicit assumption. On the contrary, it was established and acknowledged sufficiently overtly that there is little need to read between the lines. The political and intellectual climate of the time revolved around drawing lessons from a comparison of the two imperial powers (the Roman and British Empires) and the two imperial colonies (Roman Britain and British India), as exemplified by the authors mentioned earlier.[39] Professional academic historians were not isolated from the current. Although their methodological rigour and critical approach set them apart from the gentlemen scholars, to a certain extent they channelled the same understanding through their professional expertise and developed it into strands of studies in Roman history.

---

[37] Haverfield 1923.   [38] Vance 1997: 70.   [39] Lucas 1912; Bryce 1914.

Two particular areas of study, formed and flourishing in this period, heavily hinge on this identification and its assumptions: first, prosopographical studies, pioneered by Sir Ronald Syme, and, second, frontier studies, led by Haverfield. First, prosopographical studies, exemplified by Syme's *Roman Revolution* in Anglo-American scholarship, uses the network of Roman elites to explain political developments at the imperial centre and in the wider empire.[40] The underlying belief that the elites determine the course of imperial history was widely accepted during the time, not only because rigorous analysis of the network convincingly demonstrated it, but also because both historians and readers of the time – both predominantly from an elite background – shared the same worldview: that the elites dictate the course of history. In other words, the prevalent understanding that British elites determined the course of their imperial politics was projected onto Roman elites and their course of history and allowed prosopographical studies to gain sympathetic reception.[41] Second, frontier studies headed by Haverfield also benefited from the popular identification between Roman and British imperial elites. Frontier studies employed increasingly scientific methodologies of archaeology, for example to examine Hadrian's Wall and military sites in north England, and thereby transformed Roman history and archaeology from the earlier gentlemanly pursuit to an organized academic discipline. Nonetheless, the contemporary concern shared by both gentlemen scholars and professional academics fuelled the development of frontier studies: how British imperial elites should administer 'the frontier of civilization' oriented historians' and archaeologists' interests to investigate how ancient Roman elites administered their own frontiers, since they believed that Roman and British elites shared similar concerns and were thus akin to one another.[42] The identification which stems from the gentlemanly tradition of Classics continued to influence the course of Roman historiography in the first half of the twentieth century, until an intellectual backlash took place in the second half of the twentieth century.

As shown, it was not an abrupt rupture from the exemplary history of gentlemen scholars to the critical history of professional academics. Certainly there was a shift in the overall direction. The historical truth that gentlemen scholars sought was the underlying and permanent force of human nature, will, or (ir)rationality repeatedly manifested through the

---

[40] Syme 1939. Matthias Gelzer is a foundational figure in prosopography in classical scholarship, whose works include: Gelzer 1912. The later leading figures include T. R. S. Broughton, T. P. Wiseman, and Errnst Badian: Broughton 1951; Wiseman 1971; Badian 1958.
[41] Peachin 2011: 4–5.   [42] Hingley 2000.

course of history, in other words, 'History with a capital H' in the tradition of Kant and Hegel. Historical truth that professional academics pursued, on the other hand, was a systematic knowledge of the past liberated from subjective value judgements. 'All subjective elements (as they were called) in the historian's point of view had to be eliminated. The historian must pass no judgement on the facts: he must only say what they were,' as Collingwood describes the positivist history dominant during the time.[43] However, the vantage point of the twenty-first century offers hindsight that positivist history was not value-free or neutral as it claimed. Processing historical data (according to certain criteria), prioritizing historical facts (perhaps over contexts), and then asserting historical truth (however it is defined) all in itself entails implicit value judgements. As Stray analyses the transition taking place in the study of Classics and ancient history, 'this search for truth was moralized and given a reformulated cultural authority' as academic knowledge.[44] Contrary to its claim to purified and objective historical knowledge/truth, to borrow Foucault's terms, positivist history not only contained subjective elements built into its own system but also acquired authority to establish a new régime of historical truth.[45] It was the régime of historical knowledge/truth that shifted from one mode to another. Transition took place in the methodology and philosophy of historical knowledge/truth, whilst continuity prevailed in the structure and content of historical discourse. The parallel frame between the ancient Roman and the modern British empires and between civilizing mission and Romanization occupied the attention of both gentlemen scholars and professional academics. The structure and content of the discourse that persisted on the surface reveals that another régime of truth, which sustained the discourse at its root, continued to be upheld throughout the transitional period – colonialism and/or imperialism. For example, notions such as the dialectic between the civilized colonizer and the barbarian colonized and the progress of civilization through imperialism stood steadfast through the period of shift from exemplary history to critical history. The 'collusion between classics and empire', in the words of Vasunia, did not come to an end with the advent of professedly objective positivist history, but rather continued to be built into the new régime of truth for critical Roman history. As a whole, there was a shift in the régime of truth on one level and continuity on another level.

As a result, the mixture of continuity and discontinuity pervades the discourse on Romanization. The break from the gentlemanly tradition is

[43] Collingwood 1946: 131. [44] Stray 1998. [45] See Foucault 1980.

perhaps most pronounced in the general impression that 'Roman history ... has become more difficult, more full of facts, more technical', as Haverfield writes.[46] Professional academics published their historical research dense with literary, epigraphic, and archaeological evidence, developed systematic analyses of literary and non-literary evidence, and became disciplinary specialists. It was amid the professionalization of the discipline that the framework of Romanization came to appear in the British scholarship. While Mommsen first advanced his idea of 'Romanisierung' in German scholarship based on his mastery of literary and epigraphic sources in the fifth volume of *Römische Geschichte* in 1885, Haverfield brought archaeological sources to the fore and formulated the model of Romanization in *The Romanization of Roman Britain*, published in 1905. Credited with founding the discipline of Romano-British archaeology, Haverfield stresses the newfound potential of archaeological evidence:

> The field of non-literary evidence offers a still wider and more fertile area of virgin soil. That is, indeed, the chief work now to be done in Roman history, to wring life and blood out of stone.
> The more I study the ordinary written materials, the harder I find it to learn the truth from them, the more often I feel that the story which they tell is not the story which is worth telling. I would sacrifice all that tract of Arrian which Professor Pelham was discussing, for a little appropriate archaeological evidence. It is no doubt hard to construct a 'story' out of archaeological evidence, but it is certainly possible to construct history. It is possible to-day to write some sort of history of the Roman frontier in Scotland, although the facts of that history are known to us mainly through archaeological evidence: they are the fruits of the labours of Mr. J. Curle and Mr. George Macdonald and one or two others during recent years. Without these researches we should still be struggling with vague Tacitean rhetoric or should remain the victims of errors into which even Mommsen fell when he tried to tell the tale of Roman Caledonia and suggested that Septimus Severus rebuilt the Wall from Forth to Clyde.[47]

He believes that archaeological evidence is tangible, specific, and consistent: it is free from possible errors that literary evidence poses with its ambiguity, subjectivity, and inconsistency and, therefore, not only complements but also counterbalances literary evidence. Advocating the use of archaeological evidence to write history, he published many excavation reports, catalogues of archaeological objects, and monographs that heavily draw upon archaeological evidence, *The Romanization of Roman Britain*,

---

[46] Haverfield 1923: xiv.   [47] Haverfield 1923: xv–xvi.

Ancient Town-Planning, and *The Roman Occupation of Britain* to name a few.[48] Following in Haverfield's footsteps, Collingwood also made a substantial contribution that furthered Romano-British archaeology, of which the most significant works include *The Archaeology of Roman Britain* and *Roman Britain and the English Settlements*.[49]

The rise of Romano-British archaeology stood at odds with the gentlemanly tradition. When ancient Roman artefacts were unearthed and presented, the past became the present and lost the appeal of being permanently 'classic'. Archaeology, which attempts to locate the ancient past in specific time, space, and context, by implication challenged the gentlemanly tradition, which sought to learn historical lessons that transcend the specifics of time, space, and contexts. Stray describes the significance of archaeology in the British scholarship: '[t]he ancient world shifts from mirror to window, from reflection to perception; the mirror's silvering is eroded to show a past separated by the thin glass wall of history'.[50] This, nevertheless, should not be taken to imply that the parallel discourse between the ancient Roman and the modern British empires abated. Instead, this parallel discourse unfalteringly continued. With the rise of archaeology, the discourse was reframed from the mirror study of gentlemen scholars pivoting on personal experiences to the comparative study of professional academics referring to organized evidence. Romano-British archaeology, despite Haverfield's claim to be objective, was not free from the imperialist régime of truth that has underpinned the parallel discourse. In fact, it was not exempt from imperialism but founded upon it, thus argues Hingley extensively in his book *Roman Officers and English Gentlemen: The Imperial Origins of Roman Archaeology*: 'a circular process of interpretation existed … In the context of imperial discourse, archaeological narrative was drawn into the provision of useful lessons for the British Empire'.[51] Hingley debunks the scientific objectivity of Romano-British archaeology and exposes imperialist thoughts pervading professional academic scholarship. A closer look at their studies on Roman Britain and Romanization reveals how professional academic historians and archaeologists shaped the discourse with a seemingly contradictory blend of positivism and imperialism.

Positivism sparked off the rise of Romano-British archaeology, and this, in turn, launched a new branch of studies in the British scholarship of Roman history, that is, Roman Britain. Archaeology enriched the understanding of Roman Britain with systematic excavations. While

---

[48] Haverfield 1923, 1913, 1924.   [49] Collingwood 1930, 1936.   [50] Stray 1998.
[51] Hingley 2000: 1–2.

literary sources have characterized Roman Britain merely as a military frontier of the Roman Empire, newly discovered epigraphic and archaeological evidence filled the landscape of Roman Britain with towns, villas, temples, sculptures, writing tablets, etcetera. Roman Britain became an ideal field for professional academics of the time to showcase their versatility, to build their expertise, and to cultivate a cohort of specialists. They were able to demonstrate their methodical rigour with epigraphic and archaeological evidence discovered in Britain, to reappraise Romano-British heritage and promote the heritage industry, and to engage with the wider imperial discourse of the time by linking ancient Roman and modern British imperialism. In short, in the context of British scholarship, Roman Britain became more than a regional case study of Romanization and established itself as an exclusive subject of expertise. As Hingley depicts the narrow scholarship of Roman Britain, 'Romano-British scholarship has often been no less an island than its subject. By and large, [Roman] Britain has formed the preserve for a clearly defined group of scholars who conduct work of a specific type which is cut off to an extent from broader classical scholarship'.[52] According to Hingley, the fundamental reason behind the phenomenon is that British national identity was at stake in the history of Roman Britain. Instead of contextualizing Roman Britain more broadly with studies on other Roman provinces, Romano-British historians and archaeologists tended to be preoccupied with resolving the British past as the conquered in relation to the Roman Empire and vindicating the British present as the conqueror in India.[53] Although their arguments were far from homogenous, they carried similar nationalistic concerns originating from their shared social, political, and historical realities.

Above all, a lingering uneasiness in relation to the conquered ancient Britons was shared across the discipline. It became a paramount question, because racial theories in anthropology, which had been employed to justify European imperialism at the time, could imply the racial inferiority of the British. Previously, the dilemma had been dealt with mainly by two different racial myths: first, by identifying the defeated Celtic Britons with the ancestors of the marginalized Welsh and Cornish and the subsequently conquering Anglo-Saxons with the ancestors of the prevailing English,[54] or second by characterizing the Roman rule over the fiercely independent Britons as superficial and fleeting.[55] Haverfield

---

[52] Hingley 2000: 164.   [53] Hingley 2000; Vasunia 2013.   [54] Hingley 2000: 63–5.
[55] Haverfield 1923: 23.

The Rise of Professional Academics 33

then took a different approach and proposed Romanization as a key to resolve the conundrum:

> The west offers a different spectacle. Here Rome found races that were not yet civilized, yet were racially capable of accepting her culture. Here, accordingly, her conquests different from the two forms of conquest with which modern men are most familiar. We know well enough the rule of civilized white men over uncivilized Africans, who seem sundered for ever from their conquerors by a broad physical distinction. We know, too, the rule of civilized white men over civilized white men – of Russian (for example) over Pole, where the individualities of two civilized races clash in undying conflict. The Roman conquest of western Europe resembled neither of these. Celt, Iberian, German, Illyrian, were marked off from Italian by no broad distinction of race and colour, such as that which marked off the ancient Egyptian from the Italian, or that which divides the Frenchman from the Algerian Arab. They were marked off, further, by no ancient culture, such as that which had existed for centuries round the Aegean. It was possible, it was easy, to Romanize these western peoples.[56]

And he continues to build up towards the observation that 'uncivilized but intelligent' Britons learned the benefits of Roman civilization and eventually surpassed their conquerors to become even more powerful imperialists on their own (only many centuries later).[57] Hingley rightly points out that the magic formula behind Haverfield's Romanization was that it conveniently 'removed the stigma of conquest'.[58] As Hingley explains, Haverfield's argument that endorses imperialism without compromising national pride and racial superiority has unsurprisingly gained enduring and far-reaching influence. From his initial framework of Romanization onwards, Haverfield prompted the ensuing discourse on Romanization to acquire its particular relevance and significance in a British, as well as a wider Anglo-American, context.

The many editions and reprints of *The Romanization of Roman Britain* testify to the long-lived success of Haverfield's Romanization model. First proposed in his lecture in 1905, then expanded and published into a monograph in 1912, his book is still reprinted to this day. Even though his work, interspersed with antiquated ideas on race and civilization, might appear to be obsolete to many modern readers, its staggering longevity and legacy in the present day necessitates a closer look at Haverfield's original paradigm. G. D. Barri Jones aptly summarizes the significance that Haverfield holds in the Anglo-American discourse on Romanization: 'In Anglophone

---

[56] Haverfield 1923: 13.   [57] Haverfield 1923: 15.   [58] Hingley 2000: 95.

34   The Discourse on Romanization in the Age of Empires

terms ... the debate was formulated and shaped over half a century by Haverfield's study of Romanization in Britain ... Effectively, until the rise of revisionism in 1970s, it is fair to say that Haverfield's framework provided the *Leitmotif* of approaches to Romanization'.[59] It is regrettable that Haverfield's colossal presence came to obscure the contributions of other historians (a closer reading of one of them, Collingwood, will follow in order to consider counterpoints made during the period); on the other hand, his incomparable contribution to the shifting of popular perception of the Roman Empire explains his status in Anglo-American scholarship.[60] Until Haverfield, 'historians seldom praise[d] the Roman Empire. They regard[ed] it as a period of death and despotism, from which manly vigour and political freedom and creative genius and the energies of speculative intellect were all alike excluded'.[61] Aided by the thriving British Empire at the time, he succeeded in overturning the general inclination to be sympathetic towards ancient Roman imperialism and, moreover, in raising the relevance of the discipline to contemporary British imperialism.[62] He achieves it by underlining long peace, safety, and stability within the Empire secured by Romanization.

Romanization, therefore, thanks to Haverfield, became a focal point of Roman imperial success:

> The Roman Empire was the civilized world; the safety of Rome was the safety of all civilization. Outside roared the wild chaos of barbarism. Rome kept it back, from end to end of Europe and across a thousand miles of western Asia. Had Rome failed to civilize, had the civilized life found no period in which to grow firm and tenacious, civilization would have perished utterly. The culture of the old world would not have lived on, to form the groundwork of the best culture of to-day.[63]
>
> It was this growth of internal civilization which formed the second and most lasting of the achievements of the Empire. Its long and peaceable government – the longest and most orderly that has yet been granted to any large portion of the world – gave time for the expansion of Roman speech and manners, for the extension of the political franchise, the establishment of city life, the assimilation of the provincial populations

---

[59] Jones 1997: 185–6.
[60] On the other hand, Philip W. M. Freeman contextualizes the development of Haverfield's Romanization studies in the wider European scholarship of the time and investigates the scholarly pedigree leading up to Mommsen. Freeman 1997a.
[61] Haverfield 1923: 9.
[62] Haverfield 1923: 2. 'The old theory of an age of despotism and decay has been overthrown, and the believer in human nature can now feel confident that, whatever their limitations, the men of the Empire wrought for the betterment and the happiness of the world'.
[63] Haverfield 1923: 11.

The Rise of Professional Academics 35

in an orderly and coherent civilization. As the importance of the city of Rome declined, as the world became Romeless, a large part of the world grew to be Roman. It has been said that Greece taught men to be human and Rome made mankind civilised. That was the work of the Empire; the form it took was Romanization.

Employing the dichotomy between civilization and barbarism, he conjures up the Roman Empire as an enclosure that preserved civilization. This binary outlook, as a matter of course, leads him to rank his archaeological data between the hierarchical binaries of superior 'classical/Roman' and inferior 'native/Celtic' and to interpret them as evidence of a unilateral civilizing process in varying degrees – but not those of reciprocal cultural change. In this narrative, the rebellion of Boudicca serves as a moment of regression hindering the progress of civilization.[64] On the whole, Romanization, according to Haverfield, was a linear progress of civilization in which Romans handed over the torch of civilization to the 'uncivilized but intelligent' natives, or Britons. When social Darwinism seemed to explain the expanding British Empire, progressive Romanization became another parallel example in history without much question.[65]

Yet not everyone agreed with Haverfield. Collingwood, widely considered to be Haverfield's successor, after a hiatus due to the First World War, recommenced his study of Romano-British archaeology as well as philosophy. With most of his fellow students trained by Haverfield having fallen in the war, he was left alone to carry on Haverfield's legacy, 'to keep alive the Oxford school of Romano-British studies that [Haverfield] had founded, to pass on the training [Haverfield] had given …, and to make use of the specialist library [Haverfield] had left to the University'.[66] While he established himself in philosophy, he also endeavoured to fulfil his obligation to continue Romano-British studies. Inquiring into both the history of philosophy and the philosophy of history, he used history and philosophy to enlighten one another. In his autobiography, he puts his scholarly trajectory in a nutshell: 'My life's work hitherto, as seen from my fiftieth year, has been in the main an attempt to bring about a *rapprochement* between philosophy and history [italics in original]'.[67] Yet, it is worth noting that Collingwood was better known as a philosopher: he held the position of Waynflete Professor of metaphysical philosophy at the University of Oxford and wrote his tour de force in the field of philosophy, *The Essay on Philosophical Method*.[68] Additionally, his posthumously published *The Idea of History*,

---

[64] Haverfield 1923: 75. [65] On social Darwinism, see Bowler 1984. [66] Collingwood 1982: 120.
[67] Collingwood 1982: 77. [68] Collingwood 2005.

36   The Discourse on Romanization in the Age of Empires

which recounts how philosophy on historical truth (or régime of historical truth in Foucault's vocabulary) has changed over the course of history, became one of his notable works that bridge his interests between philosophy and history.[69] This piece crucially reveals that Collingwood, against the backdrop of the positivist trend, approached history not only with empirical data and positivist methodologies but also with epistemological questions on historical knowledge. His remark quoted at the beginning of this chapter captures his concerns as well as his contribution.

Likewise, the opening chapter to Collingwood's *Roman Britain*, published in 1923 and then expanded in 1932, immediately lays out his distinctive approach to Roman Britain:

> There are two sides to Roman Britain, the British side and the Roman. That is to say, it may be regarded either as an episode of in the history of England or as a part of the Roman Empire. If we wish to form a true idea of it, we must do justice to both these sides.
>
> For a citizen of the Roman Empire, Britain had no individuality of its own except a purely political individuality, like that of an electoral district. The student who approaches Roman Britain as merely an episode in English history cannot see this fact. His point of view makes him forget that England herself, at the beginning of English history, did not exist, even by the name of Britain; and that England is the product of an historical process. Thus, in his well-known *History of England*, Gardiner remarks on the melancholy fact that the Britons had no patriotism, that they did not feel called upon to 'die for Britain'. Such lack of patriotism he feels to be a reproach both to the Britons and to the Roman Empire. But the fact is that, writing from the distorting point of view of an historian of England, he expects the Britons to show loyalty to something which had not even begun to exist.[70]

Collingwood warns of anachronistic nationalism distorting the history of Roman Britain. Emphasizing that the nation as a sovereign state and the national consciousness as a coherent character are historical, not intrinsic, ideas, he exhorts his readers to refrain from projecting modern nationalist patriotism to the ancient past and from distorting the historical truth with contemporary social, political, and historical surroundings. He himself was not exempt from the influences of his own surroundings, as he betrays a hint of patriotism from time to time.[71] Still, he is mindful that the epistemology

---

[69] Collingwood 1946.   [70] Collingwood 1932: 1, 11.
[71] For instance, '[y]et, although Britain contributed little or nothing to *belles-lettres*, it was not untouched by the deeper intellectual movements of the time. The country which was so often to place the European thought on new lines of progress, the country of William of Occam, Francis Bacon, Locke and Darwin, began its philosophical history by producing Pelagianism'. Collingwood 1932: 122.

of historical knowledge/truth is founded not only on hard evidence but also on the philosophy of history governing the processing of evidence, which is a historical product as well. Since he finds it anachronistic to impose the dualist perspective fostered by modern nationalism, he rejects reading the history of Roman Britain in the framework of conquest by foreign power or conflict/competition between dialectic forces. To resolve these binary perspectives, Collingwood brings Romanization to the fore. Like Haverfield, he centres on Romanization, but veers away from Haverfield's view to form a distinct outlook from the 1930s.

In contrast to his renown as a philosopher, Collingwood has not received due recognition in Romanization studies.[72] Haverfield's monumental presence in Romanization studies effectively eclipsed the original contribution of Collingwood as a mere reflection of Haverfield's legacy. This led many to the misunderstanding that there had not been any attempt to revise Haverfield's Romanization until the wave of revisionism from the mid-twentieth century. Admittedly, Collingwood was also immersed in the imperialism of the era and challenged Haverfield's Romanization less radically than revisionist historians of the post-colonial generation. Nevertheless, as Hingley points out, 'Collingwood belonged to a less optimistic generation than Haverfield', having witnessed the First World War and the rise of Nazi Germany and Fascist Italy.[73] His contemporary circumstances as well as his academic career in philosophy prompted him to re-examine Romanization. To start with, Collingwood rejects the rigorous binary perspectives, as mentioned earlier. He contends that the dialectical relationship between the civilized, conquering Italian Romans versus the savage, conquered Celtic Britons is a myth. Such a gulf in race, language, and culture as exists in modern European imperialism between Britain and India or between France and Algeria is not applicable to ancient Roman imperialism. On the other hand, between Romans and Britons, '[t]here was no sharp distinction of race; the distinction of language did not matter; and the difference in civilization was not of such a kind that Romans could be called civilized and the Britons savages'.[74] Therefore, Collingwood does not translate Romanization into a unilateral civilizing process. Instead:

> What we found is a mixture of Roman and Celtic elements. In a sense it might be said that the civilization of Roman Britain is neither Roman nor British but Romano-British, a fusion of the two things into a single thing

---

[72] Often Collingwood is missing or mentioned briefly as a successor of Haverfield in the discussion of the historiography of Romanization and Roman Britain. The exception is Hingley's *Roman Officers and English Gentlemen* in which he recognizes Collingwood's contribution to the discourse and analyses the development of Collingwood's historical thought.
[73] Hingley 2000: 132.   [74] Collingwood 1932: 6–7.

different from either. But this is not a quite satisfactory way of putting it; for it suggests that there was a definite blend of Roman and British elements, producing a civilization that was consistent and homogenous throughout the fabric of society. The fact is rather that a scale of Romanization can be recognized. At one end of the scale of come the upper class of society and towns; at the other end, the lower classes and the villages.[75]

He neither outright rejects the model of Romanization nor puts forward a catchy term to satisfactorily replace it, which partly explains his ineffectiveness in giving currency to his idea. Nonetheless, it is worth noting Collingwood's attempt to revise Haverfield's model of Romanization. Collingwood argues that it was a process of cultural change with its scale tipped in favour of Romanization that resulted in hybrid Romano-British civilization.

Collingwood handpicks one piece among his many writings to best represent his view: 'the chapter on "Art" in the *Oxford History of England* [titled *Roman Britain and the English*]; a chapter which I would gladly leave as the sole memorial of my Romano-British studies, and the best example I can give to posterity of how to solve a much-debated problem in history, not by discovering fresh evidence, but by reconsidering questions of principle'.[76] Here, he ponders over the problem that Haverfield's unilateral Romanization encounters over how to interpret Celtic art surviving and reviving in Roman Britain. The linear understanding of the change under Roman imperial rule has divided opinion into two camps, either British artisans' failure to master the higher form of Roman art or British artistic resistance against oppressive Roman art. Looking at the same examples of Romano-British artworks, including 'the Bath Gorgon, the Corbridge lion, the Aesica brooch, Castor or New Forest pottery, or the like', Collingwood proposes a different perspective.[77] He argues that there coexisted different layers of culture. Repeatedly warning against pseudo-scientific readings of Celtic artistic expressions as racial temperament, he claims that Celtic tradition, which was the underlying cultural tradition, persisted 'behind the façade of [R]omanization'.[78] In particular, he elevates the Bath Gorgon on the temple pediment of the Roman Baths as a paragon of Romano-British art, bringing Roman demands and old Celtic styles together into a syncretic piece of artwork, rather than describing it as a 'vigorous semi-barbaric carving' as Haverfield does.[79] Collingwood argues: '[t]he artistic romanization of Britain is therefore a melancholy

---

[75] Collingwood 1932: 92. [76] Collingwood 1982: 144–5. [77] Collingwood 1936: 260.
[78] Collingwood 1936: 256. [79] Haverfield 1923: 24.

story, not because Rome failed to impose her standards – she succeeded all too well – nor because Britain lacked artistic aptitude, for she had it in plenty, but because teacher and pupil were at cross-purposes'.[80] Although Collingwood still maintains the hierarchy between Romans and Britons in softened language and assumes Roman imperialism to be benevolent, it is worth noting that he recasts linear Romanization into the bilateral synthesis of Romano-British culture. It would be farfetched to consider Collingwood a precursor of the postcolonial revisionist movement that took off from the late twentieth century onwards, since he presumes imperialism (either ancient Roman or modern British) to be normative, as it was commonly considered during the time. Still, recognizing hyphenated Romano-British culture as a valid culture of its own may have set the course for subsequent studies on Romanization. Despite all, his attempt to revise Romanization leaves a crucial lesson that resonates with the historiography of Romanization – that the set of evidence on which to investigate the same historical phenomenon has not much changed, but the epistemological questions on how to interpret that same set of evidence have changed to reshape our understanding. Collingwood's model demonstrates that recognizing Celtic elements in Romano-British art as an active force in the dynamic, rather than a passive or reactive, recasts Romanization in a different light. How the next generation of Roman historians and archaeologists read and interpret evidence to reshape the framework of Romanization will be investigated in later chapters.

Professional academic historians reframed the history of Roman Britain and Romanization with their new critical tools, including systematic analysis of literary, epigraphic, and archaeological evidence and epistemological questioning of the historical truth. Haverfield most influentially reframes Roman Britain as the frontier of Roman civilization and argues convincingly that Romanization was a civilizing process to cohere the yet-to-be-civilized natives within the civilized world of the Roman Empire. Less influentially but no less importantly, Collingwood maintains that a process of cultural exchange between unequally civilized Romans and Britons took place and envisions Roman Britain as a site of new hybrid civilization with stronger Roman influences. With their methodological rigour and epistemological questioning, they shifted Roman history from the gentlemanly tradition of exemplary history to the professional academics' critical history. Notwithstanding, the colonialist régime of truth persisted throughout. Neither Haverfield nor Collingwood fundamentally raises questions regarding their own value

[80] Collingwood 1936: 254–5.

judgements to distinguish the civilized from the barbarian and their own implicit premise that the more civilized Romans rightfully colonized the less civilized or barbarian natives. Their arguments, by implication, uphold British imperialism while excusing the failure of British assimilation, which confronted a more difficult challenge of ruling over less civilized and less intelligent races. Meanwhile, by reconstructing Roman Britain into a successful example of Romanization, they emphasize the exceptionality of Europeans in their capacity to reap the benefits of civilization (which, at the same time, contributes to justifying the perpetually colonized state of North Africa by a series of invaders in history).[81] In this way, Romanization studies came to develop hand in hand with imperialism.

The Dawn of American Scholarship

It would be useful here to take a brief pause to place Anglo-American scholarship into global perspective; overlooking the international context risks isolating Anglo-American scholarship as an independent body and giving a misleading account of it. From an international standpoint, classical studies in the early twentieth century had different dynamics from that in the mid to late twentieth century. A data sample which Chester G. Starr, the first president of the American Association of Ancient Historians, draws attention to verifies the general opinion that German scholarship blossomed while Anglo-American scholarship lagged behind in the early twentieth century. Based on the number of items published under the index of 'Histoire romaine et romanique' in *L'Année philologique*, Starr reports that: '[I]n 1924–26 works in German were by far the largest group at 44 per cent of the total – followed by English (about 20 per cent) and French (about 15 per cent)'.[82] Moreover, many scholars around the world went to Germany for their doctoral research and introduced approaches modelled after German *Altertumswissenshaft* to their countries' scholarship. Yet, 'thirty years later German titles had sunk to 17 per cent, well below English (30 per cent) and Italian (26 per cent)'.[83] The proliferation of works produced in English from the mid-twentieth century onwards owes in part to the growth of American scholarship. Although its contribution has expanded over time to become, it was rather less remarkable in the early twentieth century. Keeping this aspect in mind helps in understanding both the development of American scholarship and its growing contribution to and exchange

[81] Mattingly 2011b: 43–74.   [82] Starr 1960: 158.   [83] Starr 1960.

The Dawn of American Scholarship 41

with the wider scholarship in the following decades. A couple of episodes that Starr relates evoke the atmosphere of American scholarship in relation to its European counterpart in the early to mid-twentieth century:

> European scholars had harsh views of the early training of American scholars; A. E. Housman wrote Robert Bridges in 1924, 'I am glad you are safe home from America [where he had been a visiting lecturer at Ann Arbor University, Michigan] where I hope you have lit a candle or sown seed. They are terribly docile, but have not much earth, so it is apt to wither away.' Later, in 1949, I wrote a little book tracing the rise of Rome; for no very good reason Cornell University Press sent review copies abroad. French and Belgian critics were shocked at the limited amount of knowledge which American freshmen could be presumed to have; today, in view of the abrupt decline of Greek and Latin in European education, they could scarcely adopt such a stance.[84]

A mixed bag of feelings towards European scholarship aside, Starr here acknowledges the underdeveloped early stage of the American scholarship compared with the established European scholarship. However, lacking infrastructure alone neither defines nor does justice to American scholarship of the early twentieth century. Rather, as Richard P. Saller suggests, American historians of the early twentieth century communicating with European peers started to form 'American classical historians' self-identity ... marked by a pragmatic and anti-theoretical streak'.[85]

Tenney Frank stands for this distinctively American strand of scholarship, rather than the mainstream of overall American scholarship.[86] In his article sketching American scholarship of the twentieth century, Starr praises Frank as an outstanding figure during the earliest years of American scholarship: 'Tenney Frank, however, was so extraordinary a character as to deserve larger note.... He was perhaps a genius, if flawed somewhat in our eyes by his obsession with racial theories'.[87] Frank's presence in and contribution to the budding American scholarship was indeed noteworthy, but Saller more aptly delineates the significance of

---

[84] Starr 1991: 183.   [85] Saller 1998: 223.
[86] Saller terms it the 'native American' pragmatic thread of classical scholarship. His use of quotation marks suggest that he acknowledges his incorrect use of 'native American', since Frank was a descendant of Swedish immigrants, not a native American as a matter of fact. He seems to have resorted to the term to conveniently distinguish it from other strands of the American scholarship influenced by European scholarship. Here – particularly in the context of dealing with postcolonial questions – I do not use Saller's label in order to avoid any confusion. Saller 1998 points out that *Party Politics of Age of Caesar*, a work of Lily Ross Taylor, rather represents the mainstream of American scholarship which is written in the European style of Sir Ronald Syme. Taylor 1949.
[87] Starr 1991: 179.

Frank in the international landscape of classical scholarship. He notes that Frank was one of the few American-born and American-trained Roman historians amid a drift of European scholars crossing the Atlantic to the United States. Against the backdrop of transatlantic scholarship, Frank maintained a distinctively American perspective characterized by a pragmatic and anti-theoretical attitude. While European historians concentrated on shifting Roman history from a gentlemanly intellectual pastime/pursuit to a modern scientific discipline and on adopting methodological tools and theoretical questions for critical analysis, a group of American historians spearheaded by Frank did not share the same agenda and instead retained optimism towards their anti-theoretical and pragmatic reading of evidence. American pragmatism and optimism, which distinguished America from Europe from the late nineteenth to the early twentieth century with respect to both academic and everyday philosophy, permeated the American scholarship of Roman history and set the undertone. Starr, who is also an American-born and -trained scholar, affirms that 'generally the method of approach does subtly differ.' Compared with their European peers, American historians were less theoretical, that is, less receptive to theories from anthropology or sociology, and more pragmatic, that is, more attuned to practical concerns demonstrated in literary and epigraphic sources.[88] This tendency resulted in American scholarship gravitating towards conventional approaches. In general, it favoured literary and epigraphic sources and shunned relatively new approaches of exploring archaeological sources, sociological concepts, or epistemological questions.

Anti-theoretical, however, does not imply absence of perspective or any conceptual framework. Not sharing the same agenda or perspective with European contemporaries, Frank advances his own objective: to disentangle Roman history from the 'old-world political traditions'.[89] He contends that the old-world European politics enacted by vying imperialistic powers for centuries had shaped a historical perspective unfit to explain the new-world politics. The old-world historical perspective regards expansion and imperialism as a natural course of history and fails to grasp the new-world political history, to which the Roman Republic belonged. In Frank's framework of the binary division between the old world and the new world, the Roman Republic became the new world where the Near Eastern empires had been the old world. His further implication is not so subtle. The underlying parallel between the modern old-world Europe and the ancient old-world

[88] Starr 1991: 184.   [89] Frank 1914: vii.

Near Eastern empires and between the modern new-world America and the ancient new-world Roman Republic extends across his work. Based on this parallel, he asserts the need to shift away from the old-world European perspective towards the new-world American perspective in order to correct the misunderstanding about Roman imperialism. It almost appears that he regards himself as a historian bearing the mission of American manifest destiny to redeem the old world:

> This misconception will best be refuted by a full statement of the causes, but it may be worth while to point out that it has its origin, not in a study of Roman history, but in a misapplication of Oriental, as well as more modern ideals, to Roman methods. Before the history of the eastern states – Babylonia, Egypt, and Persia – was as thoroughly studied as it now is, the possibility existed of loosely grouping of their political ideals with those of Greece and Rome and arriving at the popular generalization that the 'ancient' state was imperialistic in a sense that, since the creation of the modern 'concert of powers,' no longer exists. Now it is true that the eastern monarchies were generally imperialistic. The empire of the East was seldom a nation of one tongue, one race, one worship; it was held together artificially by its ruler and his effective instrument, a mercenary army. Conquests which brought tribute – the sinews of the ruler's wars – were absolutely essential to the life of dynasty. How different was the Greco-Roman city-state whose very origin lay in the homogenous small group which constituted its own army, paid its own expenses, and chose its own magistrates from its own body! Even in such a state, of course, greed for conquest might arise, but it would manifestly go against the grain, for the citizen himself must shoulder the danger and the cost, and the conviction is ever present that expansion is suicidal, for the city-state constitution must go under with the acquisition of dependencies.[90]

Frank maintains his analogy based on rather optimistic and loose interpretation of literary and epigraphic sources. As Saller points out, Frank does not resort to 'any conceptual sophistication' to support his reading. Instead, '[it is] Frank's view that Americans were especially well placed to understand the early Romans of the republic, because they were kindred spirits ... Instead of theory, Frank possessed American pragmatic common sense, as evidenced in his proverbs and racism'.[91] As described, Frank readily projects Americans' self-identity of the time – particularly as simple, honourable, and pragmatic in relation to Europeans – onto Romans:

> The important point after all is the fact established by the existence of this institution that the Roman *mos maiorum* did not recognize the right of

---

[90] Frank 1914: 119.   [91] Saller 1998: 224.

aggression or a desire for more territory as just causes of war. That the institution was observed in good faith for centuries there can be little doubt. The Romans soon discovered that political and trading alliances – alliances carved on stone and based only upon a mutual consent dictated by considerations of common advantages – were the rule among civilized peoples.[92]

Reading literary and epigraphic sources through the lens of what he considers to be the modern equivalent, the American perspective, Frank portrays the Roman Republic as a law-abiding and pragmatic society of civilized people. Although Frank's bias towards an American perspective sounds peculiar in the wider scholarship of Roman history, in fact it was far from being unique within the context of broader American scholarship, according to Saller. Saller claims that 'Frank fits the broader pattern of liberal reaction of American exceptionalism to the historicist and structural intellectual currents of Europe'.[93]

The underlying parallel further dictates Frank's view on Roman expansion and Romanization. His understanding of Roman expansion and Romanization, in essence, echoes American frontier history. The undercurrents of manifest destiny, individualism, and optimism underpin Frank's narrative. As for territorial expansion during the Republican period, he argues that the senate, due to both its law-abiding integrity and practical concerns, did not have a deliberate expansionist policy. Instead, senators' efforts to preserve their peace, order, and civilization led them to gradually extend their sphere of influence and eventually their territories:

> Rome was also expanding ... Here was no overcrowding of population. She actually lacked men to settle the frontier colonies and had to borrow homesteaders from her allies to hold her acquisitions. In fact, at Rome expansion was an accident rather than a necessity,–a by-product of Rome's insistence upon good order on the frontier and perfect regularity in all international transactions. She pacified the periphery in order to protect the center, and since the new frontier exposed her to strange, lawless tribes, that is, lawless from the point of view of Rome's mos maiorum, her thoroughgoing insistence upon her conception of government drew her into a progressive game of pacification and organization.[94]

His romanticized portrayal of Roman expansion as benevolent, defensive, and civilizing imperialism echoes the early American tale of manifest destiny to civilize and organize the Wild West. Even though Frank

[92] Frank 1914: 9, 23.   [93] Saller 1998: 234.   [94] Frank 1914: 47.

acknowledges a less noble but practical aspect of Roman expansion in which people's greed for land and money propelled imperialistic expansion, he nevertheless maintains the American vision of Roman expansion. He projects American frontier expansion, which promoted the growth of the American middle class, onto Roman expansion and regards Roman expansion as a similar process which increased the number of small landowners in the Roman Republic.

According to Frank, Romanization was a natural outcome. Emphasizing that it was not a state-led policy but an organic process, he argues that each individual party, through their own will and practical interests, participated in Roman customs and thus contributed to bring about Romanization. This reveals his underlying conception of the Roman Republic – in a similar form to the federation of the United States of America, that is, different races and independent states joining under a liberal federation. Then, identifying the Roman rule with the American laissez-faire approach and 'the [antecedent] of American liberalism',[95] Frank treats Romanization as its expected consequence:

> There is not an act clearly traceable to a desire to Romanize or, as has so insistently been claimed, to 'urbanize' and thereby to civilize the natives of the provinces. [Augustus] insisted, wherever possible, that there should be some community or orderly tribe responsible for the preservation of peace – and the tax gathering – in every nook and corner of the Empire, and when this was not possible, as in Egypt, he tried to find a substitute. But after that was secured, each community was permitted to go its own way. Economic and social laissez-faire has never been more consistently practised. After all it was probably the quickest road to success if he really cared for Romanization. Peace through the Empire gave the opportunity for material development to those who desired it, and prosperity brought satisfaction and goodwill towards the government, which in turn invited closer relations and a natural assimilation of Roman customs. Prosperity also provided the means for acquiring the amenities of urban life, so that those who craved them drifted to villages and cities. It is true that many cities throughout the rural regions of the Empire dated their beginnings from the Augustan period, but this development was a concomitant, not a purposed goal of the Augustan peace.[96]

Frank's view on Roman imperialism and Romanization reflects delusive optimism from the perspective of the conqueror-ruler. It effectively precludes the conquered natives from playing any active role, either contribution or resistance, apart from following their practical interests to be Romanized and reduces the complexities in the Romanization process.

[95] Saller 1998: 224. [96] Frank 1920: 407.

Frank's attempt to dislodge the old-world political tradition from Roman history in fact incurs a series of problems. While it unburdens the American historian Frank from the stigma of conquest, it at the same time removes the little interests concerning the conquered natives, renders the narrative heavily biased towards the conquering Romans, and oversimplifies Romanization into a one-way process. He even more resolutely identifies and sympathizes with conquering Romans.

It is misleading to consider Frank indicative of the entirety of American scholarship. The presence of many European, especially British, emigrant scholars working in the United States and their intellectual ties across the Atlantic have helped to form a certain continuity across Anglo-American scholarship. Given the broader intellectual continuity, Frank illustrates a distinct strand of American scholarship, as was his objective. He intends to liberate Roman history from old-world European traditions and eventually frames it within American notions of exceptionalism. Believing that Americans are exceptional in sharing kindred spirits with Romans in the new world, he applies American pragmatism and optimism to comprehend Roman history. Accordingly, the parallel between Americans and Romans underpins his argument on Roman imperialism and Romanization: both Romans and Americans were simple, pragmatic, and honourable people of the new world, having escaped from the corrupted old world; they both expanded their frontier to safeguard civilization and peace and to stabilize through the growth of the middle classes; and they both, with their liberal approach, led the conquered to be assimilated for their practical benefits. His parallel discourse did not implant connection between America and Rome to the extent that the British parallel did in British scholarship. Yet, his identification of Americans with Romans and projection of American experience onto Roman history left behind his overly positive and simplified narrative. Not sharing the same stigma of conquest with Europeans, he was even less concerned with the question of conquered natives than his European peers and contributed to the perpetuation of colonialist history. Although his approach is said to be 'anti-theoretical', his history paradoxically demonstrates the significance of theoretical and/or conceptual framework.

Appendix 1: The Continental Factors

Today's French Classicists have a great deal to say about 'Western' thought. Unlike some of their Anglo-American counterparts, however, they tend to treat their subject more objectively as a living historical fact – not as some moribund fetish that needs to be propped up against the ever-fresh onslaughts of 'theory' or even barbarism. This book is lacking in grim exhortations that call upon Classicists to man the ramparts of crumbling empires. It is pervaded, rather, by a far more easy going atmosphere, one that fosters a general sense of intellectual optimism about 'Western' thought. The French Classicists' freedom from cultural insecurity – as Classicists – is palpable. ... In the long run, French Classicists view the term 'Western' in terms of historical contingency, not manifest destiny.[97]

This, in brief, captures how French classicists and ancient historians perceive themselves, particularly in relation to their Anglo-American counterparts. Although Nagy, Slatkin, and Loraux might not speak for the entirety of French scholarship at the turn of the twenty-first century, they still express the overall mood concerning the widening gap that has been building across the Channel over decades. This French attitude, which might sound brash, particularly to Anglo-American ears, shows that they wrote history in different contexts, such as social statuses, political roles, and intellectual traditions. Here, a brief snapshot of neighbouring French scholarship of Roman history is drawn to provide another point of comparison to contextualize the contemporary Anglo-American discourse on Roman imperialism and Romanization.

First and foremost, the pride of French classicists and ancient historians is not merely a hollow echo of the bygone glory of the nineteenth-century elitist Classics. On the contrary, it reflects a redefined prestige of the disciplines of history and Classics in the twentieth century. Compared to the sharply marginalized position of Classics in Anglo-American scholarship, the disciplines of both history and Classics have enjoyed relatively high esteem and support in wider French scholarship until experiencing some gradual decline in the twenty-first century. (Perhaps, this to a certain extent explains why their Anglo-American counterparts might find the pride of French classicists and ancient historians somewhat outdated.) When the professionalization of academia and higher education has set in France following the German model, which emphasizes disciplinary training and research in relation to the traditional public lecture from the late nineteenth century,[98] the elitism tied to classical education has faded away, but the significance of history and Classics has endured. In particular, history became the focal point of intellectual culture. The ideological influence of history during the time of rivalry with Germany reinforced its

---

[97] Nagy, Slatkin, and Loraux 2001: 2.
[98] Fritz K. Ringer's study of French academia in relation to its German counterpart provides lucid insight: Ringer 1992.

48   The Discourse on Romanization in the Age of Empires

significance and prestige. Furthermore, the trend of positivism stressing methodological rigour refreshed its direction and intellectual legitimacy in accord with the new era of professional academics.

With respect to the intellectual currents predominant in Roman history, structuralism, which swept across the French intellectual scene, presided over the disciplines of both history and Classics and, accordingly, the scholarship of Roman history. In particular, the Annales school in the discipline of history came to predominate in shaping the course of Roman historiography. Proclaiming the triad of économies, sociétés, and civilisations,[99] the Annales school of the early twentieth century pioneered an influential approach to social and economic history in the *longue durée*, which takes rigid structural factors of geography, environment, and mentalités into account. The Annales school, which had humble beginnings under the somewhat different agenda of Lucien Febvre and Marc Bloch during the interwar period, blossomed with historians of the next generation, such as Ernest Labrousse, Fernand Braudel, and many others, to achieve international distinction in the postwar era. One of the tours de force of the school was Braudel's *La Méditerranée et le monde méditerranéen à l'époque de Philippe II*, while his posthumous work *Les mémoires de la Méditerranée: préhistoire et antiquité* became a more relevant reference for later Roman historians.[100] The Annales school to a degree defined the scope of historical scholarship in twentieth-century France, whilst positivism largely governed its methodology. With the subject matter presented by the Annales school, positivism resulted in an emphasis on 'the systematic use of measurement' and 'formalization of the data and tests' to document social and economic history.[101] Roughly put, this led to prioritizing quantitative evidence over qualitative interpretation – without acknowledging subjective premises which filter and interpret seemingly objective data. The practice unmistakably pervaded Roman history as professional academics gained their authority following Mommsenian methodological rigour.

Besides the *longue durée* vision coupled with Mommsenian methodological rigour, the outlook on the ancient Roman and modern French imperialism set French scholars apart from their Anglo-American peers.

> La fonction justificatrice de l'histoire romaine, par le biais d'une filiation rattachant l'Europe à l'empire pacificateur et civilisateur, n'est nulle part plus sensible que dans le discours idéologique – et souvent dans le discours des historiens – des puissances coloniales qui avaient eu l'occasion, comme

[99] This was the title of the journal of the Annales school from 1946 to 1994.
[100] Braudel 1949, 1998.   [101] Revel 1995: 24–5.

Appendix 1: The Continental Factors 49

la France et l'Italie, mais non l'Angleterre – il lui manquait cela – de mettre leurs pas dans les pas de Rome. En Libye, l'Italie trouva, peu après la conquête, l'occasion rêvée de mettre en oeuvre la récupération de la romanité, point important de l'idéologie fasciste. Mais la France de la IIIe et de la IVe République se considérait elle-même, dans le Maghreb, comme l'héritière de Rome, et sa mission civilisatrice, comme la distance marquée à l'égard des populations locales, était, pour bien des responsables ou même des habitants d'origine européenne, cautionnée par le passé, notamment par l'imposant patrimoine archéologique du pays. Nombre de savants articles témoignent, parfois avec ingénuité, de cette filiation revendiquée.[102]

Whereas the pendulum oscillated in Anglo-American scholarship between identifying Romans with the predecessors of civilizing imperialists and referring to Romans solely for practical examples or warnings, the parallel discourse between ancient Roman and modern French imperialism took a firm hold on French scholarship. As Edmond Frézouls compares and contrasts with British imperialism, the overlap in imperial geography affirmed French affinity with Romans in their civilizing mission. It did not stop at fostering sentimental connection. It enabled French archaeologists to recover the Roman past in their North African colonies as well as France and to readily institute their version of parallel discourse into a form of historical knowledge, while British archaeologists focused on recovering Roman Britain and pondered over the question of their conquered past.

The medley of positivist methodological rigour, *longue durée* view of the Annales school, and French imperialism in North Africa reinforced the parallel discourse between ancient Roman and modern French imperialism. Frézouls notes that the overall circumstance allowed the Mommsenian view of defensive imperialism to dominate French scholarship, which came to be reformulated and transmitted through the works of Jullian and Maurice Holleaux during the first half of the twentieth century.[103] Although composed with different scopes and agendas, both Jullian's *Histoire de la Gaule*

---

[102] Frézouls 1983: 145–6. 'The justifying function of Roman history, through a lineage linking Europe to the pacifying and civilizing empire, is nowhere more evident than in the ideological discourse – and often in the discourse of historians – of colonial powers which had had the opportunity, like France and Italy, but not England – it lacked that – to follow in the footsteps of Rome. In Libya, Italy found, shortly after the conquest, the perfect opportunity to implement the recovery of Romanità, an important point of fascist ideology. But France of the Third and Fourth Republic considered itself, in the Maghreb, as the heir of Rome, and its civilizing mission, just like the distance it maintained between the French colonists and the local populations, was, for many officials or even inhabitants of European origin, endorsed by the past, in particular by the imposing archaeological heritage of the country. A number of scholarly articles bear witness, sometimes ingenuously, to this claimed lineage.' (translation by the present author).
[103] Frézouls 1983: 147.

and Holleaux's *Rome, la Grèce et les monarchies hellénistiques au III*^{e} *siècle avant J.-C. (273 – 205)* inherited contemporary European views on imperialism and imprinted civilizing and defensive imperialism on French scholarship.[104] First, Jullian, whose weight in Gallo-Roman studies is often equated with that of Haverfield in Romano-British studies, aims to recover a Celtic nation in the *longue durée* and argues that the Celts were instrumental in reaping the benefits of civilizing imperialism and spreading them over the long course of history. While projecting nineteenth-century romantic nationalism onto the ancient past, he elevates the Celts as a special ethnic group to progress human civilization through imperialism.[105] On the other hand, Holleaux in his rigorous study contends that Rome came to extend her power to the East to secure frontiers and to preserve herself. As for their long-standing legacy, Erich S. Gruen comments that 'the heritage of Mommsen and Holleaux remains pervasive' even to his day in the 1980s.[106]

Overall, French scholarship shared more or less the same early twentieth-century perspective on imperialism and history with Anglo-American scholarship. Yet, it is worth mentioning that French scholarship of Roman history seemed to have lacked the voice of Collingwood to raise epistemological questions. Only much later in the 1970s, epistemological questions were raised – and all-too-often overlooked. The forceful energy that had gathered its momentum from the nineteenth century at some points grew into perverse positivism prevalent in French scholarship, where methodological procedures were unnecessarily convoluted and data was confusingly overwhelming. It effectively stifled questions on underlying ideologies or conditions of history and quelled the philosophy of history in French historiography for the coming decades. The collapse of Marxism and the decline of the Annales school in the late twentieth century without a conspicuous trigger further highlighted the epistemological vacuum. Jacques Revel assesses that '[a]fter a period of lawlike certitude, the social sciences entered a phase of epistemological anarchy' in the second half of the twentieth century.[107] The vogue of heritage memory in French scholarship was symptomatic of the lack of epistemological questioning, resulting in critiques of nationalism and colonialism going unheard. French scholarship, where the positivist tradition brushed off epistemological criticism, became an infertile ground for postcolonial questions on historical epistemology to take hold.

---

[104] Jullian 1920; Holleaux 1921.   [105] Woolf 1998: 4–5.   [106] Gruen 1984: 7.
[107] Revel 1995: 48.

CHAPTER 2

Postcolonial Themes

The publication of Said's *Orientalism* in 1978 marks a watershed moment for postcolonial studies. From the 1980s, the triad of Said, Bhabha, and Spivak actively published and lectured on both sides of the Atlantic and effectively established postcolonial studies as an influential field of study in the Anglo-American intellectual world. Its increasing influence across academia and culture, however, was slow to reach Classical studies. Most Roman historians remained largely reserved about the wave of postcolonial thought, while some explored the possibilities of rewriting history with postcolonial perspectives. Mapping out the impact of postcolonial thought onto the scholarship of Roman history is far from straightforward: it allowed some scholars to be inspired by postcolonial thought but at the same time others remained sceptical; it provided a breakthrough to some and at the same time meant a loss of intellectual tradition to others.

The complexity of the idea of postcolonialism travelling to the discourse of Romanization is hardly unexpected. Even at first glance, the gap between postcolonial studies and Romanization studies appears to be difficult to bridge. The wide temporal and spatial gulf of their focus makes the link between them seem questionable. Having evolved from investigating the legacy of modern European colonization, postcolonial studies primarily delves into colonialism and its aftermath from the fifteenth century up until the present day and from the Western colonial powers to their decolonized countries.[1] On the other hand, Romanization studies specifically concerns the consequence of Roman imperialism from the second century BC up to the fourth century AD in the provinces of the Roman Empire. Broadly speaking, there is a common ground of focus on imperialism and its consequences. Nevertheless, doubts have been voiced as to whether these modern Western and ancient Roman imperial powers and their impact are comparable in nature and whether postcolonial

---

[1] For an overview of postcolonial studies, see Chrisman and Williams 1993; Ashcroft et al. 1994.

studies is applicable to Romanization studies. Fundamentally, the question can be formulated as: how useful is postcolonial studies as an analytical tool when used to re-examine Romanization?

The concern about a crude application of postcolonialism onto Romanization was articulated by Richard Alston. He stresses that Roman imperialism, sustained by its 'integrating' mentality, essentially differs from European imperialism with its 'divisive' mentality and, hence, doubts if postcolonial theories based on modern European imperialism can advance understanding of Romanization.[2] His reservations are valid. First, does postcolonial studies present a theoretical framework appropriate to Romanization studies? Postcolonial theories have developed from specific historical and material realities shaped by European colonization and subsequent decolonization. They do not claim to be universal or applicable to all cases of colonization, such as Roman imperialism, and cannot be automatically extended to explain Romanization. Second, does Romanization studies have evidence appropriate for postcolonial theories? While postcolonial studies has a variety of means to investigate the colonized subjects and, therefore, would have some degree of confidence to cross-examine theoretical frameworks with different types of evidence, it is more difficult to claim the same level of confidence for Romanization studies, as it often relies on material sources to access the colonized subjects. When interpreting material sources, theoretical frameworks play a more significant role than they do in conventional literary sources, because archaeological data do not articulate agency as literary sources often do. Without care, postcolonial readings of provincial material culture in the Roman Empire risk slipping into the perilous loop of theory filtering history and history reaffirming theory.[3] On the whole, these concerns point towards the same questions again: can postcolonial studies provide a new direction to improve our understanding of the Roman Empire? Or, does it simply comprise another strand of contemporary intellectual thought concerning the Roman Empire, based on modern theories rather than ancient sources, that does not get us closer to the ancient historical reality? How can we avoid such a crude application of postcolonial studies and instead benefit from it?

---

[2] Alston 1996.
[3] The late twentieth-century awareness of the importance of theory and epistemology in the Anglo-American scholarship of Roman history and archaeology resulted in the birth of the Theoretical Roman Archaeology Conferences (TRAC) in the UK in 1991.

Jane Webster tackles the question head-on: '[b]ut isn't it a-historical?'[4] She contends that postcolonial theories used with the right focus can still enlighten Romanization studies:

> The focus of post-colonial theory is such that the reader will not find direct comparisons between colonial texts . . .; what are compared are not 'colonialisms', but the *discourses* which enable colonialism. We have taken from post-colonial theory the understanding that discourse plays a crucial part in producing and sustaining hegemonic power, and we have explored the discourses of Roman imperialism from that perspective.[5]

As Webster concedes, Roman imperial discourse shaped by its specific historical context requires postcolonial approaches adapted to it. Applying postcolonial theories does not immediately offer a direct analogy with modern imperialisms or a ready-to-use strategy to destabilize Roman imperialist discourse. Instead, postcolonial studies can provide general orientations to re-examine Roman imperialism and Romanization and potential strategies to deconstruct imperialist epistemology in its discourse.

Enrico Dal Lago and Constantina Katsari present another helpful guide to bridge the gap between postcolonial theories and Romanization studies. In the Introduction to their comparative study *Slave Systems: Ancient and Modern*, they explain the purpose of comparative study between ancient and modern pasts.[6] Although each slavery institution operated distinctively in its specific historical environments, the underlying 'system' of slavery – 'a particular set of factors that allowed the economy and society of a particular historical culture to operate' – was pervasive through the course of history.[7] In order to understand the 'system' of slavery, rather than an individual institution of slavery, the project requires a comprehensive perspective to juxtapose various slave systems in history and to investigate systemic similarities and differences. Yet, Dal Lago and Katsari clarify that comparative study is not an end in itself, but 'a heuristical tool'. By comparing ancient and modern slave systems, they aim at a 'diachronic' understanding of the slave system, 'in which the dynamic process of "slaving" – rather than the static concept of "slavery" – provides the element of continuity, seen from the point of view of both the enslavers and the enslaved, while change relates to the differences in modes and strategies employed in different historical epochs'.[8] Their explanation of the diachronic view of history in relation to the synchronic view helps in understanding the merits of comparing ancient and modern systems.

---

[4] Webster 1996.   [5] Webster 1996.   [6] Dal Lago and Katsari 2008.
[7] Dal Lago and Katsari 2008: 3.   [8] Dal Lago and Katsari 2008: 13.

The difference between the two approaches is of paramount importance for the study of ancient and modern 'slave systems'. In one case, 'slave systems' can be taken and studied as relatively fixed and somewhat self-contained units of analysis – thus leading to insightful findings on the meaning of similarities and difference between them – while, in the other case, they are 'deconstructed' and stripped of their 'systemic' aspects, so to emphasize the dynamic components of the process of 'slaving' that has generated them; a process which is the actual object of the analysis. Thus, depending on which approach one takes – whether it focuses on actually comparing ancient and modern 'slave systems' or an analysing the development of the process of 'slaving' from the ancient to the modern worlds – he/she will ask different questions, will find different results, equally valid, and will have to rely on different sets of scholarship altogether.[9]

They argue that the diachronic approach is more appropriate in order to understand the system, because each institution of slavery did not take place independently. As ideas and customs travelled through history and across the globe, each institution developed interdependently with others. Therefore, a comparative study with a diachronic view of history, or *histoire croisée* in French historiography, will yield a deeper understanding of the overall system in its dynamic development.[10]

Dal Lago and Katsari's approach to the systems of slavery from ancient to modern sheds light on the relationship between ancient Roman and modern Western systems of imperialism. Despite having taken place in different social, economic, and political contexts, both empires fundamentally operated the system of imperialism. Furthermore, they were not historically independent entities, either. As detailed in Chapter 1, ancient Roman imperialism has been a constant point of reference in the discourse on modern Western imperialism, and, vice versa, modern Western imperialism was a lens through which the discourse on ancient Roman imperialism has developed. Dal Lago and Katsari's diachronic approach – to consider the dynamic development of imperial systems through history – offers a prospect of better grasping ancient Roman imperialism by investigating the intertwined histories of and discourses on two imperialist systems. When placed in the diachronic investigation of imperial systems, the role of postcolonialism becomes lucid. Even though postcolonial theories did not stem from ancient Roman imperialism per se, they provide a heuristic tool to destabilize the discourse that has sustained imperial systems through history. Hence, the concerns raised about the

---

[9] Dal Lago and Katsari 2008: 11–12.   [10] On *histoire croisée*, see Werner and Zimmermann 2003.

temporal and spatial gulf between the two imperialisms and about the hasty application of postcolonialism are resolved. Postcolonialism, instead, helps Roman historians and archaeologists to reach a deeper understanding about the dynamic process of imperial discourses and to deconstruct the imperial discourses built through the complex layers of histories.

From the late twentieth century onwards, the wave of postcolonialism became difficult to disregard even for the rather reserved scholarship of Classics and ancient history. Postcolonial studies has not only gained more prominence as an academic discipline in its own right, but has also started to offer fresh inspiration to other academic disciplines. Its influence within the wider academia began to infiltrate the scholarship of Roman history and inspired a new orientation for Romanization studies. The fundamental shift that postcolonial theories prompted in Romanization studies is rooted in their questioning of history. By challenging not only the concept but also the methodology of historical knowledge built on imperialism, postcolonial theories aim at restructuring imperialist historiography. This wave of postcolonialism has motivated Roman historians and archaeologists to question Roman history in turn: that is, to review the historiography of Romanization, to take a fresh look at the much-debated issue of Romanization, and to rewrite the history of Romanization. Since here I aim to investigate how scholars have reshaped the discourse on Romanization from postcolonial perspectives, I will take a closer look at selected themes in postcolonial studies which Roman scholars have found relevant and opted for, rather than surveying the entire body of postcolonial studies. In other words, this chapter does not deliver an exhaustive analysis or a landscape overview of postcolonial studies according to a certain order of significance or thematic categorization, as is the common practice in that discipline, for example along the triad of Said-Bhabha-Spivak or along the axis of theoretical and materialist approaches. Instead, here I explore postcolonial ideas which have influenced and reoriented Romanization studies. Therefore, among other postcolonial themes, postcolonial questions on history and historiography will be the focal point. Based on their impact on Romanization studies, here I shall broadly introduce postcolonial ideas in two strands: first, postcolonial questions on the place of the Self and the Other assumed in historiography, and second, postcolonial reconfigurations of the interaction between the Self and the Other in history. This will allow us later to perceive how Romanization studies came to change its course owing to postcolonial perspectives.

History as Knowledge and Power

I have laid out the intended scope of this chapter on postcolonial theories, but I ought to begin from poststructuralist ideas, particularly those of Michel Foucault. Given the widely acknowledged indebtedness of postcolonial studies to poststructuralist thought, starting from poststructuralist thought will facilitate the introduction of postcolonial questions on history and historiography.[11] Yet it is not the sole reason why I lead off with Foucault. It is because there are Roman historians and archaeologists who credit Foucault with ushering in new understandings of Roman history, including Romanization. Overall, Foucault has twofold significance for Romanization studies: first, he has influenced postcolonial studies, which in turn shaped the course of Romanization studies, and second, he has also influenced the scholarship of Roman history to trigger rethinking about Romanization. Either directly or indirectly he has transformed the discourse on Romanization, and thus deserves our attention here.

The principal reason why Foucault has left far-reaching impacts across disciplines is that he challenged fundamental beliefs behind the tradition of history writing. According to Foucault, the writing of history had held on to a single purpose: to discover and expound the truth which is unequivocally presiding but hidden in mundane and seemingly random events. Such an aim depends on two presumptions: that history will eventually reveal teleological correlations between seemingly separate events and reconstitute them into a total unity; and that history progresses towards a cohesive end. Foucault brings into question the well-established purpose of history as well as the implicit presumptions rooted in it. In the words of Foucault himself, he '[intends] to question teleologies and totalizations' of history.[12] He contends that the teleologies and totalizations predicated in traditional history writing confine any historical investigation to a circular argument from the onset. Since the conclusion of any history writing is already determined even before the investigation, any attempt to write history in accordance with the predetermined truth selects and filters evidence accordingly. Counter-evidence is set aside either as a dispensable counter-force to the fulfilment of Hegelian History or as a negligible factor in the total progress of History. The truth which claims to be discovered and confirmed by History in fact does not gain any more validity from historical investigations, but still precariously remains as a priori arguments. Foucault urges us

---

[11] On the relation between poststructuralism and postcolonialism, see: Gandhi 1998: 23–41.
[12] Foucault 1972: 1–19.

to liberate history from imprisoning ideas of History – teleologies and totalizations, continuity and unity – and to rediscover uniqueness, specificity, and discontinuity in history.

Nevertheless, continuity and unity in history are not entirely invalid. Foucault instead argues that these concepts are misplaced. Continuity and unity do not exist as permanent distinctive features within the essence of a historical object. Continuity and unity that we had assumed to be as such and, therefore, positively verifiable are, in fact, artificially constructed 'through error, oblivion, illusion, ignorance, or the inertia of beliefs and traditions, or even perhaps unconscious desire not to see and not to speak'.[13] Objects of historical enquiry in reality hold not only continuities and commonalities to a certain extent, but also discontinuities in time, differences in form, and dispersions in space. Continuity and unity, on the contrary, are set on the level of discourse. They do not exist in objects per se but are developed and formulated in the discourse of objects, 'in their distribution, in the interplay of their differences, in their proximity of distance – in short, in what is given to the speaking subject'.[14] Foucault's placement of continuity and unity at the level of historical discourse rather than historical reality necessitates questions on how to understand the history written thus far. Since, according to Foucault, continuous and coherent objects chronicled in history are products of discourse removed from reality, we need to treat them as discursive objects rather than verified objects. Furthermore, Foucault's exegesis on history writing demands an examination of how discursive formulations have treated discontinuities, differences, and dispersions in discourses on history. This new outlook on history then allows us to inject contradictions in history as they are 'neither appearances to be overcome, nor secret principles to be uncovered' until there is no longer an idea of contradiction in history for the sake of teleological totalizing history.[15] Foucault ultimately redefines history – from the traditional history with pre-determined orientations and pre-given answers to a new history with diverse meanings and open possibilities.

Foucault left even more striking impacts across the intellectual world, needless to say including the scholarship of Roman history, when he started to connect his work on discursive knowledge with the question of power.[16] Foremost, he restructures the conception of power and rejects its 'juridico-discursive' representation as negative, in the sense that it is

---

[13] Foucault 1972: 44–54.   [14] Foucault 1972.   [15] Foucault 1972: 166–73.
[16] The emphasis, as mentioned at the start of this section, is selective according to the influence on the development of Romanization discourse. Although not dealt with in detail here, Foucault has written extensively on power. See also Foucault 1977, 1979.

prohibitive, disciplinary, and punitive, because it reduces diverse and multi-faceted power relations into a single trajectory. This originates, as Foucault explains, from uncritical application of the much-studied and-analysed theory of power between the sovereign and the individual to explain different kinds of power relations '[b]etween every point of social body, between a man and a woman, between the members of a family, between a master and a pupil, between every one who knows and every one who does not'.[17] It thereby reduces the scope of complex manifestations of power relations, for example inter-dependence, complementarity, and selective obstruction, to an overly simplistic dimension. Most significantly, as part of his attempt to take these factors into account to advocate a new conceptualization of power, he demonstrates how resistance also takes place within power relations:

> Where there is power, there is resistance, and yet, or rather consequently, this resistance is never in a position of exteriority in relation to power. Should it be said that one is 'always' inside the power, there is no 'escaping' it, there is no absolute outside where it is concerned, because one is subject to the law in any case? Or that, history being the ruse of reason, always emerging the winner? This would be to misunderstand the strictly relational character of power relationships. Their existence depends on a multiplicity of points of resistance; these play the role of adversary, target, support, or handle in power relations. These points of resistance are everywhere in the power network. . . . [B]y definition, they can only exist in the strategic field of power relations.[18]

Locating resistance within the network of power relations, Foucault further clarifies the relation between power and resistance. Inasmuch as power takes different directions, forms, and effects, resistance is not a simple opposing force against power, but has its own diverse and multiple orientations, targets, and characters. Power and resistance, in other words, 'work in a disruptive rather than dialectical relation to each other'.[19] Foucault deconstructs 'the dominant model of inside/outside conventional [power] politics' and exposes complexity of power relations.[20]

One of the most complicated and crucial aspects of power, and also Foucault's preoccupation overarching his oeuvre, is that power and knowledge/truth are intrinsically enmeshed together. This not only resonates with, but also amplifies, his earlier elaborations on the discursivity of knowledge – for our purpose here, specifically, historical knowledge. Foucault maintains that the process of discourse formation leads to

[17] Foucault 1980: 183–93.   [18] Foucault 1979: 95–6.   [19] Young 1990: 122–4.   [20] Young 1990.

competition over what is true and false and builds into a 'régime of truth', i.e. power politics to determine and approve the truth and to accord values in society. A certain body of knowledge becomes the truth, which is neither universally nor permanently valid, but rather sanctioned, regulated, and distributed in accordance with the specific régime of truth in each society. Foucault asserts that it is futile trying to extract knowledge/truth purified from worldly or political ideologies, since knowledge/truth in itself is power. Instead '[it is] … a matter of … detaching the power of truth from the forms of hegemony, social, economic and cultural, within which it operates at the present time'.[21] Thus, Foucault warns historians – and others – to be aware of the discursive nature of history and of the régime of truth built into any given historical knowledge/truth and to prevent hegemony from perverting it.

Foucault does not deal with colonial or postcolonial issues. Nonetheless, his reconfiguration of history as discursive knowledge built through complex power relations has spurred some historians to question colonial power built into established historical knowledge/truth. First, let us take a look at how postcolonial thinkers have come forth from Foucault's poststructuralist foundations.

History of the Self and the Other

Foucault challenged traditional structures of understanding historical knowledge/truth and called for a new approach to history writing. Why then do we move on to postcolonial theories? Is poststructuralism not sufficient to reform history writing? How does postcolonial studies offer aims and approaches to writing new history different from poststructuralist thought? Robert J. C. Young advocates that postcolonial theories hold the key to effect a breakthrough that poststructuralism proposes yet fails to achieve. Although poststructuralism criticizes teleological and totalizing history, it in itself is still locked into Eurocentrism.[22] Not only spurred by its mission to break teleology and totalization but also aided by contemporary currents, that is, 'self-consciousness about a culture's own historical relativity' and 'loss of the sense of an absoluteness of any Western account of History', poststructuralism has strived to be more sensitive to the problem of alterity and sought heterogeneity.[23] However, it does so in order to deconstruct and restructure the Western theory of history – not in order to re-conceptualize history which fundamentally breaks away from

---

[21] Foucault 1980: 109–33.   [22] On Eurocentrism, see Amin 1989.   [23] Young 1990: 43–52.

Western epistemology. To go beyond Eurocentric historiography, Young argues:

> It is rather colonialism, I argue, that constitutes the dislocating term in the theory/history debate; from this perspective, theoretical and political questions are inflected towards the way in which theory and history, together with Marxism itself, have themselves been implicated in the long history of European colonialism – and, above all, the extent to which that history continues to determine both the institutional conditions of knowledge as well as the terms of contemporary institutional practices – practices which extend beyond the limits of the academic institutions.[24]

To put it another way, poststructuralism, despite its aim to deconstruct traditional Hegelian and Marxist theories of history, is enmeshed with the Eurocentric colonialist/imperialist systems of power and knowledge through intellectual and academic traditions. In contrast, postcolonial theories can work as a disruptive force between European colonial/imperial power and the Eurocentric régime of truth to dislodge its hegemony. Asking the question of alterity, initially posed by poststructuralism, directly back to poststructuralist and earlier Western theories of history, postcolonial history attempts to move beyond European self-centred or self-reflexive history and to push the epistemological boundary to colonial peripheries.[25]

Naturally, postcolonial theories set off with the agenda to challenge Eurocentrism, namely the firmly entrenched identification of the colonizing West as the Self and the colonized non-West as the Other, in history, historiography, theory of history, and beyond. Although there have been critiques of ethnocentrism built into Western epistemology and humanism, notably by Frantz Fanon,[26] it was Said's *Orientalism*, first published in 1978, that sent shock waves through the Western intellectual world about the ingrained and pandemic Eurocentrism and became 'the principal catalyst and reference point for postcolonial [theories]'.[27] Adopting Foucault's theories on discourse and power-knowledge, Said exposes the collusion between Western colonial institutions of power and academic knowledge about the colonized East.[28] In order to unveil it, Said roughly follows two steps, of which the first is to establish the discursive nature of Orientalism. Defining Orientalism as the Western system of discursive knowledge about the East, particularly the Islamic Near East, he affirms

---

[24] Young 1990: xii. See also Biel 2015.   [25] Gandhi 1998: 68–74.   [26] Fanon 1965.
[27] Gandhi 1998: 25.
[28] Said does not completely agree with Foucault and disagrees with him on some issues, which I will not delve into. On Said's view of Foucault, see: Said 1978: 3, 22–23.

that Orientalism is far from empirical or universal knowledge about the real Orient. Orientalism is essentially a discourse of, by, and for the Western Self concerning the Eastern Other, but lacking the real East. Secondly, Said delimits Orientalism as a phenomenon particular to Britain and France, because their considerable involvement with the Near East over time, which is qualitatively and quantitatively incomparable to other European countries or North America, has shaped an enduring discourse and sustained it till now.

In the long-established Orientalist tradition, according to Said, British and French intellectuals have observed the Islamic Near East while keeping their distance, analysed it with their Western epistemology and philosophy, defined it with Western concepts and terms, circulated their 'objective' knowledge to a Western audience, and made themselves ultimate authorities over it. Thus, Orientalism presents an East that the West has appropriated, reduced, and even created by and for itself. Said argues that the self-reflexive and self-serving nature of Orientalist discourse inherently keeps reinforcing the divide between the West as subject Self and the East as object Other, since the subject Western Self assumes itself to have the ability to know, understand, and penetrate the object Eastern Other and even to have the right to speak for it. As a matter of course it leads the discourse to identify the subject Western Self as rational, eloquent, and progressive and the object Eastern Other as primitive, inarticulate, and backward. Eurocentrism embedded in the discourse of Orientalism perpetuates the vicious cycle of fortifying the dialectical framework in history, contrary to its purported aim to better understand the Other and to resolve the divide. Said alerts us to the fact that the two poles of Western Self and Eastern Other in history are far from two competing forces in balance. The West's military despotism of the East is in itself a statement of Western power. Although on the surface of Orientalism the West presumes its intellectual superiority to the East, according to Said, Orientalism rather manifests Western political, military, and economic domination over the East. Based on Foucault's tenet on knowledge and power, Said maintains that there is no pure knowledge, free of political power structures. Political power is always implicated in knowledge, because political power as well as its economic or military consequences underlies the production, regulation, circulation, and exploitation of knowledge. However much the knowledge subtly or overtly professes to be political or apolitical, there is no 'distinction between pure and political knowledge'. Subsequently, it is wrong to presume that Orientalism has been unfairly tarnished and exploited by external political factors, since Orientalism by definition cannot be a pure academic knowledge, albeit it claims to be safe from power structures.[29] Ultimately, Said ascribed the power relationship underlying Orientalism to Western hegemony.

Certainly, the power dynamics between the West and the East have not always been those of colonial domination, but within varying degrees of dominance the West has maintained the upper hand and concurrently has upheld the dialectical discourse between the dominant Self and the dominated Other. Said yet warns against confusing the relationship between colonial power and knowledge as a simple causation, as if Orientalism were invented later to vindicate Western colonialism: '[w]e would be wrong, I think, to underestimate the reservoir of accredited knowledge, the codes of Orientalist orthodoxy ... To say simply that Orientalism was a rationalization of colonial rule is to ignore the extent to which colonial rule was justified in advance of Orientalism, rather than after the fact'.[30] Instead, extensive political, economic, and military predominance of the West has intertwined with the discourse of Orientalism and cemented it as an internally coherent, durable, and forceful body of theory and practice. History as an academic discipline – contrary to the belief in history as empirical knowledge on the past – was no exception to conspire with Western political, economic, and military dominance to frame its discourse along the contrast between the powerful, independent, and vocal Western Self and the powerless, dependent, and silent non-Western Other. Hence, Said argues, history written by the Western Self has produced a portrait of the Eastern Other which is paradoxically devoid of voices of the Other.

Thus, postcolonial studies raises the following questions: is it possible to retrieve the lost Other in history and how? Is it possible to write alternative narratives to the Eurocentric historiography and how? Is it possible to reproduce the Other which is not a mirror reflection of the European Self and to compose alternative histories which are not merely counter-narratives of Eurocentric historiography and how? Gayatri Chakravorty Spivak brings these questions together in her acclaimed essay 'Can the Subaltern Speak?'[31] She points out that poststructuralist thinkers, even though they address the problem of alterity and propose heterogeneous histories, assume that 'the oppressed, if given the chance ... *can speak and know their conditions* [emphasis in the original]'. Spivak thus proposes her provocative question '*can the subaltern speak?* [emphasis in the original]'.[32] Not subscribing to the Eurocentric binary framework of the Western Self

---

[29] Said 1978: 9–15.   [30] Said 1978: 39.   [31] Spivak 1988.   [32] Spivak 1988: 283.

and the non-Western Other, she realigns the divide between the powerful and vocal Self and the powerless and silent Other in accordance with political and economic circumstances. Drawing on Antonio Gramsci's notion of *subaltern classes*, she categorizes the elite – whether foreign or Indigenous, whether European or non-European – as the Self, who with power to express and exercise have monopolized historiography, and the oppressed non-elite as the Other, who without such power have been manipulated by this monopolized historiography.[33]

As Spivak notes, a group of intellectuals, including herself, called the 'subaltern studies group' has undertaken a mission to rethink imperialist historiography from the perspective of the muted subaltern.[34] She nonetheless challenges this approach, because it does not resolve the fundamental problem that subaltern experts speak for the subaltern and assume the authority to represent them in the same fashion as Orientalists have been doing. The investigating subject Self unavoidably intervenes and mediates the investigated object Other and repeats epistemic violence. No matter what attempts have been made to retrieve the unspoken consciousness of the subaltern, Spivak solemnly accepts that 'the subaltern cannot speak'.[35] However, Spivak still remains optimistic. She exhorts postcolonial intellectuals to consciously make efforts to 'unlearn' their politically instituted knowledge and 'to articulate that ideological formation – by *measuring silences, if necessary* – into the *object* of investigation [emphasis in the original]'.[36] Their continuing efforts alone can '[bring] hegemonic historiography to crisis'.[37] Such a role played by postcolonial intellectuals is vital, as Spivak contends, because hegemonic historiography upheld by colonialism and imperialism continues to persist – from old colonialist historiography to current neo-colonialist/imperialist historiography. The old liaison between Western colonial institutions and Orientalism, which had been apparent, has been refashioned into a less obvious and subtler system of power and knowledge which is sustained by international corporations, their division of labour, and Third Worldism. Terms such as globalization of capital and internationalization of division of labour, which are used to describe the contemporary system of power and knowledge, often mask neutral or even progressive tones. They, in fact, euphemize the neo-colonialist link between

---

[33] Gramsci 1975.
[34] The Subaltern Studies Group is a historiographical project mainly comprised of South Asian scholars spearheaded by Ranajit Guha. Notable works include: Guha 1983; Guha and Spivak 1989; Chakrabarty 2000.
[35] Spivak 1988.   [36] Spivak 1988: 296.   [37] Spivak 1985.

First World capital and Third World natural and human resources and discreetly reinscribe the Third World as the oppressed Other in history.[38]

It is accurate, as Young indicates, that the Third World, derived from the Third Estate within the context of the French Revolution, was originally put forward as 'a positive term of radical critique ... to incorporate equally revolutionary ideals of providing a radical alternative to the hegemonic capitalist-socialist power blocks of the post-war period'.[39] Although some, including Young, keep believing in the potential of the Third World to disrupt European hegemony, others, including Spivak, at the same time warn against the hasty use of this buzzword with the effect of obscuring the First World's hegemony of power and knowledge. For all its revolutionary ideals, 'the Third World' has undeniably become a convenient label for the First World to apply to the generally marginalized and has thereby deluded many about the persistent neo-colonialist/imperialist political-economic and epistemological structures of the First World. Like the Orient, the Third World is being stripped of its heterogeneity and being appropriated, homogenized, essentialized, and encapsulated as the opposite of the First World. Yet, Spivak adds one significant dimension to the contemporary configurations that had been absent in the former Orientalism. She warns that postcolonial Third World intellectuals who often communicate to the First World audience with words and thoughts acquired from First World education may contribute to sustaining this distorted phenomenon of Third Worldism, instead of measuring the silences of the Third World subaltern: 'It is as if, in a certain way, we [postcolonial intellectuals] are becoming complicitious in the perpetration of a "new orientalism"'.[40] Only a constant unlearning of Eurocentric systems of power and knowledge, she argues, will allow the intellectual and political project of allowing the subaltern to speak to make strides.

Postcolonial theorists, notably Said and Spivak amongst others, posed questions raised by poststructuralism, alterity, and power-knowledge directly back to Western historiography. They espouse that Western historiography, which professes its positivity, universality, and superiority, is in fact a discursive knowledge formulated in conjunction with its power in forms of colonialism and imperialism over the Other; that it has shaped the historical knowledge along the polar framework between the powerful subject Self of the West and the powerless object Other of the non-West in order to

---

[38] See Krishna 2009; Cope 2012.   [39] Young 1990: 43.
[40] Spivak 1993: 56. A few scholars have attempted to tackle the question, see Prakash 1990; O'Hanlon and Washbrook 1992.

maintain Western predominance; and that Western hegemony was not limited to political, economic, and military arenas but has stretched to shape epistemology and history of the Other. These postcolonial challenges to Eurocentrism have brought Western historiographical hegemony into crisis. Although Spivak does not give up the project of subaltern history and continues to seek ways of getting closer to the aim, in her essay 'Can the Subaltern Speak?' she accepts that the subaltern Other cannot write alternative history. Is there, indeed, any possibility left for writing alternative history?

History of the Interaction between the Self and the Other

Spivak, to a certain extent, comes to this rather bleak conclusion after having witnessed endeavours and setbacks in postcolonial restructurings of history thus far. Even though these earlier efforts contain theoretical weaknesses and are constrained by political-economic limitations, it is nonetheless worth examining them here. These earlier milestone works, which postcolonial discourse continues to develop and refine, have also ushered the scholarship of Roman history into the postcolonial age of history writing. Here we will take a closer look at postcolonial attempts to produce alternative history which centre, first, on re-examining colonial interactions between the colonizer and the colonized and, second, on inverting and/or subverting the Self and the Other implanted by colonialist/imperialist historiography. Now let us see if alternative history is indeed unattainable or not.

One of the earliest and most significant attempts was made by Fanon, before Foucault's poststructuralist treatises and far before the institution of postcolonial studies.[41] Influential in both political and intellectual arenas during the era of decolonization, Fanon's works laid the foundation for postcolonial studies. A Martinique-born psychiatrist and a vigorous supporter of Algerian independence from France, he channelled his medical expertise to expose psychological dehumanization and devastation committed by colonialism.[42] He pours out vehement indictments of European colonialism. It scarcely comes close to progress towards the professed goal of civilizing, humanizing, or enriching the colonized. Instead, it commits

---

[41] Frantz Fanon was particularly influenced by his teacher and mentor Aimé Césaire, who was a Martinique-born intellectual and led the Négritude movement. Négritude intellectuals, including Aimé Césaire, Léopold Sédar Senghor, and Frantz Fanon, tried to recover Black consciousness across the Pan-Africa and African diaspora. Important Négritude works include: Césaire 1939; Senghor 1945, 1948.
[42] In particular, see Fanon 1965.

indefensible violation against territories and properties of the local people and makes an unjustifiable equation of Europeans with humans and non-Europeans with animals into reality. His unique language of indignation in severed sentences cannot convey any more powerfully how unutterable the colonial reality actually was:

> The colonial world is a compartmentalized world. . . .
> The 'native' sector is not complementary to the European sector. The two confront each other, but not in the service of a higher unity. Governed by a purely Aristotelian logic, they follow the dictates of mutual exclusion: There is no conciliation possible, one of them is superfluous. The colonist's sector is sector built to last, all stone and steel. It's a sector of lights and paved roads, where the trash cans constantly overflow with strange and wonderful garbage, undreamed-of leftovers. The colonist's feet can never be glimpsed, except perhaps in the sea, but then you can never get close enough. They are protected by solid shoes in a sector where the streets are clean and smooth, without a pothole, without a stone. The colonist's sector is a sated, sluggish sector, its belly is permanently full of good things. The colonist's sector is a white folks' sector, a sector of foreigners.
> The colonized's sector, or at least the 'native' quarters, the shanty town, the Medina, the reservation, is a disreputable place, inhabited by disreputable people. You are born anywhere, anyhow. You die anywhere, from anything. It's a world with no space, people are piled one on top of the other, the shacks squeezed tightly together. The colonized's sector is a famished sector, hungry for bread, meat, shows, coal, and light. The colonized's sector is a sector that crouches and cowers, a sector on its knees, a sector that is prostrate. It's a sector of niggers, a sector of towelheads.
> This compartmentalized world, this world divided in two, is inhabited by different species.[43]
> [C]olonialism is not a machine capable of thinking, a body endowed with reason. It is naked violence and only gives in when confronted with greater violence.[44]

Admittedly, given the current exposure of colonial brutality, Fanon's description may not sound as shocking as it once was to the European readership. Yet, the even more deeply resounding and far-reaching shock-wave originates not from facing up to the extreme reality of appalling colonial cruelty, but from confronting Fanon's fundamental shift of what is normative of colonial reality. He awakens the world to realize that the horrifying state is not an aberrant by-product of European colonialism but a normative sequel, and thereby he re-evaluates the reality of colonial interactions and redefines the nature of colonialism.

---

[43] Fanon 1965: 3–5. [44] Fanon 1965: 23.

History of the Interaction between the Self and the Other 67

Fanon's rewriting of the history of colonialism is rooted in his switch of perspective from that of the colonizing European to that of the colonized non-European. While the object of investigation remains the same European colonialism, he relocates the position of the investigating subject Self to the colonized natives, as opposed to the colonizing Europeans, and correspondingly reorients the discourse. He still uses the dialectical framework between the Self and the Other to perceive colonialism, but flips it into one between the Indigenous victimized Self and the foreign exploiting Other:

> The ruling species is first and foremost the outsider from elsewhere, different from indigenous population, 'the others'.[45]
>
> On the logical plane, the Manichaeism of the settler produces a Manichaeism of the native. To the theory of the 'absolute evil of the native' the theory of the 'absolute evil of the settler' replies.[46]
>
> The wealth of the imperialist nation is also our wealth. ... Europe is literally the creation of the Third World.[47]

Fanon's very rewriting of colonialism from the perspective of the colonized Self, instead of the colonizer Self, is rightly seen as an effort to write new history against the hegemonic Eurocentric historiography. Well aware that history of the colonized is imprisoned by Eurocentric historiography, he cries out for its liberation:

> The colonist makes history. His story is an epic, an odyssey. He is invested with the very beginning. ... Opposite him, listless beings wasted away by fevers and consumed by 'ancestral customs' compose a virtually petrified background to the innovative dynamism of colonial mercantilism.
>
> The colonist makes history and he knows it. And because he refers constantly to the history of his metropolis, he plainly indicates that here he is the extension of this metropolis. The history he writes is therefore not the history that he is despoiling, but the history of his own nation's looting, raping, and starving to death. The immobility to which the colonized is condemned can be challenged only when if he decides to put an end to the history of colonization and the history of despoliation in order to bring to life the history of the nation, the history of decolonization.[48]

From the viewpoint of the colonized Self, he envisions political decolonization as the ultimate solution to reclaim not only territories and properties illegitimately robbed from the colonizers, but also the history of the colonized likewise being subsumed under Eurocentric historiography. Fanon claims that only when the material reality of decolonization

[45] Fanon 1965: 5.   [46] Fanon 1965: 73.   [47] Fanon 1965: 58.   [48] Fanon 1965: 14–15.

is achieved can the decolonized build their own historical reality and write their own historical narrative. In other words, only through decolonization can they understand, write, and own their history: 'Decolonization, as we know, is an historical process: in other words, it can only be understood, it can only find its significance and become self-coherent insofar as we can discern the history-making movement which gives it form and substance'.[49]

With hindsight, it has now become clear that Fanon's solution did not work out despite his revolutionary perspectives and visions. Decolonization did not put an end to colonialist enslavement but led to even more impenetrable neo-colonialist and imperialist exploitation; nor did it dissolve Eurocentric historiography, but yielded many attempts to write history which in one way or another echo Eurocentrism.[50] With respect to Fanon's attempt, its limitation is rooted in the limitation of Marxism, which overarches not only the political but also the historiographical philosophy of Fanon. He believes that the decolonization movement on the national level will mobilize the people, arouse their consciousness, and write 'collective history into every consciousness'. On the international level he believes it is the only viable route to redistribute wealth across developed European countries and underdeveloped colonized countries.[51] He therefore argues that decolonization not only accords with Marxist values, but also is a prerequisite to realize its political-economic ideals beyond the immediate scope of Europe. Naturally, Fanon formulates a Marxist history which moves forward towards decolonization. While retaining the structure of Western Marxist historiography, such as dialectic, teleology, and totalization, Fanon rearranges their components into the dialectical relationship between the colonized non-European Self and the colonizing European Other, and the telos and totalization reached by decolonization and anti-colonialism. Fanon reverses the hierarchy within the same historiography but does not overthrow the Western historiography. On that account, Fanon may be subject to the same poststructuralist critique on Western historiography that it reduces discontinuities, differences, and dispersions and seeks to replace the European hegemonic and homogenizing historiography with another. Thus, for all his intellectual breakthroughs, Fanon did not succeed in writing alternative history and is more often labelled an anti-colonialist than a postcolonial intellectual.

[49] Fanon 1965: 2.
[50] Arif Dirklik explains the struggle of writing history that breaks away from Eurocentrism. Dirlik 1999.
[51] Fanon 1965: 51, 55.

Nevertheless, Bhabha pays due credit to Fanon. Bhabha acknowledges that Fanon, like anyone else, was affected by his surroundings and was shaped by the thoughts of his own time and space. The unstable transitional phase between colonization and decolonization, as well as the intellectual predominance of Marxism, has forged Fanon's thought. It has unavoidably confined Fanon to the shortcomings of his era and inclined him to challenge the colonial hierarchy instead of questioning the Eurocentric superstructural ideas of human and history. Bhabha urges us to read Fanon more closely, because even though Fanon did not spell it out or could not find the right words to express it, he reveals much more about colonial encounters than the much-emphasized dichotomy:

> His voice is most clearly heard in the subversive turn of a familiar term, in the silence of sudden rupture: 'The Negro is not. Any more than the white man.' The awkward division that breaks his line of thought keeps alive the dramatic and enigmatic sense of change. The familiar alignment of colonial subjects – Black/White, Self/Other – is disturbed with one brief pause and the traditional grounds of racial identity are dispersed, whenever they are found to rest in the narcissistic myth of negritude or white cultural supremacy.[52]

In a way, Bhabha attempts to measure the silent pause between Fanon's disrupted sentences, as Spivak encourages. However, Bhabha does not do so in order to retrieve the muted subaltern in history. Rather, he aims at not lingering on the history professed either by the colonizer or by the colonized any longer and at moving *beyond*, not *after*, colonial historiography towards a postcolonial one.

Colonialist history revolves around the theme of civilization, and anti-colonialist history around that of exploitation. Bhabha instead advances ambivalence as one of the keys to postcolonial history. He suggests that neither ignoring the colonial past nor inverting the colonial hierarchy paves the way to move beyond a Eurocentric historiography, since both approaches, which circumvent the fundamental question of Eurocentric humanism and history, are either implicitly or explicitly haunted by Eurocentrism. Constantly revisiting colonial history and persistently questioning the Eurocentric historiography alone will lead to a new history, according to Bhabha: 'Remembering Fanon is a process of intense discovery and disorientation. Remembering is never a quiet act of introspection and retrospection. It is a painful re-membering, a putting together of the dismembered past to make sense of the trauma of the present'.[53] What he

---

[52] Bhabha 2004c: 40.   [53] Bhabha 2004c: 63.

discovers from revisiting Fanon's *The Wretched of the Earth* is that the Other as an object of colonial discourse was not constructed and stereotyped by immediate recognition and following rejection of difference from the subject Self. On the contrary, ambivalence between desire and fear towards the Other, ambivalence between identification with and alienation from the Other, and ambivalence between assertion and anxiety about the Self's origin and identity compared with that of the Other constantly vacillate in the colonial discourse of the Self and the Other. 'What [Fanon] achieves,' Bhabha believes, 'is something far greater: for in seeing the phobic image of the Negro, the native, the colonized, deeply woven into the psychic pattern of the West, he offers the master and slave a deeper reflection of their interpositions, as well as the hope of a difficult, even dangerous, freedom'.[54] Bhabha captures moments of ambivalence not only from Fanon but also from Said. Said defends the internal coherence of Orientalist discourse according to the European power and its régime of truth. Yet, Bhabha points out that Said's Orientalism also fluctuates between 'the *content* of Orientalism as the unconscious repository of fantasy, imaginative writings and essential ideas; and the *form* of Orientalism as the historically and discursively determined, diachronic aspect'. 'Manifest and latent Orientalism', in Said's terminology, is tentatively unified by Said, as long as he assumes that European power enforces itself with an unequivocal singular mind.[55]

Bhabha calls attention to Fanon's psychoanalysis of ambivalent desires permeating both the colonizing European and the colonized non-European: the colonizers want the colonized to emulate them but still want to distinguish themselves from the colonized and desire to cultivate but enslave them, whereas the colonized want to imitate the colonizers but still want to overthrow them and desire to mimic but deride them.[56] Ambivalence pervades the colonial interaction. There is no clarity, coherence, or distinctiveness to define the Self from the Other and the Other from the Self and to explain the power and régime of truth governed by whoever the Self or the Other is. Bhabha maintains that the ambivalence that prevails in the colonial interaction is why colonial discourse betrays its ambivalent state between control and anxiety, between desire and fear, and heads towards conflicting directions, integration and separation.[57] The age-old dialectics of colonial discourse between the Self and the Other, between the Subject and the Object, and between the European and the

---

[54] Bhabha 2004c: 90.   [55] Bhabha 2004f.   [56] Bhabha 2004f; Fanon 1965, 1986.
[57] Bhabha 2004e.

non-European have been reinforced only through discursive repetition over time and are somewhat symptomatic of obsessive anxiety about internal contradictions. Bhabha contends that ambivalence exposes and dissolves these dialectics.

If ambivalence can disperse the dialectics between the Self and the Other in colonial discourse by revealing their internal splits and contradictions, Bhabha convinces us that hybridity can destabilize the system of colonial power-knowledge. When Said argued that the basis of colonial discourse is the Eurocentric dialectic between the powerful Western Self and the powerless Eastern Other, which is supported by European colonial power, he was criticized for reifying the polarity and the hegemony of Eurocentric discourse, for locking himself up in the Eurocentric power-knowledge, and for 'reproduc[ing] what he has characterized as the limitations of his object'.[58] In other words, Said does not suggest a way out of the Orientalist dilemma. Bhabha, on the other hand, proposes hybridity as a key to unlock the Eurocentric hegemony of power-knowledge. To begin with, hybridity is not a euphemistic or naïve tactic to bridge the Self and the Other or to resolve tension in peaceful cohabitation. Instead, the hybrid embodies ambivalences of both the colonizer and the colonized:

> Produced through a strategy of disavowal, the *reference* of discrimination is always a process of splitting as the condition of subjection: a discrimination between mother culture and its bastards, the self and its doubles, where the trace of what is disavowed is not repressed but repeated as something *different* – a mutation, a hybrid. It is such a partial and double force that is more that the mimetic but less than symbolic, that disturbs the visibility of colonial presence and makes the recognition of its authority more problematic.[59]
>
> [C]olonial hybridity is not a *problem* of genealogy or identity between two cultures which can then be resolved as an issue of cultural relativism. Hybridity is a problematic of colonial representation and individuation that reverses the effects of colonial disavowal, so that the other 'denied' knowledges enter upon the dominant discourse and estrange the basis of its authority – its rules of recognition.[60]

Hybridity does not echo Eurocentrism by simply inverting the Eurocentric power-knowledge hierarchy, but reflects the ambivalence within the Eurocentric system of power-knowledge back to European colonizers and subverts the authority of Eurocentrism. In other words, hybridity undermines Eurocentrism by using its system of power-knowledge

---

[58] Young 1990: 197. [59] Bhabha 2004g: 159. [60] Bhabha 2004g: 162.

partially or distortedly against the very idea of Eurocentrism itself. Being a different strategy from using the master's tool to dismantle the master's house, hybridity inevitably transforms the nature of colonial discourse. There is no pure history in accordance with Eurocentric power and knowledge or with nativist power and knowledge. 'To the extent to which discourse is a form of defensive warfare, mimicry marks those moments of civil disobedience within the discipline of civility: signs of spectacular resistance. Then the words of master become the site of hybridity – the warlike, subaltern sign of the native – then we may not only read between lines but even seek to change the often coercive reality that they so lucidly contain'.[61]

Now, let us return to the original question: can we write history alternative to colonialist/imperialist history? Fanon attempts to write anti-colonialist/nativist history and Bhabha hybrid history. Both start challenging the Eurocentric discourse of history by examining the interaction between the Self and the Other, between the European and the non-European, and between the colonizer and the colonized. They reveal that the colonial encounter, contrary to the claims of the colonizers and/or colonized, has contaminated the identity and epistemology of each and has undermined the hierarchical dialectic, and, as a result, they invert or subvert the Eurocentric power-knowledge and historiography. Yet, both of them constantly receive criticism from various perspectives and do not provide the ultimate answer to alternative historiography. In fact, postcolonial studies bearing poststructuralist thought does not seek to replace one hegemonic historiography with another, but believes in multiple and different histories and historiographies. In that sense, Bhabha certainly provides one new way to write history.

Appendix 2: Postcolonialism *à la française*

In the second half of the twentieth century, views on postcolonialism in the French intellectual world swung from one extreme to another. Some accused French intellectuals and scholars of being entrenched in French exceptionalism to haughtily reject new ideas, whilst others regarded their disapproval of postcolonialism as a form of resisting Anglo-American hegemony that threatens to subsume French intellectual tradition and discourse. What can be agreed upon amidst the heated debates surrounding postcolonialism in France is that postcolonial thoughts are yet to set

[61] Bhabha 2004g: 172.

Appendix 2: Postcolonialism à la française

foot in mainstream French intellectual discourse or academia. Jean-Marc Moura sketches out the situation: '"with the exception of scholars who work in English studies departments", *most* French scholars *do* think postcolonialism is just a vague, liberal, politically correct movement that is uncritically in favour of multiculturalism [emphasis in the original]'.[62] Although postcolonial studies has been unfavourably received in France, particularly metropolitan France, there was an unexpected incident to change the mood at the turn of the century. The promulgation of the so-called Law of 23 February 2005 led to a watershed moment for postcolonial thought in France. Eventually repealed, Article 4 of the law stipulated: 'Les programmes scolaires reconnaissent en particulier le rôle positif de la présence française outre-mer, notamment en Afrique du Nord et accordent à l'histoire et aux sacrifices de l'armée française issus de ces territoires la place éminente à laquelle ils ont droit'.[63] Under the banner of 'liberté pour l'histoire', a number of distinguished French historians petitioned against the law mainly to defend academic freedom in history against any official history sponsored by the state. However, the controversy sparked by the new legislation took a twist and brought colonial and postcolonial issues to public attention. This law did not succeed at garnering support for the liberté pour l'histoire movement to safeguard academic freedom, but instead provided impetus for growing interest in postcolonialism in French academia. For example, *La fracture coloniale : la société française au prisme de l'héritage colonial*, a collective work edited by Pascal Blanchard, Nicolas Bancel, and Sandrine Lemaire and published in 2005, became a key focus of these fresh interests.[64] Furthermore, in 2006, an international conference titled 'Que faire des postcolonial studies?' was held at Science-Po, one of the grandes écoles, and one of the most prestigious intellectual hubs in France.[65] Soon '*le postcolonialisme*' and '*les postcolonial studies* (or *les études postcoloniales*)' entered the franglais lexicon.

Nevertheless, Charles Forsdick and David Murphy warn that 'it is misguided to dismiss embryonic postcolonial debates in France as pale imitations of their Anglophone counterparts'.[66] The lack of an original label derived from the inner recesses of French academia or an established

---

[62] Moura 2008: 263.
[63] 'The school programmes recognize in particular the positive role of the French overseas presence, notably in North Africa and deservedly give a prominent place to its history and to the sacrifices of French army soldiers from these territories' (translation by the present author).
[64] Blanchard, Bancel, and Lemaire 2005. Their trilogy encompassing French colonial and postcolonial history was influential: Blanchard and Lemaire 2003, 2004, 2006.
[65] Smouts 2007.   [66] Forsdick and Murphy 2009: 8.

discipline in France does not necessarily suggest absence of discourse on the colonial past and legacy. Rather, the pitfall here would be to impose the Anglo-American model of postcolonial thought to measure and analyse French thought without taking into account French social, political, and historical contexts and to deny the particularity of French discourse in this field. For our purpose at least, it is vital to understand postcolonial thought in France in the form of 'travelling ideas' and to recognize that the trajectory of French discourse took a course and a pace quite different from that of Anglo-American discourse. Let us first consider French dimensions of postcolonial discourse – in other words how social, political, and historical factors shaped French postcolonial discourse.

The prevalent French opinion of postcolonialism is, first of all, that it is foreign, that is, Anglo-American, not French. Although French schools of thought – exoticism, anti-colonialism, post-structuralism, Négritude movement, and Francophone studies – have continuously contributed to and engaged with postcolonialism, it is too readily evoked as a threat against French republicanism. The 'Anglo-Saxon communitarian model' of postcoloniality is often mentioned as a model antithetical to the French republican tradition: Margaret A. Majumber discredits it as a vague 'ideological construct … [to reassert] the primacy of "French" Republican values'.[67] Bancel and Blanchard portray the general atmosphere whereby '[t]o brandish the republican flag each time the colonial question is raised is symptomatic of the deliberately muddled thinking that attempts to shut down the debate'.[68] Furthermore, Forsdick and Murphy identify 'a certain French style of commentary … regarding commodification of difference [and] the distinction between universality and singularity' to target arguments and ideas which might potentially undermine republican ideals.[69] The other side of the coin regarding French resistance to postcolonialism is that its supporters likewise too quickly reduce French criticisms of postcolonialism to staunch and uncritical republicanism. The narrow focus of criticism from each side has disposed the debate towards a rigid dichotomy between Anglo-Saxon multiculturalist postcolonialism and French universalist republicanism. Therefore, unsurprisingly, the tension between postcolonialism and republicanism has become quintessential to the French postcolonial debate.

Accordingly, postcolonial studies *à la française* focuses on exposing schizophrenic symptoms built in the tension between French republican and

[67] Majumdar 2007: 221, 25.   [68] Bancel and Blanchard 2009: 303.
[69] Forsdick and Murphy 2009: 13.

Appendix 2: Postcolonialism à la française

colonial discourse.[70] Foremost, the contradiction concerning the Other, which French discourse exposes, is critical. The doctrine of assimilationist universalism, which advocated equality of rights and meritocracy for all in principle, led in practice to the rejection of cultural relativism and differences. The differences of the Other were suppressed in the public sphere and politics but instead found their outlets for expression in the private sphere and particularly in artistic and cultural productions. They were depoliticized mainly through aesthetic exoticization and fed the long tradition of French exoticism, which extends from the Near East, Africa, and the Far East to America and can be traced back to the early nineteenth century, as epitomized by Eugène Delacroix's violent and eroticized Oriental paintings, and up to contemporary *beur* literature and *raï* music. Essentially, French exoticism, as Majumdar points out, 'form[ed] a counterbalancing weight to the undifferentiating discourse of Republicanism, or, to use another metaphor, the other side of the Republican coin'.[71] However, postcolonial thinkers further highlight that the republican contradiction concerning the Other – universalist yet exotic and attractive yet uncivilized – has downplayed the French imperialism and Eurocentrism built into such contradiction. For example, the notorious 1931 *Exposition coloniale* at Vincennes, particularly the human zoo, was evidently not an aesthetic exoticism to celebrate diversity but an imperialist exoticism to glorify French power and civilization and to subjugate the Other. Therefore, the contradiction regarding the Other is more complex than conflicts between hierarchical binaries, the superior subject Self versus the inferior object Other, as commonly found in the Anglo-American debate. Rather, revolving around the three axes of republicanism, exoticism, and imperialism, the French debate concerning the Other is even more complex: 'the (anti-colonialist) denunciation of the exotic as ossified tradition; the exotic as defining an anti-hegemonic position; and the assertion of universalism as overriding, but also containing, the exotic'.[72] The contradictory dimensions of the Other in French discourse have thus challenged French intellectuals to forge a consistent postcolonial conception of the Other.

The complex and often paradoxical relationship between republicanism and the Other has further underpinned French anticolonial and postcolonial discourse. When the exotic, colonized Other strived for liberation from French imperial power, it demanded republican rights from the French republic itself, undermined French republicanism with its own republican ideologies, and articulated its beliefs for independence with

---

[70] Majumdar describes contradictions in French discourse as 'schizophrenia'. Majumdar 2007: 10–13.
[71] Majumdar 2007: 216.   [72] Yee 2009: 186.

republican vocabulary. In other words, the elite of the colonized Other internalized and inverted republican ideologies enough to expose the hypocrisy of French republicanism and to develop anticolonial struggle, as well as *la francophonie*, based on republican ideals.[73] Even though they themselves embodied the failure and paradox of French Republicanism, their belief in the republican ideal was often steadfast. Following the independence of colonies, the contradiction no longer remained only offshore in ex-colonies or overseas territories, but also emerged as a pressing issue in metropolitan France. When the exotic Other from the former colonies was granted French citizenship de jure, becoming a French citizen de facto was merely a mirage. A series of riots led by deprived ethnic minorities erupted in French *banlieues* in the 2000s, and the gulf between ideal and reality became an inescapable domestic problem. 'La *citoyenneté paradoxale*, une citoyenneté *colorée*... (être citoyen et colonisé)', Françoise Vergès explains, 'est un symptôme de cette relation qui produit inclusion *et* exclusion. La citoyenneté, l'égalité, la fraternité sont infléchis : citoyens mais colonisés, égaux mais pas complètement, frères mais petits frère [emphasis in original]'.[74] The urgency of problems rooted in the paradox of republicanism in the Hexagon has provoked a recent surge of interest in postcolonialism. Many French intellectuals attempted to comprehend the disintegration of contemporary French society despite the republican ideal and to discover underlying causes in the colonial past, thus giving wide currency to the arguments set forth in *La fracture coloniale* by Blanchard, Bancel, and Lemaire. However, the original raison d'être of postcolonial studies in Anglo-American discourse – to bring the hegemony of Eurocentric epistemology into crisis – did not succeed in gaining firm ground across the Channel in French discourse. Criticisms regarding the paradox in French republicanism, the gap between its ideal and reality, and the ensuing social problems did not result in a critical challenge to republicanism itself, that is, the Eurocentric foundation of republicanism.

Similarly, postcolonial studies *à la française* reveals the schizophrenic symptom built into French historiography in the republican tradition as well, but has yet to question the very essence of republicanism. The starkest contradiction underscored by postcolonial intellectuals in French historiography is a strong tendency to remember and, at the same time, to forget. In

---

[73] Majumdar 2007: 12–13.
[74] '*Paradoxical citizenship*, a *coloured* citizenship (being a citizen and colonized) is a symptom of this relationship which produces inclusion and exclusion. Citizenship, equality, fraternity are inflected: citizens but colonized, equal but not completely, brothers but little brothers'. Vergès 2005: 73 (translation by the present author).

particular, the post-Second World War zeitgeist following the shame of the Vichy régime crystallized into attempts to rebuild and reconstruct French republican memory and heritage while downplaying or muffling any potential disruptions of the republican narrative, most notably at the cost of French colonial history. 'Vichy syndrome' – a term coined by Henry Rousso to illustrate the French postwar preoccupation and anxiety about the Vichy collaboration – in short, encouraged a resurgence in republicanism, overshadowed other significant contemporary issues, and therefore obfuscated colonial history from mainstream discourse and consciousness.[75] Pierre Nora's monumental *Les lieux de mémoire* notably exemplifies this.[76] A grand collection of 133 articles in seven volumes compiled from contributions by many eminent historians and intellectuals contends that the postwar French state took control of *mémoire patrimoniale* (heritage memory) by means of public monuments and commemorations and 'reinforce[d] "a certain idea of France"'.[77] The vast anthology did not draw upon any legacy of French imperialism, except one article by Charles-Robert Ageron that touches upon the 1931 Exposition coloniale.[78]

The virtual silence on the colonial past betrays that there exists a suppressed dark side of republican heritage memory which is equally substantial: what is not celebrated in public monuments and commemorations, what is forgotten from heritage memory, and what is excluded from French national consciousness. Recently, the paradox between collective memory and collective amnesia of the past has posed pertinent questions to French scholarship. French intellectuals have 'questioned the validity of the argument that claims that some things are best forgotten in the name of national reconciliation'.[79] Furthermore, Marc Ferro calls out the issue as '*les tabous de l'histoire*' and warns of its gravity:

> On peut faire le parallèle avec les manuels scolaire japonais, où pratiquement tout est faux, car ces ouvrages reposent sur un système de légitimation de la tradition impériale. Encore, aujourd'hui, il est très difficile au Japon de réviser cette histoire, car toutes les élites ont baigné dans ces visions apologétiques. C'est un peu la même chose en France en ce qui concerne la colonisation, ce qui rend difficile l'approche de l'histoire coloniale dans sa complexité, même si l'anticolonialisme constitue l'une des familles de pensée les plus anciennes dans ce pays.[80]

---

[75] Rousso 1991.   [76] Nora 1984.   [77] Vergès 1999.   [78] Ageron 2005.
[79] Majumdar 2007: 180.
[80] 'One can draw a parallel with Japanese school textbooks, where practically everything is false, because these works are based on a system of legitimization of the imperial tradition. Even today, it is very difficult in Japan to revise this history, because all the elites have been immersed in these

Even when French intellectuals address the schizophrenic attitudes towards colonial history, commemorating French imperial grandeur while overlooking anti-colonial movements and, notably, Haitian independence, they portray the contradiction as the historical fracture disintegrated from *Histoire* with a capital H. Hence, they urge a reintegration of fragmented histories and memories and a restoration of the grand narrative of *Histoire de la France*. This indicates that the underlying assumption about *Histoire* as universal progress in the *longue durée* remains largely unchallenged, which the popularity of *La fracture coloniale* by Blanchard, Bancel, and Lemaire also demonstrates. Yet, Margaret Majumdar further argues that the contradiction in French historiography is rooted in deeper and more complex tensions between republicanism and history which is particular to the French context:

> There is one further contradiction in French Republican ideology that needs to be tabled at this stage. This concerns the contradiction within the notion of history itself, which has assumed such importance in the legitimation of the French state. History, usually written with a capital H in French, provides the material for the foundation of the French Republic. As such, it relies heavily on the notion of tradition; *la tradition républicaine* ('the Republican tradition') is one of the stock-in-trade phrases of French political discourse. Yet, at the heart of this 'tradition', indeed as its founding principle, one finds a basic discontinuity, a rupture with the past, dramatised in the French Revolution. On the one hand, this is the modernist notion of history as progress, looking to the future; on the other, the historical legitimacy of the French state relies on its root in the past. The ambivalence implicit in the notion of history has been further accentuated in recent years by an increased importance given to the notions of memory and heritage, particularly in connection with issues of national identity. The future project contained in the Revolutionary view of history has largely disappeared from the mainstream political discourse.[81]

The internal paradox of *Histoire à la tradition républicaine* is articulated as a universally progressive vision harking back to the fragmented past. Nonetheless, some critical questions are yet to be raised, which include Eurocentric definition of universal progress, republicanism, and therefore of history. For the moment, the postcolonial history project *à la française* focuses on recovering the forgotten and erased parts of history and

---

apologetic visions. It's a bit similar in France with regard to colonization, which makes it difficult to approach colonial history in its complexity, even if anti-colonialism constitutes one of the oldest families of thought in this country.' Ferro 2005: 132 (translation by the present author).

[81] Majumdar 2007: 28.

restoring history from the schizophrenic realities of republicanism. But it is another matter altogether whether the retrieved histories will lead French historians to challenge the Eurocentric notion of history and republicanism in future.

A final schizophrenic symptom of French republican discourse raised by postcolonial studies *à la française* is its contradictory claim to universalism and multiculturalism on a global plane. The core claim of French language, culture, and republicanism has been universalism. However, from the 1990s onwards, a new twist on strategies to advance French influence has been adopted. The new approach promoted French language and culture as a significant counterweight to the dominance of Anglo-American influence, in other words homogenization under the English language, American popular culture, and mass consumerism, and as the best avenue to stimulate diversity in Anglo-American-led globalization. Mujumdar points out that 'the French language began to be portrayed, not just for its universality, but more specifically for its equality and appeal to the elite of the French-speaking world as the "language of the culture", by which was meant a highbrow, intellectual culture, far removed from the popular mass culture of the "Anglo-Saxons"'.[82] Branding itself as a token of intellectual culture, French language and culture adopted a niche-marketing strategy on the global stage, notwithstanding its claim to universalism. Likewise, the Francophone movement, which used to give prominence to universality in different corners of Francophone countries, shifted its emphasis to celebrating linguistic and cultural diversity. The new direction was to transfer its focus away from forming a meaningless rivalry with Anglo-American influence towards further championing French influence as a leading force to achieve global diversity in the face of global uniformity. 'Then', in Majumdar's analysis, '*Francophonie* was increasingly represented not just as the champion of the French language and culture alone, but as a major global site for the defence of cultural and linguistic diversity worldwide. No longer was it a case of French against English, or even French (high) culture against American dumbing-down. *Francophonie* now adopted a more pluralist line, in which the right of all languages and cultures to exist in a celebration of multilingualism and cultural diversity'.[83] The Francophone movement's new slogan, 'Unity in Diversity', betrayed an effort to bring contradictory concepts of French republican discourse into uneasy coexistence.

---

[82] Majumdar 2007: 167.   [83] Majumdar 2007.

The three principal themes which create contradictions with republicanism – exoticism, collective amnesia, and multiculturalism – underpin the postcolonial debate in France. There is certainly a risk involved in prematurely capturing a landscape overview of fledgling studies with ongoing attempts to answer questions and resolve inconsistencies. There is also a danger in oversimplifying the complexity and diversity of the French debate into the conflict with republicanism. Nonetheless, it is important for the purpose of our study to understand the different trajectory and pace of postcolonial studies *à la française*. The widespread scepticism towards postcolonialism in France, and particularly towards the Anglo-American model of multiculturalist postcolonialism, is unmistakable. Jean-Francois Bayart's fierce indictment of postcolonial studies is indicative of the general sentiment, derived from a cocktail of peripheral exposure to, and misunderstanding of, postcolonial theories: 'La révolution copernicienne qu'entendaient incarner les *postcolonial studies* est encore devant nous. Si l'on veut comprendre l'historicité propre des sociétés en s'émancipant de l'« historicisme » de l'*épistème* occidentale – et jamais cette tâche n'a été aussi impérative –, il faut d'abord libérer nos problématiques de l'interaction coloniale dans laquelle elles persistent à les consigner [emphasis in original]'.[84] However, it was not the case that all French intellectuals dismissed the merits of postcolonial studies that had developed in the Anglo-American context wholesale. It was clear that some intellectuals strived to shape their own strands of thought applicable to the French context, where frequently they posed key questions with regard to republicanism from a postcolonial perspective in order to expose internal paradoxes of republicanism.

As French intellectuals grapple with defining and understanding postcolonialism vis-à-vis republicanism, it may be premature to pass judgment on French intellectuals for being too insulated or arrogant, as some do. Nonetheless, it is clear that the key objective of postcolonial studies to bring Eurocentric epistemology into crisis has not yet been assertively voiced. Thus far, French intellectuals have attempted to deconstruct republican discourse within the same Eurocentric system of power-knowledge. Their efforts in this sense echo poststructuralism and hold the same limitations of being enclosed in Eurocentrism.

---

[84] 'The Copernican revolution that postcolonial studies intended to embody is still before us. If one wants to understand the specific historicity of societies by emancipating ourselves from the "historicism" of the Western episteme – and this task has never been so imperative – we must first free our problems from the colonial interaction in which they persist in confining them.' Bayart 2011: 97 (translation by the present author).

CHAPTER 3

Postcolonial Questions in the Age of Decolonization

The lingering shadow of Western imperial glory that had endured up until the early twentieth century plunged into turbulent uncertainty in the midtwentieth century. A series of events irrevocably redrew the global political, social, and economic landscape. High hopes fuelled by British and American territorial expansion, political dominance, and economic growth no longer deluded the new generation in the face of the Great Depression, the Second World War, and decolonization. The United States of America survived the turmoil to become one of the leading world powers of the Cold War, leaving Europe behind in the shadows of bygone glory. Nevertheless, it became undeniable that Western values and thoughts cradled in Europe also reached a crisis in the United States. Mounting doubts about traditional Western values and ideals made a sea change in the intellectual landscape unavoidable. Meanwhile, Marxism became a buzzword that uniquely penetrated the era. In one form or another (e.g. orthodox, derivative, or reactionary), it swept across Europe and America. In academia, it contributed to the rise of social sciences established by the triad of Karl Marx, Max Weber, and Émile Durkheim. As for the discipline of history, their rise, in turn, steered mainstream studies away from political history to social and economic history. Focus was drawn to social structures and economic forces, and methodologies were borrowed from various disciplines within the social sciences, such as sociology, economics, and anthropology, to name but a few. In particular, Marxism as well as the Annales school and the cliometrics revolution stood out as influential intellectual movements to drive the scholarship of history to this new stage.[1] Among many works composed during the period,

---

[1] The cliometrics revolution, which began in the late 1950s and early 1960s in America, had a decisive impact on economic history. Landmark works in cliometrics, also known as 'The New Economic History', include: Meyer and Conrad 1957; Fogel 1974; North 1990. For further insight into the influence of cliometrics on the scholarship of Roman history, see Hobson 2018.

E. P. Thompson's *The Making of the English Working Class* in 1963 was hailed as the *pièce de résistance* of the historical scholarship of the era.[2] The impact of Marxism on the Anglo-American sphere was less extensive in comparison with most other Western countries, but Marxism's grand theories in the academic world and Marxist student revolts in universities still had a profound impact on the Anglo-American intellectual world. Many professional academic historians in tumultuous universities believed that their role was to intellectually lead 'the age of revolution' and decisively restructure the field of modern history along the tenets of Marxist historiography.

Not only these external changes, but internal changes within the discipline also played their parts in shaping the course of diffusion of travelling ideas. Particularly in the postwar Anglo-American academia, interconnected and ultimately inseparable processes of professionalization, democratization, and marginalization reconstructed the discipline of Roman history. Professionalization, which had begun during the first half of the twentieth century, intensified in the second half, and the distinction between gentleman/politician scholars and professional academics, which had been rather negligible, became more substantial as the discipline was increasingly professionalized. As more professionally trained classicists, historians, and archaeologists moved away from general studies to specialized areas of research, they found their academic positions and research bases in institutions other than Oxford or Cambridge, such as University College London, King's College London, Durham University, the University of St Andrews, and American universities. This diminished the dominance of Oxonian Classics in Roman history and gradually democratized the culture of the discipline. For instance, the Society for the Promotion of Roman Studies (The Roman Society) and its *Journal of Roman Studies*, which in effect had been an extension of Oxford Classics until the first half of the twentieth century, started to attract diverse scholars from outside Oxford with the help of 'friendship between Hugh Last, Frank Adcock of Cambridge and Norman Baynes of London', and relocated its base from Oxford to Bloomsbury Square, London, in 1954.[3]

Yet, the decline of Oxford Classics turned out to be double-edged. It meant losing its privileged position not only to non-Oxford Classics, but also to other Oxford disciplines. In particular, Oxford's new programme entitled Philosophy, Politics, and Economics (commonly known as PPE) superseded the crucial role of educating and consolidating the elites in

---

[2] Thompson 1963.   [3] Stray 2010: 7.

Oxford and accelerated the marginalization of Classics and ancient history.[4] The marginalized position of Classics and ancient history within the socioeconomic and political strata inevitably repositioned Roman historians in the system as well. The old ties between imperial elites and Roman historians consolidated within Oxford became memories from the bygone golden age. As Roman scholars began to lose their privileged authority to educate and advise the elites, they found an acute need to promote Classics and ancient history and make the ancient world relevant to the modern public. The changed circumstances surrounding the scholarship, along with the overall wave of Marxism, contributed to shifting the next generation of scholars' historical interests and perspectives and, ultimately, to shaping the postwar historiography of Roman imperialism.

However, the scholarship of ancient history, as described previously, in general maintained some sceptical distance from the scholarship of modern history. Alston relates that the scholarship of ancient Roman history was prone to remain 'rather insular' from developing intellectual movements including Marxist historiography.[5] Differences not only in the subject matter, but also in their institutional tradition played a part in keeping this tendency. Many ancient historians voiced reservations about applying modern social sciences, arguing that the models designed to understand modern societies are often anachronistic and problematic when used to explain pre-modern societies. They instead adhered to the empiricist and/or antiquarian traditions, which continued from earlier generations. Moreover, the position of ancient history in academic institutions set ancient historians further apart from modern historians with regard to their intellectual environment. As Ian Morris points out, '[a]ncient historians are still found chiefly outside university history departments'. Somewhat awkwardly placed between Classics departments and history departments, depending on institution, ancient historians 'tend to go to different conferences than the ones attended by modern historians, to publish in different journals, and almost to speak a different language'. Patchy exposure to and communication with the currents in the scholarship of modern history unsurprisingly contributed to slowing down ancient historians from tuning into the rapidly changing intellectual climate of the time. 'As late as the 1970s, the vision of historiography as the handmaiden of philology still dominated the field'.[6] It is worth noting that Moses I. Finley's interests in social structures and economic forces,

---

[4] Stray 1998: 282–3.   [5] Alston 2001: 28.   [6] Morris 1999: xxiv–xxv.

which might appear unrevolutionary nowadays, were in fact not shared by many at the time.

Despite the delay in comparison with the scholarship of modern history, the intellectual shift propelled by Marxism eventually emerged in the scholarship of ancient history. It may sound obvious, but it is worth reminding readers briefly here that Anglo-American scholarship of our interest spans across the Atlantic. Thus far the main focus of the discussion has been scholarship in Britain, because Classics and ancient history in Britain, particularly at Oxford, dominated Anglo-American scholarship of the discipline until the first half of the twentieth century. However, since the discipline became democratized from the second half of the twentieth century, with many competing institutions, the scope is to be widened to include British and American scholarship. It would be fair to say that British and American institutions inherited and worked within more or less the same intellectual traditions of the discipline, since many British scholars moved and worked across the Atlantic. Yet, they were situated in different social, political, and historical realities and were exposed to different environmental factors, the most crucial of which was the understanding and application of Marxism. It provided a marked point of diversion between the courses of British and American scholarship.

Saller aptly describes the discipline of the time:

> To simplify, the politics in European classical historiography was organized around the axis of Marxism and its critics. In the Marxist historical-developmental scheme, of course, classical antiquity was characterized as dominated by the slave mode of production; consequently, the significance of slavery in antiquity became a central issue in the debate. As late as the 1980s, fierce arguments over the explanatory value of the slave mode of production for the decline of the Roman Empire were going on in England and on the Continent. In England the focal point was G. E. M. de Ste Croix's *Class Struggle in the Ancient Greek World* (1981).[7]

Under the sweeping influence of Marxism, many ancient historians turned their attention to slavery as a key to grasp ancient social and economic structures.[8] The counterpart to de Ste Croix's oeuvre in Roman history was Finley's *Ancient Economy*.[9] Finley was an American historian who was purged by the Red Scare and emigrated to Britain. But even during his

---

[7] Saller 1998: 226; De Ste. Croix 1981.
[8] There is an extensive bibliography on Roman slavery, but to name just a few works of the time: Finley 1960, 1983; Hopkins 1978; Bradley 1984, 1994.
[9] Finley 1973.

time in New York he maintained close relationships with the Frankfurt School in exile and was influenced by European historical theories. He did not explicitly give credit to Marxist historical thought in his works, but the influence was apparent.[10] He contended that the ancient economy was fundamentally different from the modern economy – not governed by a capitalistic mode of production. This so-called Finley's model of ancient economy was built upon the underlying current of structuralism underpinning Marxism. Marxism did not convert as many ancient Roman historians as modern historians, nor to the same degree, but gradually developed to form a strand of debate in the British scholarship of Roman history. By utilizing Marxist historical thought, Roman historians in turn redefined their own social and political position as intellectuals and professional historians. They, to a certain extent, began to move away from elitist classicists to social historians to join the wider intellectual discourse.

In the United States, by contrast, with Finley being exiled, McCarthyism effectively suppressed Marxist historical thought from taking roots in the scholarship of Roman history. It was not only in the scholarship of Roman history, but also in the overall intellectual world, that the Cold War and its proxy wars left little room for any studies evoking Marxism even slightly to be accepted in American academia. Nevertheless, American historians did not linger on the traditional elitist political history either. Instead, '[i]n the United States', Saller relates, 'contemporary political issues other than Marxism – especially problems of minority rights – have stimulated the most heated debates among classicists … The three political rights movements in the United States – feminism, the gay/lesbian activism, Afrocentrism – have inspired new histories that have challenged the standard narrative of American's European cultural heritage in different ways'.[11] Whereas feminism and LGBT activism kindled new interests in ancient Roman women and sexuality, Afrocentrism of the time stirred some to raise a fundamental question about Eurocentric historiography in Roman history. Martin Bernal's *Black Athena*, which argues that modern Eurocentrism obscured Afro-Asiatic influence, Egyptian and Phoenician, on ancient Greek civilization, became a phenomenon.[12] The controversy over *Black Athena* was international, but in the United States the political sensitivity concerning racism and Afrocentrism was so sharp that it politicized the debate. Mary Beard encapsulates the nature of the controversy: 'Almost equally politicised were debates in America over Bernal's *Black Athena*, with its claims for a black ancestry underlying

---

[10] Harris 2013b. [11] Saller 1998: 227, 32. [12] Bernal 1987.

achievements of classical Greek culture. This was ignored or suppressed by generations of western scholars. The question within the American academy is not just "Was Bernal correct?", but "How far were those who rejected Bernal's claims racist?".[13] Even though Bernal's claim was largely dismissed, the merit of his challenge to classical scholarship was still noted. He revealed that academic debates in Roman history are not simply about disputing historical facts, but are intrinsically linked with historical perspectives formed through contemporary social and political circumstances. Confronting normative perspectives rooted in classical scholarship, he challenged classicists and ancient historians to question their Eurocentric tradition. Hence, although not substantially moved by the role of Marxism in the intellectual mise en scène, Roman historians in the United States were compelled, in the face of contemporary multiculturalism in its various manifestations, to reconfigure the social and political positions implicit in their histories.

The wave of Marxism and multiculturalism surrounding the British and American intellectual world in the latter half of the twentieth century has left indelible marks on the classical scholarship of each country. It is undeniable that classical scholarship remained relatively entrenched in the empiricist and antiquarian traditions and was insulated from the new tides of modern theories, such as from the emerging disciplines of sociology or anthropology. '[B]y the late 1960s, social history had come to be an established and influential movement in the world of historical scholarship altogether' – except ancient Greek and Roman history.[14] Nevertheless, the marginalized position of classicists and ancient historians in the second half of the twentieth century gradually induced them to explore beyond their familiar comfort zone. It became difficult for classicists and ancient historians to identify themselves as gentlemen scholars embodying the elitist ideal rather than as professional academic historians in universities which were in the midst of social and political activism. Michael Peachin explains the late blooming of social history in Roman history from the 1970s: '[p]erhaps, then, it was the social ferment of the 1960s and early 1970s, more than scholarly trends in the wider field of history, that cause[d] Roman historians to turn toward society as an object of study. Be that as it may, the 1970s witnessed an explosion of interest in social-historical issues concerning the Roman world, and ever since, Roman society has been a focal point of vibrant research'.[15] The changing milieu surrounding the scholarship of Roman history steered historical interests and perspectives

---

[13] Mitra Das 2014. [14] Peachin 2011: 7. [15] Peachin 2011: 7.

from elite-driven political history to more everyday social history, including 'women, the family, slaves and freedmen, patronage, law and society, urbanism, leisure and entertainment, and so forth'.[16] The application of modern theories to Roman history in the second half of the twentieth century could be understood as part of a wider attempt to counter the elite-driven tradition in Roman history.

This process, nevertheless, did not simply result in a 'delayed' mirroring of the scholarship of modern history. Morris recounts that the internal politics in academic communities has shaped a distinct course of historiography for ancient history:

> Ancient historians effectively skipped the stage in the development of modern historiography when social and economic questions dominated the agenda and moved straight from philology and politics to cultural poetics. Most departments contain a substantial group of (now aging) radical economic and social historians hired in the 1970s and early 1980s who defend their turf against the cultural historians. The slow spread of ancient economic and social history, the small scale of most ancient history programs, and the demographic structure of the profession – which made 1970s and 1980s lean years for new appointments – combined to create a situation in which very few classics departments hired in social and economic history. One result of this dearth of social and economic historians is that the shift toward cultural history in classical studies has been defined not against social and economic history but against more traditional philological scholarship.[17]

In other words, while social and economic history was established securely enough to mobilize a new generation of cultural historians to critique its limits in the scholarship of modern history, social and economic historians of ancient history instead cooperated with cultural historians to carve out a share of mainstream discourse from the first generation of professional ancient historians.[18] Therefore, in the scholarship of ancient history, cultural history positioned itself as a branch or an extension of social history, rather than as its critique.[19] Not long after Marxism, the Annales school and the cliometrics revolution in social and economic studies entered the scholarship

---

[16] Peachin 2011: 11. [17] Morris 1999: xxv.
[18] Mikhail (Michael) I. Rostovzeff, a Russian émigré historian, was one of the pioneers of social and economic history in Anglo-American scholarship of Roman history. His magnum opus *The Social and Economic History of the Roman Empire*, first published in 1926 (Rostovzeff 1926), was at the crossroads between the tradition of composing a grand political narrative and the innovation of conducting an analysis of social and economic structures. Rostovtzeff 1926. On discussion of his legacy, see: Reinhold 1946; Momigliano 1966; Bowersock 1974; Potter 2006.
[19] Peachin 2011: 12.

of Roman history. Soon after, poststructuralism and postcolonialism, which became dominant movements in cultural studies, followed suit to penetrate Romanization studies.

The discourse on Romanization, accordingly, took a turn. Decades of effective hiatus in the wider scholarship brought by the Second World War, along with overall acceptance of Haverfield's paradigm of Romanization as an orthodoxy in the meantime (which works on Roman Britain and Romanization during the mid-twentieth century such as *Roman Britain* by Ian A. Richmond and *Britannia: A History of Roman Britain* by Sheppard Frere had consolidated) meant that rather an abrupt shift, instead of a gradual transition, followed.[20] The war took the lives of a generation of prospective young historians and archaeologists who would have shaped the course of historiography, and its aftermath irrevocably altered the historical perspective of survivors in many ways. Besides, generous funds from American institutions after the war, compared with their impoverished European counterparts, to a certain degree contributed to transferring the weight from Europe to America. American institutions attracted many European scholars and replaced European institutions in directing substantial archaeological projects.[21] Against the backdrop of overarching transformations, William V. Harris' *War and Imperialism in Republican Rome, 327 – 70 B.C.*, first published in 1979, became 'pivotal to this rejuvenation in interest'.[22] As Phillip W. M. Freeman observes, '[t]his debate originally concerned the Roman actions under the Republic, but its effects have had their consequences for the Principate and Roman provinces, their archaeology, and so Romanization studies'.[23] Harris' work, in a way, pulled the trigger for a new strand of discourse on Romanization that engaged with new intellectual movements of the time.

Influential thoughts from Marxism, the Annales school, and the cliometrics revolution to poststructuralism and postcolonialism subsequently travelled to and infiltrated Romanization studies. This not only helped to enrich the discourse, but it allowed the posing of meaningful questions. Applying contemporary studies on social structures, economic forces, and cultural politics, historians and archaeologists were able to gradually raise

---

[20] Richmond 1947; Frere 1967. During the mid-twentieth century, the questions that Collingwood raised mostly disappeared, and Romanization came to be understood as a natural progress of history.
[21] Dyson narrates how the Second World War had brought a generational void in scholarship, particularly of classical archaeology, and therefore had an impact on historiography. See Dyson 2006: 173–254.
[22] Harris 1979.   [23] Harris 1979: 27; Freeman 1997a.

questions concerning the traditional models of parallel discourse, defensive imperialism, and civilizing Romanization. Nonetheless, Romanization studies was yet to witness a breakthrough with regard to imperialist epistemology. Yet to challenge the underlying Western historiographical hegemony, the Romanization discourse largely preserved the backbone of traditional Western historiography and epistemology. An epistemological paradigm shift, or the Kuhnian Revolution, brought about by postcolonialism, was yet to be articulated in the Romanization discourse. Rather, it might have been the time when the Early Adopters, who started to tinker with the seed of postcolonial ideas, published a few key works that circulated the seed across the discourse. This chapter will discuss those key works of the Early Adopters to trace the course of postcolonial ideas that travelled to the Romanization discourse. It illustrates how the postwar generation of historians and archaeologists has enriched the Romanization discourse with social, economic, and cultural histories and started to question the imperialist epistemology upon which the discourse was built.

Othering Romans: Destabilizing the Parallel Discourse

The initial shift was not yet a shift from imperialist to postcolonial epistemology and history per se. Instead, it can be traced back to the Foucauldian epistemological shift which later formed a critical basis of postcolonialism, that is, a shift away from seeking historical truth, preordained by teleologies and totalizations, towards investigating historical discourses in order to explore alterity and heterogeneous meanings. The Early Adopters of the Foucauldian epistemological shift in the scholarship of Roman history internalized it and, in turn, prompted a kindred shift in Roman history, that is, Romans were not a historical parallel to the modern European Self, but rather the Other. Not every work of the Early Adopters addresses the issue of Romanization per se, but their destabilizing of the parallel discourse, deep-seated in the modern historiography of Roman history, made the first significant step towards making way for the postcolonial epistemological shift to take hold in the discourse on Romanization.

To follow how the Foucauldian epistemological shift came to initiate a shift in the paradigm of Romanization, we need to look into the work of the Early Adopters. One of the pioneering Early Adopters who articulated the otherness of Romans was Finley. Although nowadays honoured as one of the pillars in the scholarship of Roman history, he was an émigré iconoclast and an eclectic intellectual during his time. Many would agree that his intellectual journey tallies with Gladwell's description of Early Adopters:

'they were opinion leaders in the community, the respected, thoughtful people, who watched and analyzed what those wild Innovators were doing and then followed suit ... [They] are visionaries. They want revolutionary change, something that sets them apart qualitatively from their competitors'.[24] Indeed, engaging with extensive interdisciplinary intellectual innovations of the time, Finley broadened the scope of ancient history and ushered Roman history into the post-Foucauldian intellectual landscape.

Yet, before delving into Finley's well-recognized contribution, I would like to introduce one of the earlier and lesser-known pieces by Stephen L. Dyson, 'Native Revolts in the Roman Empire', published in 1971.[25] This particular piece, which does not always make an appearance in the bibliography on Romanization, may be an unexpected mention as one of the significant steps towards a shift in the understanding of Romanization. Although Dyson is a well-established and widely respected figure in American scholarship, it may still sound unusual to identify him as one of the Early Adopters, like Finley, who fits into Gladwell's description without question. He understandably lacked a background in Romanization studies which a defined group of Romano-British archaeologists and historians could claim in Anglo-American scholarship. Partly for that very reason, despite his article 'Native Revolts in the Roman Empire' being rather radical for the time, it has largely remained on the fringes of the mainstream discourse on Romanization, save for occasional mentions in References. Nevertheless, his article deserves fresh attention as one of the earliest attempts to destabilize the parallel discourse and to redefine Roman imperialism accordingly.

Dyson published his article in the early 1970s in Northeast America. At the time, within classical scholarship philology still prevailed, and outside scholarship people only started to question American exceptionalism and neo-colonialism during the Vietnam War. Dyson's approach, in fact, captures elements of the old and the new competing at the time. Dyson explores social, economic, and cultural aspects in accordance with the rising interest in these topics, but overall follows the literary tradition of narrative framework to chronicle the five revolts in the Roman Empire in the first part of his article.[26] In the second part, on the other hand, he diverges from the traditional framework and analyses the wider implication of revolts to re-evaluate Roman imperialism. The second part, in

---

[24] Gladwell 2000.   [25] Dyson 1971.
[26] Dyson acknowledges the importance of adapting to the changes brought by the social sciences; Dyson 1971: 274.

particular, is an innovative work for the time, but comprises seven rather short pages and remains underdeveloped. Having said that, the format and objective of Dyson's work was set out to discuss a narrowly defined subject; he addresses isolated events of five uprisings in the Western Roman Empire in thirty-five pages to point out a blind spot in the contemporary discourse on Roman imperialism and Romanization. Dyson's article does not aim to bring a full-scale paradigm shift, more to highlight this gap in Romano-centric perspectives.

Naturally, the question follows: what is the point of delving into Dyson's article 'Native Revolts in the Roman Empire'? What does he contribute to diffusing the poststructuralist and/or postcolonial seed of epistemological shift into the discourse on Romanization? Some might question why we look into Dyson's article instead of a more influential work of the time in American scholarship, for example Ramsay MacMullen's *Enemies of the Roman Order: Treason, Unrest, and Alienation in the Empire*, published in 1966.[27] Indeed, it would be fair to acknowledge that Dyson to a certain extent owes an intellectual debt to MacMullen's reconceptualization of Roman power relations: that the Roman system of power involves both power and resistance. Although MacMullen mainly recounts the parallel vulgarization of Roman power and resistance from top to bottom of the ladder of power, his underlying notion of power and resistance that chimes with that of Foucault's theory on power relations shifted understanding of Roman power relations. Nevertheless, it was Dyson who extended the Foucauldian idea of power and resistance into the understanding of Roman *imperial* power relations in order to destabilize the parallel discourse. He brings not only the colonizing Romans but also the colonized natives under the power network of Roman imperialism and, thus, inscribes not only the history of the conquering Romans but also that of the rebelling natives into Roman historiography. The colonialist dialectical framework between the colonizing Romans and the colonized natives undeniably governs Dyson's narrative. Yet, his article merits our attention because the blind spot that Dyson diagnoses still haunts us to this day as a blind spot in the discourse on Romanization. He maintains the binary perspective; however, he inverts it and exposes that the Romano-centric parallel discourse has dominated the discourse on Roman imperialism and Romanization.

Albeit limited to the five instances of riots, Dyson sheds new light on Romanization from a radically different perspective – neither of the colonizing Romans nor of the submitting natives nor of the cooperating

---

[27] MacMullen 1966.

local elites – in other words, the Romano-centric perspective – but of the rebelling natives.[28] He flips the dialectical relationship and assumes the perspective of the colonized and insubordinate natives to reorient the history of Roman imperialism and Romanization. In this sense, it is not entirely unfeasible to consider that Dyson chimes with Fanon in his anti-colonial writings. To write the history of Roman imperialism and Romanization, Dyson does not assume the point of view of Caesar and other Roman generals to trace their triumphs and their setbacks, but reverses the point of view to that of Vercingetorix, Bato the Daesitiatian, Arminius, Boudicca, and Julius Civilis. Like Fanon, he still uses the dialectical relationship but repositions the investigating subject Self to the indigenous colonized British, Gallic, or Germanic Self in relation to the foreign colonizing Roman Other. Then, he integrates ambitions and compromises of the colonized Self into the history of Roman imperialism and Romanization.[29] For instance, Dyson overturns Vercingetorix from an unenlightened agitator to the Roman civilizing mission to a shrewd leader defeated by the Roman military might:

> Vercingetorix would seem to display qualities that allow him to be typed as this kind of charismatic leader.... [H]e came from a distinguished family, but had not apparently played a major role previously in the anti-Roman resistance. Suddenly he emerges as the leader of a rebellion that sweeps much of Gaul and threatens to topple Roman domination ... Romans were massacred and soon the whole country was engulfed by rebellion. Only Caesar's rapid return and some desperate military action saved the situation.[30]

Dyson's inversion of perspective unmasks the identification that has been hitherto taken for granted. The historiography of Roman imperialism and Romanization has so far defaulted to identifying with the colonizing Romans as the Self and with the colonized natives as the Other. Despite the conflicting patriotism to manoeuvre the stigma of conquest from ancient Britons, Gauls, and Germans, the overriding identification with the so-called civilizing force of Romans as the Self has sustained the discourse on Roman imperialism and Romanization in Western scholarship. Like Fanon, without any theoretical basis of poststructuralism or postcolonialism, Dyson brings in the colonized Other to the discourse on

---

[28] Outside Anglo-American scholarship, Marcel Bénabou most notably brought resistance to the forefront of studies on Roman imperialism and Romanization. He conceives of Roman culture as a product of dialectical force between Romanization and Resistance: Bénabou 1976.
[29] These include 'the revolt of Vercingetorix, the Pannonian-Dalmatian revolt, the revolt of Arminius, the revolt of Boudicca and the Batavian revolt'. Dyson 1971: 239.
[30] Dyson 1971: 247, 249.

Othering Romans: Destabilizing the Parallel Discourse 93

Roman imperialism and Romanization and pioneers postcolonial writing of Roman history.

In addition, bringing the five cases of rebellion in the western part of the Roman Empire together into a comparative study, Dyson contends that these incidents are by no means isolated events, which modern scholars often characterize them as in order to demonstrate national spirit and to preserve national pride.[31] As he stresses, 'they have generally been considered in the individual context of particular provinces, which has often led to a nationalistic or partly nationalistic interpretation. Comparative study is necessary to change this tendency and allow these movements to be seen as the outcome of a more general social development.' Comparing the five examples of revolts, he concludes that there is an identifiable pattern that is shared not only with the Roman provincial revolts but also with the modern colonial equivalents. Both in ancient and modern imperialism, a new generation of the colonized population, who experienced fewer inter-tribal conflicts and more foreign oppression, united under a charismatic commander, who is versed in both native and foreign culture, to stir up a sweeping movement against the imperial power:

> [W]e are dealing here with more than a mere political action, but an event that is in part political, but in part socio-psychological, what is called in modern anthropological studies a nativistic or revitalization movement. . . . By it, I mean an effort by a native people whose cultural and political identity is under assault by a superior culture to assert its independence and self-identity. Such movements are very common in contact situations when the 'native' group realizes the potential finality of their subjugation. This often leads to a sudden, massive effort to expel the invader, many times accompanied by evidence of a changed, disturbed psychological state which sometimes displays itself in the rise of new religious movements.[32]

Dyson lays a paradox bare. Each revolt against the Roman Empire has manifested the British, Gallic, or Germanic strength 'clouded with many pseudo-historical assumptions prompted by modern nationalism';[33] on the other hand, revolts in modern European colonies in Africa, North and South America, and Oceania are historically compared and analysed as one of many examples of the established pattern of native movement. He exposes modern European nationalism and imperialism implicated in Roman historiography. Eurocentric imperialist historiography has deflated modern non-European

---

[31] Later scholars have further explored how the ancient past has been appropriated to construct modern national identity: Dietler 1994, 2010; Champion and Díaz-Andreu García 1996; Graves-Brown, Jones, and Gamble 1996; Mouritsen 2009.
[32] Dyson 1971: 246.   [33] Dyson 1971: 253.

revolts as ordinary incidents, but at the same time has celebrated ancient European revolts as evidence of extraordinary British, Gallic, or Germanic spirit. Dyson reveals that scholars have projected the teleology of European progress onto these revolts and interpreted them as the early signs of European potential. Recognizing the double standard, he turns these five revolts into a normative phenomenon in the history of Roman imperialism and Romanization. Without using theoretical terms, he shows that Eurocentric as well as Romano-centric perspectives have skewed the history of anti-Roman resistance, particularly in the western provinces.

Partly due to the limited impact of Dyson's article on wider scholarship, the implications of his work have not been fully explored. Although his article rather marginally swung the course of the discourse on Romanization, it is worthwhile contemplating its further significance, which has been so far overlooked. When Dyson reconstructs the five revolts in the western provinces from isolated events into a recurring phenomenon throughout the history of the Roman Empire, these revolts no longer merely represent sporadic outbreaks of the colonized's discontent or 'ethnic spirit' that do not interrupt the historical telos of Romanization. He re-evaluates resistance as an integral part of Roman imperial history. Its significance is twofold. First, Dyson internalizes anti-Roman resistance into Roman imperial history. He conceives anti-Roman resistance as a force within the Roman network of power relations, not an external force. In no way does this suggest that the colonized subjects revolted with a view to advance on the Roman ladder of power, an idea based on the traditional conception of power relations. On the contrary, Dyson employs the Foucauldian significance of power: 'These points of resistance are present everywhere in the power network. Hence there is no single locus of great Refusal, no soul of revolt, source of all rebellions, or pure law of the revolutionary'.[34] Even though Dyson's article is contemporary with Foucault's works, it is uncertain whether Foucault influenced Dyson. They do, however, share the same ideas and vocabulary. As Foucault integrates resistance within power relations, Dyson integrates the history of resistance within the history of imperial power. Provincial revolts in the history of the Roman Empire are no longer an alien factor that is too quickly dubbed 'barbarian uprisings' or British, Gallic, or Germanic 'spirit', but an inherent element in the constitution of the Roman imperial power network. Incorporating revolts into the history of Roman imperialism, Dyson proposes a new way to write imperial history that does not think from the centre of imperial power but broadens the scope to the wider

---

[34] Foucault 1979: 1, 95–6.

imperial power network. In other words, he offers a possibility of writing a history of the Roman Empire that is not imperialist. In Foucauldian vocabulary, he writes a history of Roman imperial power detached from the hegemony of Roman imperial power-knowledge. Second, Dyson uncovers an integral part of Roman imperial history that contradicts the predominant Romano-centric historiography. According to him, the series of violent revolts illustrate that the colonized population fundamentally rebelled against the Roman imperial rule – not to pour out discontent about unfair treatment, but to overthrow the foreign imperial rule as a whole. Dyson puts his finger on the blind spot long-ignored in the discourse on Romanization: the teleology of Romanization and the totalization of the Romano-centric perspective, coupled with modern imperialist historiography and the Eurocentric perspective, have for centuries obliterated and/or distorted the historical significance of revolts. For a long time, historians have failed to question and perceive the revolts as frustrated attempts to topple the Roman rule. Instead, investigating based on the assumption, conscious or unconscious, of the teleology of Romanization and European dominance, they have interpreted the revolts as negligible disruptions of ethnic vigour to the historical force of Romanization.

The historiography of the resistance exemplifies how the teleology of Romanization and the totalization of the Romano-centric perspective have for a long time framed Roman history according to the imperialist epistemology. Against the imperialist epistemology and historiography, Dyson introduces a point of rupture to the teleology of Romanization and a point of contradiction to the totalization of the Eurocentric and Romano-centric epistemology – through the colonized Other. Unfortunately, his thesis was not further developed, and MacMullen's contribution in introducing the subaltern Other into Roman history eclipses that of Dyson. However, like Fanon's work, Dyson's piece deserves to be reconsidered as a unique prototype of postcolonial history in the scholarship of Roman history which challenges the hegemony of Romano-centrism as historical epistemology. Without any specific reference point to trace back travelling ideas of poststructuralism or postcolonialism, Dyson may well be an Innovator himself or an Early Adopter of poststructuralist or postcolonial epistemological shifts in the scholarship of Roman history.

Whilst Dyson destabilizes the teleology and totalization of Romano-centrism by introducing the colonized Other, Finley destabilizes the teleology and totalization of the parallel discourse by *othering* Romans from the modern Western Self. His seminal piece *The Ancient Economy*, published in 1973, does not address Roman imperialism per se, but the epistemological shift that Finley builds upon the works of MacMullen and Dyson came to form a critical basis of the paradigm shift in the discourse on Romanization.[35] Being one of the Early Adopters to shape the course of the scholarship, Finley envisioned a prospect of ancient history radically different from his predecessors or peers. By the mid-twentieth century, while the discipline of modern history had internalized many approaches and perspectives from emerging disciplines of the social sciences, such as anthropology, economics, and sociology, the discipline of ancient history, mostly situated outside the department of history, still remained a literary activity or 'the handmaiden of philology'.[36] Finley sought to break the old ties. Against the established academic structure, Seth R. Schwarts recounts, he 'largely devoted [his academic life] to the project of decoupling ancient history from the canon of classical literature. He adamantly argued that it should be considered a subfield of history, not an ancilla to the writings of classical Athens and late republican and Augustan Rome'.[37] He urged ancient historians to push boundaries and to branch out further afield. His own scholarly path echoes his belief. His educational background before embarking on a PhD in ancient history at Columbia University touched on psychology and public law.[38] Also, during his early career in New York City, before his exile to England due to McCarthyism, he associated himself with the Frankfurt School, housed in the Institute for Social Research at Columbia University, and the Columbia group, a group of scholars with interdisciplinary interests led by Karl Polanyi.[39] Engaging with diverse intellectual communities aside from classicists and ancient historians, Finley strove to break away from the parochialism of the discipline. Eventually he ventured to rejuvenate ancient history in conversation with the wider contemporary intellectual currents:

> At Columbia University I first studied ancient history ... Those were years of considerable tension ... the Nazi seizure of power ... the Spanish Civil War ... As I think back on this period, I have the firm impression that the lectures and seminars were pretty severely locked in an ivory tower ... I ...

---

[35] Finley 1973.
[36] The vestige of the old vision and structure of ancient history still lingers, particularly in American scholarship, from my personal observation. Ancient historians frequently form a distinct minority in the department of Classics, which is dominated by philologists and classicists.
[37] Schwartz 2013: 46.
[38] Finley finished his BA in psychology at Syracuse University at the age of fifteen and received his MA in public law at Columbia University in 1929. In 1937 he completed his PhD in history at Columbia University.
[39] For the detailed academic prosopography of Finley, see Harris 2013b. As to the wider legacy of Finley, see Jew, Osborne, and Scott 2016.

refer to the irrelevance of [our professors'] work as historians. The same lectures and seminars could have been given - and no doubt were – in an earlier generation, before the First World War ... We, who were growing up in a difficult world ... sought explanation and understanding ... And so we went off on our own to seek in books what we thought we were not getting in lectures and seminars.

We read and argued about Marc Bloch and Henri Pirenne, Max Weber, Veblen and the Freudians, ... Marx and the Marxists ... not just *Das Kapital*, not even primarily *Das Kapital*, but also Marxist historical and theoretical works.[40]

Inevitably, the storm of Marxism of the mid-twentieth century affected Finley.[41] Although it might be too crude to reduce various studies of the time to the axis of Marxism, at the same time it would make Marxism an elephant in the room not to discuss it in the context of the intellectual history of the mid-twentieth century. Without exception, Finley's *The Ancient Economy* was also a product of the Marxist thought of the time, in a way a response to Marxist historical materialism. Nonetheless, make no mistake, Finley neither wholly approved nor wholly disapproved of applying Marxism, or other related contemporary social and economic theories, including the Annales or the cliometrics revolution, to ancient history.[42] The unending debate over whether Finley was Marxist or not, despite evident contacts and references, seems to be failing to grasp an essential aspect of travelling ideas: a critical distance between the point of departure and the point of arrival.[43] Besides, Finley was even more keenly aware of the critical distance to be taken into account between contemporary modern thought and the ancient Roman past. According to Saller, Finley shunned causal application: 'Finley was prepared to insist both on precision of use of modern economic concepts (as opposed to non-scientific, casual usage) and on the inapplicability of those concepts as universal laws'.[44] Finley himself devotes his first chapter of *The Ancient Economy* to warning against hasty application of modern social and economic theories:

> Marshall's title [*Principles of Economics*] cannot be translated into Greek or Latin. Neither can the basic terms, such as labour, production, capital,

---

[40] Finley 1967.
[41] This does not imply that Finley converted to Marxism. Rather, the current Marxist thoughts sweeping the intellectual scene broadened the scope of Finley's historical scholarship. As Harris points out, Finley did not employ concepts such as 'means of production, alienation, or class struggle'. For the impact of Marxism on Finley, see Harris 2013c; Nafissi 2005.
[42] See Hobson 2018; Frederiksen 1975.
[43] Without being exhaustive, the most notable intellectual influences on Finley include Karl Marx, Max Weber, Karl Polanyi, and Georg Lukács.
[44] Saller 2013: 56.

investment, income, circulation, demand, entrepreneur, utility, at least not in the abstract form required for economic analysis.

Ancient historians are not immune from current number fetishism. They are beginning to claim quantitative proof where the evidence does not warrant it, or to misjudge the implications that may legitimately be drawn from their figures. Patterns, modes of behavior, are at the heart of any historical inquiry such as the present one. 'Apart from a presupposed pattern', said Whitehead, 'quantity determines nothing'. Statistics help both to uncover and to elucidate the patterns, but there are also facets susceptible to quantification.[45]

There was no lack of critiques of the use of methodologies borrowed from modern social sciences instead of traditionally philology-driven methodologies, as Brent D. Shaw describes: '[w]ithin the discipline of ancient history, grown to a stunted maturity under the paternalistic aegis of classical philology, approaches to history that stress the techniques and methodologies of the social sciences (e.g. primacy of theory, model building, conceptual sophistication, quantification) rather than those of the mainstream tradition (e.g. linguistic categorization, literary source criticism, citation of authority) must expect to meet with more than a slight suspicion of illegitimacy'.[46] What makes Finley's *The Ancient Economy* a landmark in Roman historiography is that he proposes a new solution, an alternative paradigm which neither withdraws from the contemporary intellectual currents nor straitjackets the ancient past into modern frameworks. He engages with modern social and economic theories, models, and concepts, but maintains that they cannot immediately explain the ancient past. His solution was in part indebted to one of his intellectual mentors, Polanyi, who had led the Columbia group, which included Finley.[47] It was a tour de force of Polanyi, *The Great Transformation: The Political and Economic Origins of Our Times*, first published in 1944, that provided a key link for Finley to connect ancient history with modern social and economic theories while maintaining critical distance.[48]

In essence, Polanyi calls teleology and the totalization of capitalism in history into question. He repudiates a prevailing 'Marxist' idea of the time that the natural, consistent, and universal law of human rationality as a matter of course led to the development of capitalism.[49] Instead, he

---

[45] Finley 1973: 21, 25.
[46] Shaw 1982. For further information on the reception of social sciences in the discipline of ancient history, see Morley 2004.
[47] As for the influence of Polanyi on Finley, see Morris 1999; Nafissi 2005.   [48] Polanyi 1944.
[49] Here I am pointing to the prevailing 'Marxist' idea of the time. It is largely agreed that Marx did not extend his theory to the ancient past, as Finley points out that 'Marx never really devoted himself to

propounds that the market economy is a historically contingent product which radically transformed the human attitude towards economic activities. Rejecting the teleology and totalization of Marxist historiography, he turns his focus to rupture, change, and difference. The radical difference between ancient pre-capitalistic society and modern capitalistic society is further explored in *Trade and Market in the Early Empires: Economies in History and Theory*, published in 1957.[50] It would be farfetched to call Polanyi a poststructuralist, since he was mostly working while Marxism was still exerting a predominant force and poststructuralism just budding. Foucault and other poststructuralists' ideas emerged in the public sphere in the 1960s, only after Polanyi's major works. However, Polanyi shared common ground with poststructuralist thinkers: to challenge teleology and totalization predicated in traditional history.[51] Polanyi's epistemological shift from traditional history was further developed and organized in theoretical terms by poststructuralist thinkers, but Polanyi may as well be one of the Innovators to affect his contemporary scholars with more or less the same epistemological shift as poststructuralist thinkers. With regard to the impact of Polanyi, Sarah C. Humphreys states that 'although the essence of these views had been presented by Polanyi in 1944 in *The Great Transformation*, they did not reach anthropologists and ancient historians until the late 1950's [sic], when the collective volume *Trade and Market in the Early Empires* was published and other researchers inspired or influenced by Polanyi began to appear'. Then she adds: 'Polanyi's ideas have been transmitted through two ancient historians who took part in the Columbia research project, Moses Finley in Greek history and A. L. Oppenheim in Assriology'.[52] Yet, according to Finley, Polanyi's words mostly fell on deaf ears, except on his: 'Most recently the inapplicability to the ancient world of a market-oriented analysis was powerfully argued by Max Weber and his most important disciple among ancient historians, Johannes Hasebroek; in our own day by Karl Polanyi. All to little avail'.[53]

In the Anglo-American scholarship on Roman history, in effect Finley alone adopted Polanyi's view on the rupture between the ancient pre-capitalistic and the modern capitalistic mentalities. This bears twofold significance. On an immediate level, Polanyi provided a key for Finley on how to resolve the critical distance in the application of travelling ideas – between the point of departure, the modern theories, and the point of arrival, the

---

the problem of class relations in pre-capitalist societies'. Finley 1973: 184. As for Marx on pre-capitalist societies, see Hobsbawm 1964.
[50] Polanyi 1957.   [51] On the similarity between Polanyi and poststructuralism, see Holmes 2013.
[52] Humphreys 1969: 167, 179.   [53] Finley 1973: 26.

ancient past – distinct mentalities. Pivoting on different mentalities that govern the modern theories and the ancient past allowed Finley to avoid conflating ancient societies with modern societies on application of the modern theories. When it comes to more subtle but profound influence, by way of maintaining the critical distance via distinct mentalities, Polanyi transmitted the seed of destabilizing the teleology and totalization of traditional historiography to Finley. While Polanyi destabilizes the teleology and totalization of Marxist historiography, Finley destabilizes those of the parallel discourse in Roman historiography. Following Polanyi, Finley became an Early Adopter of the seed of the poststructuralist epistemological shift.

To demonstrate the necessity of maintaining critical distance in applying modern social and economic theories to the ancient past, Finley argues for the alienness of the ancient mentality. It was imperative for Finley to demonstrate that ancient Greeks and Romans operated with a mindset fundamentally foreign to modern people in capitalistic societies in order to declare the modern social and economic theories inapplicable straightaway.[54] Searching literary texts to conjure up the ancient mindset, he concludes that status was a key to the ancient mind. Status determined modes of behaviour for the ancients, in particular their social and economic behaviour. The social structure of differentiated statuses between masters and slaves, citizens and *peregrini*, and urban consumers and rural producers dictated the ancient societies in a way radically different from the modern capitalistic societies. Finley carefully distinguishes the ancient status-driven mindset from the modern class-driven mindset:

> Half a century ago Georg Lukács, a most orthodox Marxist, made the correct observation that in pre-capitalist societies, 'status-consciousness ... masks class consciousness'. By that he meant, in his words, that the 'the structuring of society into castes and estates means that economic elements are *inextricably* joined to political and religious factors'; that 'economic and legal categories are objectively and *substantively so interwoven as to be inseparable*'. In short, from neither a Marxist nor a non-Marxist standpoint is class a sufficiently demarcated category for our purpose – apart from the safe but vague 'upper (or lower) classes' to which I have already referred – and we are still left with the necessity of finding a term that will encompass the Spartan 'Inferiors' (citizens, technically, who had lost their holdings of land), and the nobility of the late Roman Republic, the early Hellenistic Kings, the

---

[54] Paradoxically, the idea of ancient Roman mentality incomprehensible to the modern Western mindset has its root in one aspect of modern French thought: the idea of *mentalité* in the Annales school. See Alston 2001: 11. Furthermore, according to Oswyn Murray, Finley was one of the few scholars of the time to be aware of French thought, including Jean-Pierre Vernant's idea of ancient Greeks' impregnable mentality, and to introduce it to younger scholars. Vernant 1965; Murray 2020.

men Cicero had in mind when he allowed the professions of medicine, architecture and teaching to 'those whose status they befit', and Trimachio.[55]

One of the starkest contrasts that sets the ancient mentality apart from the modern mentality is that ancient Greeks and Romans of a certain status, as a rule of thumb, sought wealth from the political or military arena, rather than commercial or industrial activities. It follows that the ancient economy was qualitatively incomparable with the modern capitalistic economy. Finley rejects modern economic analyses which assume profit-driven agents to be rational as anachronistic as a means to explain the ancient economy which was operated by status-regulated agents. He thus cuts off the continuum of capitalistic economy progressing from the ancient economy on one end to the modern economy on the other. What is perhaps less overt, but no less significant, about Finley's alien ancient mentality and economy is that he crucially destabilizes the teleology and totalization of the historical narrative that the Western Self progressed from the ancient classical to the modern capitalistic society.

Furthermore, Finley presents another striking phenomenon to illustrate the foreignness of the ancient mentality, which is one of the most profound legacies of his scholarship: war and imperialism.[56] He does not shrink from rebuking ancient historians with the observation that 'there is and has been a powerful reluctance among historians to discuss ancient warfare and its consequences with a steady eye, undistorted by anachronistic ideological or psychological considerations'.[57] Surrounded by rampant glorification of ancient Greek and Roman 'civilization', Finley argues, ancient historians dodged addressing the nature of the ancient war and imperialism, which would tarnish the lofty ancients when judged by modern moral standards. Finley wants the naked truth to be spoken: war was a part of their everyday life and business as usual. He stresses that continuous war was the most prominent example of ancient Greeks and Romans pursuing profits through political and military exploits instead of commercial or industrial activities.

The social structure of differentiated statuses embedded war and imperialism into the Roman economy as a collective economic enterprise. Yet all too often, prolific studies on ancient warfare have failed to grasp this fundamental quality, according to Finley: '[i]n their account of ancient

---

[55] Finley 1973: 50.
[56] Though Harris, who has only made a single contribution on the topic, does not credit Finley with his influence on the paradigm shift, Finley has undeniably had a profound impact on the topic. Without being exhaustive, on war and imperialism, see Garlan 1975; Garnsey and Whittaker 1978; Rich and Shipley 1993; Alston 1995; Mouritsen 1998.
[57] Finley 1985: 71.

wars, modern historians fully acknowledge honour and fear, but too often not the profit-motive ... Instead one finds a continuous succession of diplomatic and political events ending, for no sufficient reason, in a resort to arms'.[58] Without fully reassessing the ancient mentality towards warfare in both social and economic terms, any attempt to comprehend Roman society and economy would therefore be doomed. Furthermore, Finley cautions us not to confuse the profit-motive of the ancients with that of the moderns. He explains that ancient war and imperialism have been too often cast in the modern framework of mercantile war and imperialism. It needs to be established that the former advanced to gain profits from political and military exploits, whereas the latter sought to gain profits from capitalistic or commercial exploits:

> What is missing in this picture is commercial or capitalistic exploitation. The ancient economy had its own form of cheap labour and therefore did not exploit provinces in that way. Nor did it have excess capital seeking the more profitable investment outlets we associate with colonialism. The expanded commercial activity of the first two centuries of the Empire was not a Roman phenomenon. It was shared by many peoples within the empire and was no part of imperial exploitation; there was no competition between Romans or non-Romans for markets. Hence, there were no commercial or commercially inspired wars in Roman history, or at any time in antiquity. They exist in our books, to be sure: the seventh-century B.C. war over the Lalantine Plain in Euboea, the Peloponnesian War, Rome's wars with Carthage, even Trajan's badly miscalculated and expensive assault on Parthia have all been attributed to commercial conflicts by one historian or another. On investigation, however, it becomes evident that these historians have been bemused by the Anglo-Dutch wars ...[59]

Modern Europeans castigated war and imperialism based on moral or ideological grounds, at least in theory, and disputed any religious or economic reasons to justify it; by contrast, ancient Greeks and Romans celebrated it as an opportunity or a position to earn honour and wealth and competed in political or military tactics. Through his study of war and imperialism, Finley again demonstrates that the ancient mind is incomprehensible to modern eyes. The ancients are not to be understood through the modern social and economic theories rooted in modern society and economy. The bizarre ancient mentality regarding war and imperialism came to harbour perhaps a less lucid but far-reaching implication: Finley again destabilizes the teleology and totalization of the historical narrative that the

---

[58] Finley 1985: 77. [59] Finley 1973: 158.

Western Self proceeded from ancient Roman imperialism to modern capitalistic imperialism.

Under the influence of Polanyi, Finley came to be an Early Adopter of the seed of the poststructuralist epistemological shift. Adapting the seed to the context of Roman historiography, he circulated it to the scholarship of Roman history – to alienate ancient Romans as the Other and, in turn, to destabilize the teleology and totalization of the parallel discourse between ancient Romans and modern Europeans. Unfortunately, this aspect of Finley's legacy has been too frequently overlooked due to the contentious debate on models of Roman economy. Since its publication, Finley's *The Ancient Economy* has occupied the centre of the polarized debate, namely, the 'primitivist-modernist' debate on the ancient economy.[60] For proposing a non-capitalistic model of the ancient economy, Finley's thesis earned an ill-defined epithet 'primitivist' – which sits *at odds* with his original intent to epistemologically break away from the continuum of Western Self from primitive to modernist. Critiques were made that Finley neglects the industry and commerce of the ancient economy, which is substantiated by archaeological evidence but concealed from ideologically charged literary texts. Prioritizing literary evidence, Finley laid himself bare to critics equipped with the archaeological evidence.[61] In the midst of the heated debate on economic models, the poststructuralist epistemological shift of Finley to shape ancient Romans as the Other and to destabilize the teleology and totalization of the parallel discourse has failed to seize much attention. Finley's poststructuralist seed did not catch on with the Majority, yet.

---

[60] The discourse on Roman economy has undergone a full swing from Rostovtzeff's 'modernist' model to Finley's 'primitivist' model over a few decades – regardless of the authors' original meanings. It was characterized in bipolar terms: modernist model (growth, markets, trade, rational agents) versus primitivist model (subsistence agriculture, marginal growth, low trade, and irrational agents). In contrast to Finley, Rostovtzeff controversially insists that the Roman economy was qualitatively the same as the modern capitalistic economy, only quantitatively smaller in its scale. Placing the ancient Roman economy in the same continuum as the capitalistic economy, along with the modern European economy, Rostovtzeff conceives of a paradigm which later historians dub the 'modernist' Roman economy. By the 1970s, while Rostovtzeff's model became widely anachronistic and discredited, Finley's model had gained ground. It came to be established as the orthodoxy at Cambridge, until the former students of Finley, most notably Keith Hopkins, brought the modernist model back. On the historiography of the Roman economy, see Scheidel, Morris, and Saller 2007; Morley 2006; Hobson 2018.

[61] Martin W. Frederiksen, as one of the vocal critics of Finley's model at the time, encapsulates Finley's contribution and limitations in the context of the discourse on Roman economy: 'Not only in trade and industry, but also in agriculture, we may freely admit that some scholars, following in the wake of Rostovtzeff, reacted too enthusiastically to new archaeological discoveries, and may have read too much modernity into ancient remains. Correctives are always useful, but Finley's models, based as they are on selected utterances by senators in Rome, or literary sources, seem to float before us in curious isolation.' Frederiksen 1975: 169–70.

Hobson also enquires, 'How then did this orthodoxy at Cambridge [of Finley] come to be so thoroughly disregarded?,[62] Although Hobson's enquiry pertains to the discourse on Roman economy, it also partly answers why Finley's epistemological shift did not spread immediately. In short, the former students of Finley reversed the tide shortly after, in the 1980s. First, Keith Hopkins signalled a departure. Stressing, as Finley did, how the scholarship of ancient history isolated itself from the currents of contemporary thought, Hopkins endeavours to close the gulf and to keep ancient history afloat as living history. He holds that '[a]ll history is contemporary history and reflects not only the prejudices of the sources but current concerns and concepts . . . History is conversation with the dead.' Giving weight to modern readers as well as ancient Romans, he advocates that '[t]he achievements of the Roman world need to be interpreted with empathetic understanding of what the Roman themselves thought and with concepts which we ourselves use'.[63] In *Trade in the Ancient Economy*, published in 1983, which is somewhat ironically dedicated to Finley,[64] Hopkins reinstitutes modern socioeconomic concepts, such as economies of scale, capital investment, and economic growth. As a result, he brings the Roman economy back into the domain of modern social and economic theories, particularly cliometrics. Following this lead, Peter Garnsey and Richard Saller also adopt modern terminologies and formulate the ancient economy into 'an underdeveloped economy' in *The Roman Empire: Economy, Society, and Culture* published in 1987.[65] Under the overarching analysis of development economics and the universal solution of economic growth, the Roman economy lost the peculiarity of its mechanism and ethos and was reduced to an underdeveloped, crude, and backward economy. Hobson encapsulates the change of tide:

> Naturally it is also at this historical conjuncture that the word 'poverty' begins to appear in ancient history. One can compare, for example, Finley's statement that the 'widespread prevalence of household self-sufficiency in necessities was enough to put a brake on extensive production for export' (1999:138), with Garnsey and Saller's assertion that 'the poverty of the masses restricted demand' (1987:52), or with Hopkins's variation, that 'the market for such prestige goods was necessarily limited by the poverty of most city-dwellers and peasants' (1983: xii)[66]

---

[62] Hobson 2018: 17.   [63] Hopkins 1978: 1, ix–x.
[64] Hopkins writes, '[m]uch is unknown, much disputed. The contributors to this book do not all agree with each other, even about fundamental elements in the ancient economy. But then controversy and debate seem a suitable tribute to Sir Moses Finley, to whom this book is dedicated.' Hopkins 1983.
[65] Garnsey and Saller 1987.   [66] Hobson 2018: 19.

The underlying consequence was to overturn Finley's epistemological shift. The critical distance that Finley had inserted between ancient Romans and modern Europeans on account of their distinct mentalities was closed once again. Whether Hopkins, Garnsey, and Saller agreed with Finley's poststructuralist epistemological shift – otherness of the Romans – or not, they effectively made the ancient Romans comprehensible again through the lens of modern social and economic theories and placed the ancient Romans on the same continuum with modern Europeans. The blatant parallel discourse of the early twentieth century, which posits the ancient Romans as a mirror rather than a subject to be investigated, had undoubtedly become a thing of the past by the mid-twentieth century. However, the poststructuralist seed to epistemologically destabilize the underlying parallel course through the alterity of the ancient Romans did not take hold immediately.

In the broad scheme of Roman historiography, Finley, despite his scholarly distinction, appears to be an interruption in the overwhelming tide to identify continuity with the modern Western Self and, hence, to explain the ancient Romans with modern social and economic theories. Nonetheless, the changing tides of competing models belie a vital question penetrating the discourse at its root: where the ancient Romans stand in relation to each modern historian, as the parallel Self or the Other. At its root, this question has continued to shape not only the epistemological basis of discourse on Romanization but also the *raison d'être* of the wider discipline of Classics and ancient history, as Alston describes:

> [f]rom the early nineteenth century to the present day, Classics has had to compete and justify itself in a world self-consciously different from the ancients by arguing either that we are very similar to the ancients and thus we are studying ourselves in a rather peculiar context (Livingstone 1916), or that they differed from us in a certain respects and by studying the similarities and differences we can understand our culture better (Cromer 1910; Bryce 1914), or that we are very different from them but studying their culture helps us reflect on our culture (Fustel de Coulanges 1980, James Bryce, 1914; Murray 1990), or that we are very different from the ancients but they are part of our heritage, the roots from which our civilization is sprung, and thus we should study the heritage that is Classics (Beard and Henderson 1995; Grant 1991; Griffin 1986; Mackail 1925: 3–4; 219).[67]

Subsequently, more related questions ensue: is it ahistorical to apply modern social and economic thought to the study of the ancient world?

---

[67] Alston 2001: 7; Livingstone 1916; Cromer 1910; Coulanges 1877; Murray 1990; Beard and Henderson 1995; Grant 1991; Griffin 1986; Mackail 1925.

Is it not enlightening to apply new perspectives and methodologies leading to a breakthrough and wider communication? If we historians cannot escape our own currents of contemporary thoughts, how do we exercise and moderate modern perspectives and methodologies? Finley introduced the seed to make a paradigm shift in Roman history, to alter the epistemology – to recognize the ancient Romans as the Other and to destabilize the teleology and totalization of the parallel discourse. Although Finley's seed of the poststructuralist epistemological shift did not immediately gain ground amongst the Majority, it reached another Early Adopter.

Roman Imperialism: Defensive or Aggressive?

The moment of the Kuhnian revolution, a paradigm shift, in the discourse on Roman imperialism would be without difficulty agreed to be Harris' *War and Imperialism in Republican Rome, 327 – 70 B.C.*, first published in 1979. When the impetus towards social and economic history started to pick up momentum in the scholarship of ancient history, Harris harnessed the contemporary intellectual zeitgeist to challenge one of the most firmly established historical concepts in Roman scholarship – defensive imperialism.[68] Investigating the social and economic dimensions of Roman war and expansion, he challenges one of the most enduring paradigms in Roman historiography, defensive imperialism, to advance aggressive imperialism. In essence, Harris argues that the Romans did not seek defensive frontiers from war and expansion, but wealth and power: the Romans expanded their imperium aggressively. 'The major achievement of *War and Imperialism*', as John A. North succinctly expresses, 'is surely that it makes [defensive imperialism] virtually untenable . . . : at the very least, defensive imperialism will need to be restated in a new form to deal with Harris' critique'.[69] While appreciating his innovation, it should be also acknowledged that Harris' radical shift from defensive imperialism to aggressive imperialism did not happen in an intellectual vacuum. The intellectual currents in and out of the scholarship of Roman history – the legacy of Finley and the 'Vietnam Syndrome' – contributed to Harris' paradigm shift taking place. Seen from the other side of the coin, it could be also said that Harris was one of the Early Adopters to channel the shifting intellectual currents to make his new paradigm tip. Then, let us bring ourselves into the intellectual context of the time.

---

[68] In the second half of the twentieth century, Ernest Badian most notably composed *Roman Imperialism in the Late Republic* to espouse defensive imperialism: Badian 1968.
[69] North 1981: 1.

First, in the wider intellectual world, Marxism has in general lost its peak moment. Nevertheless, the vestiges of Marxism still loomed large over the new generation of scholars. Even though turbulence from Marxist movements in most of the Western world had dissipated, the Marxist divide in the form of the Cold War and the subsequent proxy wars, particularly the Vietnam War (otherwise known as the American War), still continued to cast a cloud over the intellectual world. The Vietnam War in particular swept across American politics, academia, and culture, culminating in Ronald Reagan coining a term to describe its pervasive impact as 'the Vietnam Syndrome'.[70] Questions about American imperialism mushroomed in every corner. The shift in American attitude towards war and imperialism was compelling enough to institute a new paradigm in American historiography. While pre-Vietnam American scholarship had upheld the orthodoxy of American military intervention as being just and effective, post-Vietnam scholarship effectively turned the tables and (paradoxically) established a new orthodox school of thought that castigates American military campaigns and intervention as either doomed efforts or sheer imperialistic exploitations.[71] Gabriel Kolko's *Anatomy of a War: Vietnam, the United States, and the Modern Historical Experience*, published in 1985, became an iconic text to reflect the changing mood.[72] He comprehensively articulates the new orthodoxy emerging from the 1960s. It is not clear whether Harris was aware of this particular sea change in the scholarship of American history, but there is no question that the Vietnam War marked a historiographical threshold in the wider American scholarship.

Across the Atlantic, away from the heated debates surrounding the United States' Cold War policy, the impact of the Vietnam War on Harris' *War and Imperialism* seems to have often escaped the attention of his European colleagues. Saller, an American historian, on the other hand is one of the few to remind us of the American context underlying Harris' work:[73]

> In the 1960s and 1970s the war in Vietnam stood at the center of the political storms in the United States. The parallel between American intervention in Southeast Asia and Roman wars of expansion seemed apparent to some ancient historians: like Rome, the United States intervened far from its borders on the pretext of a local invitation, but in reality on account of its own amoral, material interests. In the wake of the Vietnam War were

---

[70] Reagan 1980. [71] Hess 2009. [72] Kolko 1985.
[73] Saller is one of the eminent American historians, as well as a leading member of the Stanford school and the Chicago school, known for his cliometrics approach to the Roman economy. Nonetheless, having earned his PhD at Cambridge University under the supervision of Finley, he is also acquainted with the British scholarship.

published two major studies of the Roman imperialism by historians in the United States: W. V. Harris's *War and Imperialism in Republican Rome, 327 – 70 B.C.* (1979) and Erich Gruen's The Hellenistic World and the Coming of Rome (1984). The debate over Roman motives for expansion was international. An evaluation of a Roman history course written by an America student in the early 1970s bluntly protested that the professor should 'get the Romans out of Vietnam'.[74]

Harris does in fact allude to the Vietnam syndrome: '[t]he presumption that people naturally dislike war seems to be widespread among Roman historians ... Revulsion against war was intensified in many of us by Vietnam. But these twentieth-century attitudes can make it more difficult to grasp the mentality of the Romans of the middle Republic'.[75] At a glance, it may be confusing that Harris appears to distance himself from his historian contemporaries. As a matter of fact, on the contrary, he immerses himself in the current of American historiography. To unpack his arguments: the Vietnam War sharpened modern American morals against war and imperialism, and this, in turn, reoriented the American history of war and imperialism from noble defence to predatory enterprise. Harris' thesis of aggressive Roman imperialism runs parallel to this new orthodox school in the American historiography. Setting ancient Roman imperialism side by side with modern American imperialism, he urges readers to realize that the Romans also pursued aggressive and exploitative imperialism. Harris, therefore, introduces a paradigm shift to the scholarship of Roman history that echoes the shift in the scholarship of American history. Meanwhile, he also puts his finger on the fault line between ancient Roman and modern American imperialism. It does not lie in the distinct nature of ancient and modern imperialism per se, but in the different ancient and modern mentalities regarding war and imperialism: the modern mentality rebukes war and imperialism, whereas the ancient mentality championed it. American conduct surrounding the Vietnam War might provide a mirror to the aggressiveness and exploitation of Roman imperialism, but it would be a fatal misunderstanding to consider that the Vietnam Syndrome also reflects the ancient mentality. The blind spot, according to Harris, is to conflate the two mentalities. Instead, he contrasts the prevailing American mood with the ancient mentality to stress its foreignness.

In the context of Roman historiography, the foreignness of the ancient mind harks back to Finley. As mentioned earlier, Finley has touched upon

---

[74] Saller 1998: 227. [75] Harris 1979: 47.

Roman war and imperialism to illustrate the foreignness of the ancient mind, a thread that Harris continues to explore. Still, it is correct that Harris, like most post-Finley scholars, objects to Finley's model of the Roman economy mainly on the grounds of Finley's neglect of archaeological evidence. At times, Harris bluntly criticizes Finley: 'Moses Finley's famous synthesis, which is cited in almost every chapter in this book – usually in disagreement – was a terrific tour de force, but it was not a history because it did not attempt to explain historical change'.[76] Still, he simultaneously acknowledges his intellectual debt to Finley: '[s]peaking as one who has often expressed basic disagreements with *The Ancient Economy*, I gratefully recognize that it stimulated my mental activity as few other ancient history books have ever done'.[77] Finley, in fact, appears to be more than a mere source of inspiration for Harris. While responding to Finley's model, Harris as a matter of course adopts some of Finley's views and inherits some of his assumptions. For example, Harris follows Finley in condemning historians, especially after the collapse of Marxism, as being 'in danger of rejecting [Marxism] too much' by rebuffing economic motive in Roman behaviour too quickly.[78] Most significantly, like Finley, he ventures to retrieve the ancient perception, expectation, and mindset with regards to war, 'which often, when it was concerned with gain, thought in terms of pillage and seizure than production'.[79] While Finley emphasized the profit-oriented Roman belligerency to restructure the understanding of the Roman economy, so does Harris in order to reorient our understanding of Roman war and imperialism. Harris may not have adopted Finley's model of ancient economy, but he no doubt became an Early Adopter of Finley's seed of the poststructuralist epistemological shift via the alterity of the ancient Romans. While Finley's argument hinged on the alterity of the ancient Romans to destabilize the teleology and totalization of the parallel discourse, the progress of the Western Self from ancient Roman to modern capitalistic imperialism, Harris develops it further to destabilize the hegemony of a paradigm of defensive imperialism.

Based on the alterity of the ancient Romans, Harris concludes that the Romans collectively, both the senate and the people, pursued aggressive and interventionist imperialism. His refutation of defensive imperialism, above all, centres on the foreignness of the ancient mentality – an idea which can be traced back to Finley and, in turn, to the Annales school. Building on this, Harris further de-familiarizes the Roman mentality from modern preconceptions that the Romans disliked war. To challenge and

[76] Harris 2011: 11. [77] Harris 2013a: 2. [78] Harris 1979: 84. [79] Harris 1979: 83–4.

replace the modern bias, he attempts to concretize the Roman mentality based on both political ideology and economic structure. As for political ideology, not only the military-oriented virtues of *laus* and *gloria* cultivated the Roman belligerence, but also the legal concepts of *bellum iustum* and *ius fetiale* conveniently professed pretexts to justify war and expansion. Furthermore, the potential enrichment from successful warfare, public and private, galvanized the Romans collectively into war and expansion. The regular influx of slaves, land, and booty, as well as the well-trodden path from battlefields to political and economic ascendancy, induced both the senate and the people to promote war and expansion, despite risks and costs. Belligerence, Harris asserts, cuts through the Roman mentality, culture, and civilization:

> The significance of Roman ferocity is hard to gauge. In many respects their behaviour resembles that of many other non-primitive ancient peoples, yet few others are known to have displayed such an extreme degree of ferocity in war while reaching a high level of political culture. Roman imperialism was in large part the result of quite rational behaviour on the part of the Romans, but it also had dark and irrational roots. One of the most striking features of Roman warfare is its regularity – almost every year the legions went out and did massive violence to someone – and this regularity gives the phenomenon a pathological character. As far as the symptoms are concerned, Polybius gave an accurate description: writing about the First Punic War, but using the present tense, he says that it is a Roman characteristic to use violent force, βία, for all purposes.[80]

Harris then addresses the core tenet of defensive imperialism, that the Roman senate and the people did not seek an empire deliberately. With regards to the senate, Harris contends that it 'did not *plan* the expansion of the empire over long periods, which is true in a sense ... but irrelevant'.[81] In other words, the absence of a long-term imperialistic vision among the Roman elite does not vindicate their aggressive behaviour as a series of defensive campaigns. Likewise, with respect to the people, he maintains that their political and economic subjugation does not automatically make them passive agents or innocent participants in Roman war and imperialism. Had they not been attracted to the spoils of war and lent their support, the Roman Republic would have been unable to either wage regular warfare or to extend its imperium. Harris admonishes that '[h]istorians', despite having suffered from the traumas of the First and Second World Wars, 'should resist the presupposition that the citizens were generally reluctant to serve'.[82] In conclusion, he argues that the Roman minds,

[80] Harris 1979: 53.   [81] Harris 1979: 107.   [82] Harris 1979: 46.

fundamentally alien to the modern 'Vietnam Syndrome' mentality, celebrated war and expansion. On the whole, that is good enough to contend that the Romans collectively sought to expand their imperium irrespective of their conscious plan.

We should concede, however, that the very cornerstone of Harris' paradigm of aggressive imperialism – the Roman mentality – is double-edged. On the one hand, its weakness is its inherent intangibility. The elusive nature of the Roman mentality in itself makes it particularly susceptible to an individual historian's interpretation. As Adrian N. Sherwin-White writes, '[Harris] was not writing of the formal votes but of mental attitudes'.[83] Furthermore, it is Harris' own contention of the Roman mentality, that is, the Roman appetite for war and expansion, based on which Harris selectively accepts, modifies, or refutes Polybius' account of the Roman intention. Sherwin-White rightly makes the criticism that '[Harris] can only maintain his simplistic theory of Roman motivation in the great wars by an eclectic valuation of Polybius and the rejection of pragmatic explanations ... When Polybius proposes less aggressive explanations of particular wars his evidence is regularly rejected'.[84] For instance, when Polybius and Zonaras disagree on whether the Gallic wars of 237 BC are a provoked or unprovoked Roman invasion, Harris, against his overall trust of Polybius, prefers Zonaras' version of history. On this occasion he supposes that Polybius was possibly misled to regard it as a defensive operation partly because of the Senate's 'natural' aggression against the Gauls, 'virulent enemies whom it would be natural to attack on any occasion'.[85] As shown in this example, the causality dilemma between the evidence and the ancient mentality exposes Harris' circular argument: based on selective ancient sources he restores the ancient mentality, according to which he, in turn, accepts or rejects the ancient evidence. Sherwin-White's counter-proposal of the Roman mentality sharply criticizes this causality dilemma: 'the reader is not informed that, whatever their past aggressiveness, the Romans in the third century endured the historical experience of great defensive wars in which, whatever the nominal origins of the wars, the existence of Rome was at stake, so that the Roman mentality acquired a neurosis of fear'.[86] Also, North, despite his broad approval of Harris' project, agrees with Sherwin-White on the weakness of Harris' theory: '[the final chapter] surveys methodically the origins of all the major wars of the period, seeking to show that in

---

[83] Sherwin-White 1980: 181. [84] Sherwin-White 1980: 180. [85] Harris 1979: 193–94.
[86] Sherwin-White 1980: 178.

virtually every case the Romans were the aggressors. Sherwin-White is here quite right to object that the arguments are sometimes strained, the analysis at a superficial level and the author too close to his subject, losing the overall development of policy while grinding through war after war'.[87]

Yet, the circular argument does not invalidate Harris' thesis (or Sherwin-White's, for that matter) wholesale. The Roman mentality, in reality, is not a one-dimensional definite whole, but a multi-faceted, fluid, and fragmented composite. It is not artificially constructed to be continuous and coherent, but organically grown with contradictions, differences, and discontinuities over centuries. In Foucault's vocabulary, it is historians, like Harris and Sherwin-White, who formulate continuities and unities in the discourse of the Roman mentality by the circular process of selecting evidence and dismissing counter-evidence to deconstruct existing paradigms and to construct new ones. Therefore, given the broader complexity of the Roman mentality with contradictions, differences, and discontinuities, Sherwin-White's and Harris' discursive continuity and unity concerning the Roman mentality do not necessarily have to be mutually contradictory. What Harris achieves, regardless of critiques from Sherwin-White and others, is that he presents an alternative discursive coherence of profit-driven aggressiveness that disrupts the monolithic discursive coherence of anxiety-driven defensiveness.

The legacy of Harris' work somewhat poetically echoes his own words. Whether he intended or not, he eventually came to use the seed of poststructuralist epistemological shift to destabilize another hegemony in Roman historiography, the paradigm of defensive imperialism. When writing and understanding the history of Roman imperialism, the perception of the Roman mentality is one of the cardinal premises, but the abstract Roman mentality has been less often articulated and more often assumed. In particular, the question of where to place the Roman mentality in relation to the modern Western mentality – as the parallel Self or the Other – has underpinned the epistemology of discourse, as Harris stresses:

> Scholars' opinions about this problem of Roman history are in most cases more or less closely linked with their feelings about the politics of modern imperialism. We are deplorably slow to admit that this is so, with the result that historians of various political persuasions – in the English-speaking world, it must be said, mainly those of the right – have succeeded in distorting the Roman past in conformity with their views about the modern world.[88]

[87] North 1981: 2. [88] Harris 1979: 55.

Without exception, Harris' paradigm shift is also a reflection of his feelings towards contemporary politics about modern imperialism. In his case, the Vietnam Syndrome, namely the critique of modern Western imperialism, underlies his paradigm shift on Roman imperialism. He himself was assisted by the shifting contemporary mood towards imperialism to reveal that the modern imperialist powers have ingrained a régime of historical knowledge/truth sympathetic towards ancient imperialism. However, the fact that contemporary politics is implicated in Harris' régime of truth does not undermine it. In Foucault's poststructuralist vocabulary, knowledge/truth by nature is power. It is formed, determined, and circulated through power politics and, thereby, cannot be distilled from contemporary politics. Given that susceptibility to contemporary politics is inescapable, what Harris accomplishes is that he deploys the shifting contemporary politics to subvert the hegemony of one form of régime of truth, that is, imperialist historiography – what Foucault champions.

Certainly, Harris cannot be labelled as Foucauldian per se. He does not allude to Foucault or even vaguely resort to his conceptual language. Yet, the general intellectual atmosphere of the time shared the reflective mood not only on the threatened collapse of Western imperialism, but also on a Foucauldian challenge to the Western system of power and knowledge/truth. It prompted intellectuals, including Harris, to be self-reflective about their own history, culture, and beliefs, and to be self-conscious about their own relativity. In the overall wave of poststructuralism, Harris exposes that the Western apologetic attitude to its own imperialist past had shaped and fortified a régime of historical knowledge/truth expedient to its own imperialism, passing down the imperialist historiography of Roman imperialism. In this way, he deconstructs one of the central hegemonies of imperialist ideology ingrained in Roman historiography. Still, a more concrete poststructuralist seed can be also identified by tracing back to Finley. When Harris adopts the rupture between the Roman mentality and the modern mentality, he effectively inherits Finley's foundational argument – the alterity of Romans – that destabilizes the conventional historiography. While Finley destabilizes the teleology and totalization of the Marxist historiography during the era of Marxism, in the post-Marxist age Harris moves on to challenge the teleology and totalization of the imperialist historiography. First, Harris exposes the long-held presupposition on the Roman mentality rooted at the fundamental premise of Roman historiography thus far. It is the cherished belief that the Romans were the noble, just, and civilized predecessors of the modern West that upheld the parallel discourse between ancient Roman and modern Anglo-American imperialism. Likewise, it is the tacit assumption that the civilized Romans accrued wealth from farming and trading, unlike the barbarians who took wealth from warfaring, that has sustained the continuing discourse of defensive imperialism.

Despite his logical slip, Harris' radical proposition that the Romans – contrary to modern expectation – aggressively sought war and expansion lays these previous suppositions bare. By challenging them at their root, he then effectively calls the entire interlocked discourses into question, from the 'civilized' Romans (as opposed to the 'barbarians') to the parallel between ancient Romans and modern British/Americans to defensive imperialism. Harris' alternative premise of the Roman mentality not only betrays but also challenges the premises upon which the régime of historical knowledge/truth has been built thus far. The prospect that the 'civilized' Romans did not differ much from the 'barbaric' Goths, Huns, Vikings, or modern aggressive colonialists is indeed ground-breaking; it is threatening to the established Western system of knowledge/truth. Harris' revolutionary thesis does not hinge on new data unearthed from archives or archaeological sites. Instead, he excavates the age-old epistemology fossilized at the foundation of modern Roman historiography and implants Finley's poststructuralist seed of epistemological shift. North explicates the provocative question presented by Harris' paradigm of aggressive imperialism:

> The achievement of the book should not be under-estimated, nor its implications missed. Our whole understanding of imperialism and its origins is in question. The effect of the 'defensive imperialism' hypothesis has been to remove the need for explanation. The idea has been that the wars happened piecemeal without intention or purpose; in particular, there was no search for wealth or slaves, except as an incidental consequence of the fact of the wars. The whole problem has been reduced to one of the analysis of the causes of individual conflicts; since the circumstances were always different and the initiatives either external or provoked by external developments, there was nothing left to be explained. The wars became a sort of absolute, defying coherent analysis. What Harris has done is to restore the problem.[89]

Nevertheless, inheriting poststructuralist thought implicated Harris in its drawbacks as well, as he echoes the limits of poststructuralist thinkers. When Harris recognizes the fundamental difference between the ancient Roman and the modern Western mentality, he identifies the ancient Romans with the Other in relation to the modern Western Self. Taking this further, he subverts the interlocked discourses that hitherto hinged on the implicit identification of

---

[89] North 1981: 3.

the Romans with the past Self, that is, the parallel discourse between ancient Romans and modern British/Americans and defensive imperialism. Inevitably, as predicated by poststructuralist deconstructions, Harris' account is also inflected towards the modern Self. He raises questions while firmly rooted in the perspective of the modern Western Self. From the position of the modern Western Self, he challenges to reposition ancient Romans as the Other and to reorient the historiography of Roman imperialism. He attempts to disrupt the imperialist historiography, but the discourse keeps referring back to the modern Western Self as a point of epistemology. Hence, the self-reflexive discourse is unavoidably locked in the epistemology of the modern Western Self. The colonized Other required to deconstruct the imperialist epistemology is still absent in the discourse of Roman imperialism and Romanization. The epistemological boundaries are yet to be pushed to the colonized peripheries to destabilize the imperialist epistemology.

There was an overarching intellectual trend within and outside the scholarship of Roman history, from the Vietnam Syndrome to Finley's poststructuralist ideas, to challenge the traditional historiography. Yet, the travel of poststructuralist ideas to the Anglo-American scholarship of Roman history has not been conspicuous. Rather, it is accurate to state that the Majority of the scholarship were insulated from the contemporary intellectual currents, as Finley laments. It would be misleading to imagine that the historians discussed at length here – Finley and Harris – were well-embraced mainstream voices within the Anglo-American scholarship of Roman history. Contrary to the impression that the kudos attributed to them later as spearheads of the modern Anglo-American scholarship of Roman history might suggest, they were rather the Innovators against the mainstream orthodoxy of the time (the modernist model of Roman economy and defensive imperialism). Only a few Roman historians, including those mentioned above, engaged with the wider intellectual movements and employed them to push the epistemological boundaries long-held within the scholarship. We know that Harris did not engage precisely with poststructuralist theories per se. However, the intellectual influences he draws on within and outside the scholarship certainly imbue these important poststructuralist undercurrents. Doubts about the absoluteness of Western knowledge and history, questions about the relationship between power and historical knowledge/truth, and awareness of historical relativity and alterity defined the post-Vietnam American intellectual milieu in which Harris completed *War and Imperialism*. Not only the contemporary American intellectual environment, but also the influence of Finley allowed Harris to share more or less the same objective with the poststructuralist movement: to deconstruct teleology and totalization in traditional historiography. Thus, Harris became another Early Adopter of the poststructuralist seed of epistemological shift. By *othering* Romans, he deconstructs the fossilized notion which the modern Western imperialist epistemology has constructed of an ancient Roman historiography apologetic towards imperialism, that is, defensive imperialism.

Romanization: Negotiation, and a Tipping Point

Harris' *War and Imperialism* ushered Romanization studies into its renaissance after a decade-long hiatus.[90] Romanization has become an amphitheatre for various discourses to collide, compete, and/or collaborate. Contending discourses ranging from Roman social and economic structure, war and imperialism, identity and culture to contemporary thoughts on Marxism, cliometrics, sociology, and postmodernism all in play simultaneously to refresh the discourse on Romanization. As mentioned previously, in the overall scholarship of history, cultural history came to critique and ultimately outshine the waning Marxist social and economic history. In the scholarship of Roman history, on the contrary, cultural history incorporated and built upon social and economic history. Becoming a crossroads for social, economic, and cultural history, the discourse on Romanization came to occupy the central ground once again. Even at a glance, studies across many sub-disciplines, such as frontier, law, religion, economy, and urbanization to name but a few, proliferated to improve the understanding of Romanization from diverse aspects and perspectives.[91] In shaping this resurgence of interest in the topic, the contribution of the Early Adopters – Harris' *War and Imperialism in Republican Rome* and, in turn, that of Finley's *The Ancient Economy* – cannot be overemphasized. In essence, they distanced Romans from the modern Western Self as the Other and destabilized the parallel discourse which had underpinned the discourse on Romanization thus far. Engaging with the modern social science studies, Finley argued that the Romans' mentality favouring war and expansion governed their social and economic structures, not industrial capitalism. Then, drawing on contemporary thoughts on war and

---

[90] Freeman 1993.
[91] Far from being exhaustive, to mention a few, on frontier: Whittaker 1994; on religion: Price 1984; on law: Johnston 1999; on urbanization: Fentress and Alcock 2000.

imperialism, Harris brought together both the Roman mentality championing war and expansion and their social and economic structures, built around war and expansion, to shift the paradigm of Roman imperialism from defensive to aggressive. Changing outlooks on both the Roman and contemporary worlds, accordingly, prompted revisionist approaches to Romanization studies. This section will investigate how not only the poststructuralist but also the postcolonial seeds of epistemological shift have diffused into the discourse on Romanization to trigger a sea change.

Indeed, this volume cannot do full justice to the diverse perspectives developed in the rich discourse on Romanization. Nonetheless, for our purpose of tracing the travel of postcolonial thought into the discourse on Romanization, it would be neither practical nor useful to provide a survey of each subfield and to examine differences among prolific literature. Rather, here I will focus on the prominent paradigm of Romanization developed in the late twentieth-century age of decolonization: negotiation. It should be stressed that this is only a rudimentary description to facilitate the illustration of a broader trend. The negotiation model has not been firmly established or clearly delineated. The broad trend of the negotiation model encouraged scholars to illuminate overlooked aspects, question old and new perspectives, and revise frameworks. Hardly static, this paradigm of Romanization evolved over time. Among many works operating within this model, I will focus on a key text that produces a synthesis of scattered studies to articulate the paradigm: Martin Millett's *The Romanization of Britain: An Essay in Archaeological Interpretation*, a monograph published in 1990.[92] This may be disappointing to some readers who might be expecting an overview that broadly covers the works published in each subdiscipline of the Romanization studies. However, a close reading of this crucial text on Romanization will better show us the route which the poststructuralist and postcolonial seeds have taken to travel into the discourse on Romanization and to prompt a paradigm shift.

Nowadays Millett's *The Romanization of Britain* has become such a standard work in Romanization studies in Anglo-American scholarship that it hardly requires any introduction. Widely acknowledged as a landmark work in Romanization studies, it synthesizes a vastly growing number of excavation reports into an updated overview of Romano-British history. What should be taken into account in assessing his success is that Millett is firmly rooted in the tradition of Romano-British studies well established by his time in Anglo-American scholarship. Romano-British studies, founded

---

[92] Millett 1990; Dyson 1971.

by Haverfield and Collingwood, who were once rebels against the gentlemanly tradition of scholarship, acquired more ground thanks to the succeeding generation of Romano-British professional archaeologists and historians, such as Ian Richmond, Sheppard Frere, and Peter Salway.[93] Millett follows in the steps of these great British academics to spearhead Romano-British archaeology and history, with the help of expanding heritage studies.[94] Within the cohort of Romano-British scholars, Millett emerged as one of the leading scholars of the first post-imperial generation by publishing the up-to-date synthesis of the field.[95] While continuing the intellectual tradition of Romano-British studies, Millett enriches, modifies, and refines Romanization studies to meet the changing intellectual climate. He refreshes the tradition of Romano-British studies, which had been the mainstay of British scholarship since the professionalization of the discipline. Rather than simply an updated version, Miguel John Versulys deems Millett's *Romanization of Britain* to be a 'point of departure' from his predecessors to rewrite the history of Roman imperialism and Romanization in the new age of decolonization.[96] Gardner also observes that 'critical reaction to *The Romanization of Britain* opened the way for many new ideas in Roman archaeology in the 1990s'.[97] Millett's pièce de résistance led Roman scholarship to 'the moment of critical mass, the threshold, the boiling point' to engage with postcolonial thought.[98] That is to say, it became a Tipping Point, '[when] the unexpected becomes expected, [when] the radical change is more than a possibility' in the discourse on Romanization.[99] Thenceforth any study on Romanization from postcolonial perspectives owes an honourable mention to Millett's *The Romanization of Britain* at some point.

As to the question of why Millet's work made postcolonial perspectives tip in the discourse on Romanization, another concept from Gladwell's *The Tipping Point* – the Power of Context – might provide a clue. It may seem obvious, but Gladwell emphasizes that: 'the lesson of Power of Context is that we are more than just sensitive to changes in context. We're exquisitely sensitive to them. And the kinds of contextual changes that are capable of tipping an epidemic are very different than we might

---

[93] Haverfield 1923; Collingwood 1932, 1936; Richmond 1947; Frere 1967; Salway 1981.
[94] After the collapse of the British Empire, interest in the past was reoriented to the British Isles. Indigenous finds not only supported Romano-British archaeology, but also filled the British Museum. See Champion 1996; Bradley 2010.
[95] Richard Hingley identifies Millett and himself as 'the first English generation after the decline of the Empire': Hingley 2000: xiii.
[96] Versluys 2014: 2.   [97] Gardner 2013: 2.   [98] Gladwell 2000: 12.   [99] Gladwell 2000: 13–14.

ordinarily suspect'.[100] In other words, the environmental factor is critical for an idea to tip and to 'infect' the wider audience. In fact, Millett, in his introduction, describes how the intellectual context has changed and how it made the time ripe for a paradigm shift in the Romanization discourse:

> A review of evidence seems especially important since members of the post-imperial generation (to which I belong) are seeking new explanations for cultural change in the Roman world: they are unwilling to accept the paternalistic view that 'the Britons did what they were told by the Romans because it represented *progress*'. I have thus attempted to provide one alternative explanatory framework.[101]

Furthermore, at a symposium organized not long after Millett's *The Romanization of Britain* in 1994, Webster concurs that the postcolonial intellectual context demands a major overhaul of studies on Roman imperialism and Romanization — not only its paradigm but also its epistemology:

> ... to explore some of the central themes of post-colonial theory, and their implications for the study of Roman Empire. These are, necessarily, themes which particularly concern the Roman scholars who have grown up in what Martin Millett (1990a) calls the 'post imperial age'; and most of those present at the symposium belonged to the first (and the second) generation of 'post imperial' Roman scholars. ... In what ways, we asked, is our position within the 'post imperial' condition causing us to reassess not only *Roman* imperialism, but the epistemological basis of our discipline (the *study* of the Roman Empire), which developed in the context of Western imperialism?[102]

The Power of Context, in this case the postcolonial generation of scholars, helped Millett's *The Romanization of Britain* to reach a Tipping Point in the discourse on Romanization.

Nevertheless, the scholarship of Roman history, particularly Romano-British scholarship, has been rather insulated from contemporary intellectual currents. The cherished tradition survives from Haverfield to Millett and harbours a couple of distinctive characteristics through the postcolonial generation of scholars — despite the shockwaves from the fall of the British Empire — such as heavy reliance on archaeological data and heritage studies to shape a cloistered niche of scholarship.[103] As David Braund portrays it, the intellectual environment of Romano-British scholarship was, indeed, unique:

> A new book on Roman Britain has been no small undertaking. The history of Roman Britain has often been written, and written well. However, for the

---

[100] Gladwell 2000: 140.   [101] Millett 1990: xv.   [102] Webster 1996: 1.   [103] See Hingley 2000.

most part scholarship on Roman Britain has been no less an island than its subject. By and large, the island has been the preserve of a quite sharply defined group, though it is one that is quite extensive and impressive. Many budding historians of antiquity (as once the present writer) have been kindly advised by their sage seniors not to make the academic crossing to this island: in part through awareness of the demands of the crossing itself, in part through fear of natives, and in part through anxiety that the young will be lost there, engulfed by a mass of regional detail, never to return.[104]

Given its peculiarity, the intellectual context of Romano-British scholarship should be sufficiently factored in to understand Millett's paradigm of negotiation and the epidemic curve it tipped. The words of R. J. A. Wilson aptly portray the context of Romano-British scholarship which Millett led to a Tipping Point:

> If Cunliffe was even partly right eight years ago to claim (Antiquity 58 (1984), 178) that Romano-British studies were like an 'aged, cossetted old lady sitting immobile in an airless room reeking of stale scent, fawned on by a bevy of tireless dedicated servants', books published in recent years, of which M[illett]'s is among the most distinguished, should have dispelled any doubts about the health of the subject. Far from being immobile, Britannia is vigorous, fit, and extremely active; indeed so fast is she on the move, fed by a continuous stream of astonishing fresh discoveries, that for those with interests elsewhere in the Roman world she is proving increasingly difficult to keep up with.[105]

Indeed, the pedigree of Romano-British scholarship should not be overlooked, as it has influenced the trajectory of the discourse on Romanization in Anglo-American scholarship. First, the development of Romano-British studies fuelled by archaeology played a part in reinforcing the empiricist tradition in the discourse on Romanization. From the mid-twentieth century, benefiting from the momentum gained by social and economic history in the scholarship of Roman history, Romano-British scholars earned sympathetic ears to demonstrate social, economic, and cultural changes with a rich collection of archaeological data. The social, economic, and cultural changes they illustrate primarily centred on Romanization. Meanwhile, the surge of social sciences incurred another consequence. While its influence on Roman scholarship had been previously confined to a shift in the subject matter from political history to social and economic history, it began to equip Roman historians with positivist methodologies derived from social sciences to write history. It de facto implanted positivist history as *the* régime

[104] Braund 1996: 179. [105] Wilson 1992: 291.

of historical truth.[106] According to the standard procedure of social sciences, Romano-British scholars also attempted to substantiate, debunk, or modify different models of Romanization based on the newly acquired set of empirical data. Yet, inasmuch as there was increasing attention directed towards the analysis and interpretation of new archaeological data, the attention required to systematically question the epistemology underpinning theories, paradigms, or models to interpret data had not built up.

Empirical data by itself does not tell history. From the outset, to acquire empirical data, the search itself is based on theoretical judgements, on questions asked, methodologies undertaken, selections made, and conclusions drawn. For instance, Millett mentions that 'the question should not be why Claudius invaded Britain, but why it had not happened earlier'.[107] Later, he puts forward another question of a similar note, 'what differed in the north that led to its failure?'.[108] In other words, he questions the Roman failure to conquer the north, rather than the British success in repelling the invaders. Even for positivist enquiry, the two aforementioned questions already harbour distinct presuppositions on a number of complex issues, from the Romano-British relationship, Roman and British mentalities, and Roman and British society, to modern imperialism and national identity. Then, each question respectively contains certain embedded perspectives which determine the enquiry's objective, scope, and methodologies. In this case, Millett's question is posited on the historical telos of Roman conquest and Romanization, that is, the Romans could have conquered Britain earlier and further. He interrogates how and why the empirical data do not correspond to the telos of Roman conquest and Romanization at a certain point, in other words, how and why Roman power foundered in Britain. Nonetheless, he does not dispute the telos of Roman conquest and Romanization rooted in these questions. The historical epistemology of the telos of Romanization and the totalization of Roman imperialism still underlies Millett's empiricist investigation. Although Millett claims that he pursues fact-based archaeology immune to 'factoids', the questions he starts with show that positivist history is not immune to the question of epistemology.

---

[106] In Anglo-American scholarship, without any epistemological (or anti-positivist) tradition as strong as the one witnessed in French scholarship, critiques of positivist history were in general thin on the ground. Only a few Roman historians in Anglo-American scholarship, namely Finley, engaged with the continental European theories to confront the positivist tide in Anglo-American scholarship. Epistemological critiques of positivist history, which began to flourish recently at the turn of the century, were limited until then. See Young 1990.
[107] Millett 1990: 40.   [108] Millett 1990: 99.

Contemporary epistemological shifts prompted by poststructuralism and postcolonialism encouraged Romano-British archaeologists to update the Romanization model, but the positivist tendency in Romano-British scholarship circumscribed the influence of poststructuralism and postcolonialism on the surface. The epistemological shift of poststructuralism and postcolonialism made little headway in questioning Romano-British archaeologists' empiricist approach. As Greg Woolf points out, Millett, too, in his mission 'to be on the look out for "factoids", opinions so hallowed that they were treated as established facts, ... sometimes underestimates both the complexity and controversy of current debate'.[109] His positivism becomes more marked when compared with Finley and Harris' approach. While Finley and Harris make the poststructuralist epistemological shift to distance the Romans as the Other and, hence, to reinterpret the same set of given data into a new paradigm of aggressive imperialism, Millett draws on newly available empirical data to test against the existing model of Romanization and to modify it accordingly. At the risk of overgeneralization, in the archaeology-driven Romano-British scholarship, poststructuralism and postcolonialism were yet to spark a wider discourse to question the epistemology of how to the interpret the empirical data against the model of Romanization.

Despite the overarching empiricist tradition of Romano-British scholarship, in the second half of the twentieth century, Romano-British scholarship underwent a significant change mainly from two fronts to form the context in which Millett's *The Romanization of Britain* was written: first, the rise of field survey, and second, the rise of prehistoric archaeology. The changing intellectual current as well as the continuing empiricist gravitation of Romano-British scholarship has conditioned the environment where Millett's piece could tip the epidemic curve with his new paradigm of Romanization.

That said, let us first look into the rise of field survey in Romano-British studies. It is needless to repeat that Roman Britain is one of the most poorly documented provinces of the Roman Empire in surviving literary sources. It is also difficult to refute that Roman Britain holds rather unimpressive architecture and artefacts compared to the splendidly adorned and scrupulously chronicled provinces around the Mediterranean. The paucity of conventional literary and archaeological evidence in Britain has meant that Roman Britain had been cast aside as a barren province for both ancient Roman and modern British historians. However, from the mid-twentieth

---

[109] Woolf 1991: 342.

century onwards a medley of internal and external impulses drove the explosion of Romano-British archaeology. The collapse of the British Empire reoriented the interests of many British amateur and professional archaeologists from their imperial predecessors, including Romans, to their national ancestors.[110] The overall circumstances have steered Romano-British scholars to develop their own niche archaeological methodology suitable to Roman Britain – that is, the field survey, also known as the landscape survey. The field survey allowed British archaeologists to elicit fruitful analyses from small finds and structural remains. Thereafter, British archaeologists have yielded numerous reports of field surveys detecting distribution patterns of settlements, forts, temples, inscriptions, coins, pottery, etcetera in Roman Britain. A quick scan of Millett's *Romanization of Britain*, which is filled with distribution maps and charts that he assembles for in-depth analyses, gives a glimpse into the sheer volume of surveys executed over a couple of decades. The extensive field survey has altered the perception of Roman Britain. For a long time, the cognitive map of Roman Britain had been a damp and foggy island at the far end of the Roman Empire that was dimly lit by the remote beacon of civilization. Then field surveys started not only to fill up but also to brighten the cognitive map of Roman Britain as an island with its own distinct civilization. The acquisition history of the British Museum also reflects the gradual change, as Mark Bradley points out: when 'the influx of antiquities – classical and non-classical – in the [British] Museum slowed to a steady trickle ... [f]ollowing the collapse of British imperial authority and the gradual dismantlement of the colonies by the middle of the twentieth century ... Romano-British archaeology continued to furnish the Museum's collections with important indigenous finds'.[111] Romano-British archaeology, propelled by field surveys from the mid to late twentieth century, recast Roman Britain little by little from a pale shadow of Roman grandeur to an island with civilization, culture, and history in its own right. The enduring model of Romanization passed down from Haverfield appeared out of date.

Secondly, the rise of prehistoric archaeology has reconfigured the intellectual context surrounding the discourse on Romanization. Hitherto, the pre-Claudian Britons had been rendered as intelligent barbarians or noble savages who benefited from Romanization. As Millett suggests, historical

---

[110] Hingley narrates how the interests of British scholars have shifted back and forth between imperial predecessor and national origin. Hingley 2000.
[111] Bradley 2010: 8.

narratives based on literary sources have reinforced 'the Roman perspective, expressed by Tacitus that "one must remember we are dealing with barbarians"'.[112] Yet the growth of LPRIA [Late pre-Roman Iron Age] archaeology made the idea no longer tenable. An increasing number of LPRIA archaeological reports filled with photographs and distribution maps illustrated the social, economic, and cultural achievements of the LPRIA Britons prior to the Claudian conquest. The LPRIA archaeological remains materialized their civilization to the modern mind. Ancient Britons were no longer a monolithic group of uncivilized warriors and farmers; LPRIA archaeology retrieved the stable hierarchy, sophisticated craft and art, and geographical diversity of their civilization.[113] Thereby LPRIA archaeology recovered ancient Britons from an inert pre-historical state to a dynamic historical force.[114] It effectively put Britons on the historical map.[115]

A cocktail of ingredients ensured warm, if not swift, reception of the contribution of LPRIA archaeology to the restoration of ancient Britons in the history of the Roman Empire. Not only academic interests – that is, both the age-old concern of Romano-British studies to tackle the stigma of conquest and the contemporary influence from postcolonial studies to reconfigure the colonized subjects – but also public concerns about British identity welcomed the redemption of Britons from pre-historic barbarity. In the midst of this environment, the rise of LPRIA archaeology provided a key to trigger a comprehensive re-evaluation of Britons in the Romanization process and, as a consequence, a revision of the Romanization paradigm itself – that Britons were no longer merely colonized subjects.[116] A combination of circumstantial factors within and outside Romano-British scholarship suggests that the time was right for a paradigm shift in the discourse on Romanization. The post-imperial generation of scholars with postcolonial awareness has sprung up; the rise of field survey and LPRIA archaeology in Romano-British scholarship has recast the British Isles with its own distinct culture and civilization. When Millett

---

[112] Millett 1990: 18.; Tacitus, *Agricola*, 11. Ancient literary sources that have been instrumental in shaping the notion of the ancient Britons include: Caesar, *de Bello Gallico*, V. 12 –14. Strabo, *Geography*, IV. 5. 2.

[113] To name just a few works on LPRIA Britain, Cunliffe 1974; Miles and Cunliffe 1984; Haselgrove 1982, 1987.

[114] 'Although studies of the historical context of prehistoric archaeology have been popular since at least the 1950s, Roman archaeologist have rarely indulged in this type of analysis', as Hingley states. Hingley 2000: xi.

[115] See Fleming and Hingley 2007.

[116] Peter S. Wells notably changed the notion of LPRIA communities based on LPRIA archaeology: Wells 1999.

proposes his alternative model of Romanization, he pledges to align it with the post-imperial intellect and to reject the blatantly imperialistic structure of Roman superiority. The Power of Context was instrumental in tipping Millett's paradigm of Romanization to 'infect' the scholarship to rethink Romanization further.[117]

Now, let us take a closer look at Millett's paradigm of negotiation. Millett's solution was to rearrange the balance of power in the Romanization process in favour of Britons. While '[sharing] a common analytical framework with Haverfield's earlier study', he grants Britons more leverage in the Romanization process.[118] He deploys fundamentally the same framework of a binary hierarchical relationship between the colonizers and the colonized at each end, but turns it into a negotiation process where the ancient British elites, albeit colonized, played a pivotal role. Millett argues that, since Romans ruled indirectly via the local elites, the local elites commanded a crucial position of negotiation between colonizing Romans and colonized Britons: to bridge communication in administration, to transmit Roman values in lifestyle, and to construct an urban and rural landscape. He transforms the ancient Britons from 'uncivilized yet intelligent' barbarians to civilized members mediating between Roman and British cultures. Millett remodels the paradigm of Romanization accordingly. While Romano-British scholars of the preceding generation had conceived of Romanization as a one-way process in which colonizing Romans civilized colonized Britons, Millett redefines it as 'a process of dialectical change ... [in which] Roman culture interacted with native cultures to produce the synthesis that we call Romanized'.[119] The dialectical process, according to Millett, hinged on the local elites; the local elites emulated colonizing Romans and spread the practice to colonized Britons.[120] The continuity from Haverfield – binary hierarchy between colonizing Romans and colonized Britons – lurks beneath Millett's model, but what Millett accomplishes is to empower the subjected elites of Roman Britain in his paradigm.

As flagrant praise of imperialism had no place in the late twentieth century intellectual world, a certain progressive shift has been achieved in tandem with the contemporary mood. However, breaking away from the

---

[117] Other paradigms of Romanization which followed to complement or critique Millett's model will be discussed in Chapter 4. In the meantime, a few works produced in response to the epidemic curve that Millett tipped include: Jones 1991; Woolf 1992, 1997; Hanson 1994; Webster and Cooper 1996; Mattingly and Alcock 1997; Keay and Terrenato 2001.
[118] Hingley 1996: 41. Also, see Freeman 1993.   [119] Millett 1990: 1.
[120] Millett's framework of elite-led society harks back to a couple of influential works from the early twentieth century which have ingrained the elite-driven model for later Roman scholars to adopt: Rostovtzeff 1926; Syme 1939. On their legacy, see Potter 2006.

centuries-old imperialist epistemology entrenched in the framework of Romanization was not to be fulfilled all at once. Just as Eurocentric epistemology still dominates contemporary intellectual thought despite postcolonial thinkers' efforts to counter it, Romano-centric epistemology ingrained in the discourse on Romanization proved to be difficult to remove. In fact, Millett's paradigm of Romanization attests to its very difficulty and demonstrates how deep-rooted the Romano-centric perspective is. The analytical framework of Haverfield has bequeathed the built-in Romano-centric epistemology to its adopters. To unravel the deep-seated Romano-centric epistemology, it would be useful to break down Millett's treatment into two: Romans and Britons. If we can recognize how Romano-centric epistemology continues to influence the way Millett perceives Romans' and Britons' respective positions, the Romano-centric perspective shaping the understanding of their interaction, i.e. Romanization or otherwise, shall be clearer.

First, let us start with Millett's presentation of Romans. The belief that the Romans were the bearers of civilization and progress was no longer unassailable by the late twentieth century. Finley and, more decisively, Harris left an indelible impact on the scholarship of Roman history that successive historians and archaeologists could not overlook. In one way or another, scholars are now expected to accommodate into their framework both Finley's and Harris' views that the Romans actively sought to gain wealth from war and expansion. It entails that revisionist models of Romanization should reconcile with the idea that Romans were raiders, sackers, and exploiters across the Mediterranean and Europe, rather than defenders of civilization.[121] Millett's solution is to separate the Imperial administration from the Republican conquest. He carefully distinguishes that while the Republican elite's competition for wealth and power fuelled exploitation and subjection of their neighbours, the Imperial decentralized government depended on incorporation, prosperity, and cooperation of the provincial elites:

> The shift in administrative system from Republic to Empire may thus have diminished the centrally exploitative rôle of the imperial system, with consequent benefits for the provinces.

---

[121] For instance, in his influential work on the origin of Roman imperialism, Kurt A. Raaflaub confines the Roman pathological character as developed by Harris to the mid to late Republican period. He argues that the constant conflict and competition with neighbouring powers over centuries in the region shaped the Romans' so-called aggressive pattern of behaviour, or 'mentality', a term which he adopts. Emphasizing the geopolitical environment in which Rome became an imperial power, Raaflaub carefully removes the Romans' active agency in their aggressive imperialism. Raaflaub 1996.

Romanization: Negotiation, and a Tipping Point 127

We can draw these strands together to see Roman imperialism as an extension of the competitive structure of the élite in Rome itself. Expansion was not planned in relation to any grand strategy, and was executed piecemeal. Similarly, the advantages accruing from this expansion were not systematically organized and their exploitation was circumscribed because of the moral and ethical constraints of Roman society. These constraints did break down in the late Republic, but the Augustan administrative system deflected any emergence of systematic economic imperialism.[122]

He stresses that the economic drive for the Republican expansion did not translate into the same economic motivation sustaining the Imperial administration. He argues that unless the economic principles of the Republican expansion and the Imperial administration are separated, it would lead to the error of conflating the Roman Empire with the modern mercantile empires. On the one hand, he accepts the merits of Harris' argument while taking care not to overstretch it and not to make an error of anachronism. Yet, this approach relegates social and economic exploitation to the early phase of conquest and, instead, promotes social and economic collaboration in the later phase of Roman rule. This approach may evade the anachronistic error, but also circumvents the issue of imperialistic exploitation.

'A good shepherd shears his sheep, he does not skin them', as Millet quotes Suetonius' *Tiberius* on the imperial policy of provincial taxation.[123] Here, Millett assumes the Romano-centric apologetic attitude towards imperialistic exploitation: Romans were 'the good shepherds'. He reaffirms the literary source produced under the imperialist perspective, instead of approaching the history of Roman imperialism narrated from Roman imperialist perspective with scepticism. This suggests that the questioning of sources and interpretative framework seems to be limited: how the Roman imperial hegemony governed the production of literary, epigraphic, and archaeological data and, in addition, how 'the historiographical tradition out of which Roman archaeology developed' during the imperial period continues to influence methodology or interpretation.[124] At times, Millett recognizes instances where the Romans fell short of being 'the good shepherds'. The presence of the Roman army on foreign soil unavoidably 'destabilized' the local economy, land distribution, sex ratio, and social structure, and the occasional corruption of a few governors fomented 'discontent' among the locals.[125] Yet, it is difficult not to notice that the negative impacts of Roman imperialism on Britons seem downplayed. Compared with contemporary postcolonial writings, expressions

---

[122] Millett 1990: 6, 8. [123] Millett 1990: 57. [124] Freeman 1993: 443. [125] Millett 1990: 56–69.

such as 'destabilizing' rather than demolishing, or 'discontent' rather than grievance, inevitably understate the extent and degree of effects. More importantly, they circumscribe the phenomena to a necessary evil, an unfortunate outcome, or a bad apple against the overarching teleology of Romanization and totalization of Roman imperialism:

> [W]e need to examine the process of the conquest, not as a problem of gaining and controlling ground, but as one of winning over the peoples of LPRIA Britain.
> The complexities of supply were even greater if we are correct in assuming that the conquerors tried to ensure that unnecessary discontent was not created by making excessive demands on the native population. The self-interest in this is evident and would have combined to with the desire not to antagonize native populations, whether allied or defeated, with an imperative not to over-exploit the supply base and thus threaten future years' harvests by lack of seed corn. These considerations suggest that native supplies would have been carefully exploited and supplemented by import where necessary.[126]

According to Millett's empirical investigation, Romans were rational, mindful, and effective imperialists. His portrait of the Romans lays bare the weakness of the empiricist tradition without due epistemological consideration. In the continuing tradition of positivist history, surviving pro-Roman evidence is too often and too quickly validated without fully taking into account two intertwined imperialistic epistemologies at its foundation: ancient Roman imperialistic epistemology hegemonized the production of most surviving literary evidence, and modern Western imperialist epistemology has for a long time promoted apologetic interpretation via the paradigm of defensive imperialism and civilizing Romanization. The teleology of Romanization and totalization of Roman imperialism continue to underlie Millett's paradigm and, as a matter of course, fail to contextualize anti-Roman factors in the same way Dyson does. Anti-Roman factors are again reduced to an interruption either due to a lack of evidence or an anachronistically misplaced critique of modern imperialism. Indeed, there are differences to be recognized between modern and ancient imperialisms. The analyses of modern imperial exploitation of colonies should be applied to the ancient Roman exploitation of colonies with caution.[127] Nevertheless, literary sources produced under a Romano-centric perspective, as exemplified by Suetonius' comment on Roman taxation as 'a good shepherd' policy, do not prove that Roman

---

[126] Millett 1990: 44, 56.
[127] Richard Hingley applies Immanuel M. Wallerstein's World-systems theory to explain Roman imperial exploitation: Hingley 1982.

imperialism was not exploitative. In addition, it is difficult to infer from the sources grounded in Romano-centric epistemology that the Roman Empire was any less exploitative (given the relative scale of the ancient economy) than the modern empires and, therefore, that the comparison of exploitation anachronistic or unsound. Fundamentally, the fault line lies in the awareness of how much imperialism exploits not only the economy but also the epistemology of the subject territory – whether modern or ancient. Without sufficient epistemological consideration of the interpretative framework, a positivist investigation would conveniently fall back on the conventional imperialist epistemology to interpret the empirical data. An emphasis on 'facts', in other words the positivist methodology at the cost of epistemological questioning, would add to the effect of creating another 'factoid' that the empirical data substantiate. The consequence of this will echo the nineteenth- and early twentieth-century hegemony of the imperialistic epistemology when empirical sciences systematically legitimized European imperialism and historical knowledges vindicated Eurocentric epistemology.

Next, let us move on to Millett's treatment of the Britons. Millett recasts ancient Britons in a radically different representation. First, he reclaims the entitlement to civilization for pre-Claudian Britain. With numerous discoveries about LPRIA Britain, he establishes a new representation of civilized Britons prior to the conquest. Consequently, Millett elevates the post-conquest British ruling elites from passive adopters of Roman civilization to active adapters to Romano-British civilization. They are no longer merely colonized subjects, but resourceful mediators. Millett redefines the British elites as key contributors along with other provincial elites to shift the axis of Roman civilization from central Italy to peripheral provinces in administrative, military, and cultural spheres and, eventually, to reformulate what *romanitas* is. Yet, in Millett's paradigm, Britons do not become historical agents in their own right. In short, the position of Britons hinged on the Romans. Both before and after the Claudian conquest, British elites exercised their influence and maintained their status principally through their control of contact channels between the Roman world and their local sphere. As for pre-conquest Britain, Millett refers to Haselgrove's article, 'Romanization before the Conquest: Gaulish precedents and British consequences', published in 1984.[128] Haselgrove argues and Millett concurs that:

> [T]he social leaders of the south and east held a monopoly of trade in raw materials passing to the Empire from their territories and those further

[128] Haselgrove 1984.

inland. Through their trade contact with Rome they acquired scarce imported goods for themselves, which were held as monopoly. They thus attained additional value as symbols of prestige. The monopoly of such goods enabled the élite to maintain and enhance their power over society through control of these prestige goods, their conspicuous consumption and their proposal to clients within or beyond the social system.[129]

Essentially, according to Millett, the place of British elites in the increasingly Romanized world depended on their access to the Roman world. He defines LPRIA Britain – prior to the conquest – not as an independent domain in trade and communication with the Roman Empire, but as a 'sphere of [Roman] influence' economically and culturally, 'a pale reflection' of Romanized Gaul, and a province *to be* Romanized sooner or later.[130] The understanding certainly is not colonialist in the manner of those from the nineteenth and early twentieth century which perceived Britons as intelligent barbarians or noble savages to benefit from Romanization. However, the teleology of Romanization predetermines how to approach and understand the LPRIA Britons and brings LPRIA Britain under Roman imperialism even before the conquest. Hence, in this paradigm of Millett, the historical status of Britons changes from the barbarian to the civilized because of their continental contacts and influences formed thereby – that is, from the Romano-centric perspective.

The Romano-centric perspective still persists in explanations of post-conquest Britain. Before moving on to post-conquest Britain, Millett revises the significance of the conquest. As mentioned above, the colonialist interpretation of the previous generations, eulogizing the conquest as the dawn of civilization in Britain, became untenable in the late twentieth century. In the wave of the postcolonial revisionist movement, Millett points out the inescapable consequences of foreign invasion and garrison in the form of destabilization and discontent. However, the Romans were not completely 'foreign' to Britons in Millett's model, as he has established earlier in the explanation of LPRIA Britain. He accordingly argues that although the Claudian conquest may have temporarily disrupted political, military, and social structures in Britain, it in time fortified and stabilized the social, economic, and cultural structures that had previously existed under Roman influence. The Claudian conquest does not signal a point of discontinuity and interruption by colonization, but a point of continuity and acceleration of existing Romanization. Just as the LPRIA British elites prior to the conquest maintained their status through their access to the

[129] Millett 1990: 38.   [130] Millett 1990: 40, 30.

Roman World, Romano-British elites after the conquest continued to utilize their access to the Romans, more and better than before:

> Political positions within the new structure may have conferred their own status both through access to the new supra-tribal source of power and the knowledge of Roman ways, together with the associated material attributes. This access to things Roman, both materially and in the abstract, would fulfil an important rôle in social competition. ... In the early years after the conquest this process was vital, as shown in the words of Tacitus (*Agricola* 21): 'competition for honour proved as effective as compulsion ... ' ... [T]he process of portraying oneself as Roman – wearing the toga and speaking latin – became a 'prestige good' in its own right.[131]

Romanization, essentially the same in kind and only intensified in degree, ensued 'by passive encouragement' and 'without coercion'.[132] Given their higher level of Romanization, Millett changes our understanding of Romano-British elites, elevating their status from that of colonized subjects in earlier models to productive co-operators in his new model. Millett takes Romano-British elites' increased purchase of Samian ware and wine, increased construction of villas, and increased use of Latin as evidence of the British aspiration to emulate Romans and to participate in *romanitas*, rather than evidence of cultural exchange or spillover.[133] This again relates that the theoretical premise is critical in interpreting empirical data. In his interpretative framework where the elites determine the social, economic, and cultural structure and trickle them down, the Roman elites are the determinants across their provinces and the visionaries to spread their system and values.[134] The provincials are instantly relegated to the emulators of their colonizers' civilization and the agents to realize their colonizers' vision. It is this Romano-centric perspective that underlies whether we interpret the Romano-British data as evidence of voluntary emulation of Roman identity rather than, for example, that of political and economic calculation.

Despite the Romano-centric underpinnings, which became perceptible only after further development of postcolonial thought in the discourse on Romanization, Millett's *Romanization of Britain* in 1990 marks a Tipping Point in the Anglo-American scholarship. Encouraged by both the postcolonial wave to challenge the colonialist historiography and the rise of LPRIA archaeology, Millett took the first step towards

---

[131] Millett 1990: 68.   [132] Millett 1990: 101, 168.   [133] Freeman 1993.
[134] Millett 1990: 151. 'The prime elements in society were the elites who maintain a strong control over social and economic exchange.'

dismantling the age-old colonialist structure of the Romanization model in which the civilized Romans enlightened the barbaric Britons. Bringing numerous recently published excavation reports and landscape surveys of small finds and structures into a synthesis, he argues that Britons had their own civilization in contact with Roman civilization and were Romanized not in unilateral but in dialectical acculturation. The LPRIA British elites established a stable hierarchy, a refined culture, and geographic diversity as a result of their continental contacts, and the Romano-British elites flourished by strengthening their ties to the Roman world and emulating *romanitas*. The elite-driven social and economic structure naturally manifested itself in intensifying Romanization in Britain; Roman elites transmitted their civilization, Romano-British elites mediated it to the ordinary Britons, and the ordinary Britons aspired to it. Millett transforms Romanization from a one-way acculturation to a dialectical exchange, albeit between asymmetrical parties of unequal power, and promotes Romano-British elites from conquered savages to valuable negotiators. The trickle-down paradigm of Millett hinges on Romano-British elites. They are the key to understanding Romanization and to interpreting the vast amount of Romano-British data.

Yet to have a moment of epistemological shift in the discourse on Romanization, the imperialist epistemology – teleology of Romanization and totalization of Roman imperialism – proved to be too deep-rooted to dismantle with the first revisionist model of Millett's. Archaeological sources that offer a possibility of mitigating the perspective embedded in traditional elite-driven literary sources do not necessarily counterbalance or question but could easily consolidate the Romano-centric and elite-driven perspective. Notwithstanding an irrefutable fact that colonial rule dictated an asymmetrical relationship between Romans and Britons, a Romano-centric perspective perpetuates a particular reading of Romano-British archaeological data and defines the Britons in relation to their agreeability to the Romans. Nonetheless, there is no question of Millett's contribution to raising awareness about the colonialist system of knowledge underlying the discourse on Romanization and revising the colonialist power structure in the old Romanization framework. He tuned Romanization studies into the changing intellectual climate of questioning imperialism. Even though it may sound patronizing nowadays, his lifting of Romano-British elites from the intelligent barbarians unilaterally benefiting from civilized Romans to the cooperative negotiators bridging Romans and Britons in dialectical acculturation was a big stride in Romanization studies. Millett's reframing of Romanization as a process of delicate negotiation, based on the revised power structure, brought a Tipping Point to move the discourse on Romanization towards the postcolonial age.

Becoming Roman: Power and Knowledge

In 1998, Greg Woolf published a seminal work that pushes the boundaries of how we understand Roman imperialism and Romanization, *Becoming Roman: The Origins of Provincial Civilization in Gaul*.[135] His pioneering thesis was a product of his individual insight to revise the paradigm of Romanization, but also a product of the intellectual climate of the time. As a late twentieth-century historian, Woolf shared an intellectual environment with Millett and Dyson in a broad sense. Yet, the world has hardly stayed still since Millett's last landmark work in 1990. The on-going process of decolonization had settled in to consolidate a new world order, divided into the three worlds.[136] The Berlin Wall fell in 1989 and Germany was reunified in the following year. Not long after, in 1991, the mighty Soviet Union was dissolved. The age of Cold War – and arguably by extension the age of empire – had come to a grand finale. For some, the world as they would have understood it had piece by piece fallen apart. The collapse of existing orders one after another gave more credibility and wider currency to a set of 'post-isms' that tried to make sense of the new world – postmodernism, poststructuralism, and postcolonialism. These ideas travelled further and deeper. Gradually changing the landscape of academia, these new schools of thought sent shockwaves that the rather insulated scholarship of Roman history could no longer shrug off as irrelevant. Naturally, Roman historians enjoyed more exposure to them and gradually absorbed these new intellectual influences.[137] Woolf decisively signalled that the tides of these intellectual currents were strengthening in Romanization studies. Going further than previous historians who had

---

[135] Woolf 1998; Mouritsen 1998.
[136] Alfred Sauvy, a French historian, coined the term third world (*tier monde*) to refer to the countries that largely share a colonial past and remain unaligned with the capitalistic and communistic bloc. Sauvy 1986.
[137] With the rise of poststructuralism in the scholarship of Roman history, culture became a primary focus for the analysis of the network of power relations and the process of power negotiations. Scholars explored discourses of power embedded in various aspects of imperial culture, from art and architecture to urbanism and munificence. In particular, Zanker's work achieved a monumental success to establish Roman art and architecture as a form of power discourse: Zanker 1988. Also, see Boatwright 1987; Wallace-Hadrill 1993, 2008. For a detailed discussion on how the discourse on the city of Rome has become a scene to understand the power network, see Patterson 1992.

touched upon the issues raised by poststructuralism and postcolonialism, such as teleology, totalization, and the dialectics of imperial power, Woolf addresses the fundamental issue – that is, the imperialist system of power-knowledge entrenched in the discourse on Romanization. He develops a revisionist model of Romanization that tackles the epistemological problem at the root of the discourse. Focusing on the issue of power and knowledge, Woolf approaches Romanization in a radically different way. In fact, asserting that 'the notion of Romanization itself is fundamentally flawed as an heuristic tool', he aims to redress and reconceptualize the process of cultural change in imperial power dynamics and to explores what it meant to become Roman in a complex system of provincial culture and imperial power. With this context in mind, let us delve into Woolf's model.

Woolf's *Becoming Roman* has become a modern classic in Romanization studies, after Millett's *The Romanization of Britain*. Like Millett, with his versatile command of literary, epigraphic, and archaeological sources, Woolf has had an enduring impact on the discourse. Yet, compared with Millett, Woolf took a different scholarly trajectory and accordingly moved the discourse on Romanization to a new plane mainly in two ways. First, Woolf extends the focus of the discourse from Roman Britain to Roman Gaul. The discourse on Romanization in the context of Anglo-American scholarship, particularly in British scholarship, has unsurprisingly revolved around Roman Britain; and Romano-British scholarship from Haverfield to Millett has maintained a special place in the discourse.[138] In Romanization studies dominated by Roman Britain, Woolf brings a fresh focus of study to the forefront. By extension, he also introduces a different scholarly tradition embedded in the study of Roman Gaul to the Anglo-American discourse on Romanization, which will be discussed further. Second, he shifts the discourse on Romanization firmly into the post-Foucauldian and post-Said intellectual landscape. While previous historians have explored concerns widely expressed and publicized by poststructuralist and postcolonial movements, Woolf is one of the first historians to engage with the question that sits at the core of poststructuralism and postcolonialism, that is, the system of power and knowledge. With these two moves, he decisively brings the discourse on Romanization to an intellectual context different from before. Hitherto, the discourse has permitted many different sub-discipline studies and contemporary thoughts to collaborate and compete – within the boundaries of the conventional system of knowledge/truth, that is,

[138] Hingley 2000.

Eurocentric and Romano-centric. However, Woolf opens the door for new threads of thoughts to push the epistemological boundaries.

Let us first enquire into the significance of his choice of study, Roman Gaul. Of course there has been an array of regional studies across the Roman Empire from the East to the West, including Roman Gaul.[139] Yet, as mentioned above, in Anglo-American scholarship, the archaeology-led Romano-British scholarship has been the primary driving force behind the Romanization studies. Other regional studies have largely been tucked away on the back shelf for a small group of specialists. Gallo-Roman studies has been no exception in remaining out of the limelight in Anglo-American scholarship. Only when it comes to the discourse on Romanization in French scholarship did Gallo-Roman studies serve as a cornerstone in the same way that Romano-British studies did in Anglo-American scholarship.[140] For this reason, the success of Woolf's study on Roman Gaul resonates differently from that of Millett's study on Roman Britain. While Millett updates the repertoire of Anglo-American scholarship for the new generation, Woolf leads the Anglo-American readership to an unfamiliar territory.[141] It was not only the province of Roman Gaul that the wider Anglo-American scholarship was unaccustomed to, but also the French thoughts embedded in Gallo-Roman studies (on which detailed discussion will follow). Woolf presents a province composed of ideas unexplored by Anglo-American scholarship. His success of a Gallo-Roman study paved the way for French thoughts to travel to the Anglo-American discourse on Romanization, providing a fresh source of inspiration.

There was also a critical view on Woolf's focus on Roman Gaul. Clifford Ando, in his review of Woolf's *Becoming Roman*, warns readers to be sceptical about Woolf's perspective, which is rooted in his choice of study:

> [L]et me urge those investigating other provinces to study Woolf's methods and arguments with care. This advice is in some ways paradoxical, for if

---

[139] Elizabeth W. B. Fentress and Susan E. Alcock compiled various regional studies on urbanization in the context of Romanization: Fentress and Alcock 2000. On Romanization in the Western Empire, see Blagg and Millett 1990.

[140] Anglo-American scholarship is not a monolithic cluster. Yet, at least when it comes to the discourse on Romanization, Anglo-American scholarship shared research to make a continuous discourse because many scholars worked across Britain and the United States.

[141] Roman Gaul mostly had a small portion in empire-wide studies, rather than standing alone as an area of study in Anglo-Saxon scholarship. Before Woolf's *Becoming Roman*, there were not many studies on Roman Gaul in Anglo-Saxon scholarship. John F. Drinkwater and Colin C. Haselgrove are two of the few Anglo-Saxon scholars to have explored Roman Gaul extensively: Drinkwater 1983; Haselgrove 1990.

Becoming Roman has a serious flaw, it lies in Woolf's obsessive concern with Gaul. Although Woolf acknowledges that the boundaries of Roman provinces were political constructs, he nevertheless adopts them as his own. He also follows Braudel in endowing France with a singular and unique identity that is simultaneously uniquely diverse. Time and again Woolf could have bolstered his argument or asked his questions with greater nuance by casting his gaze beyond the boundaries of Gaul. It is in matters outside the chronological and geographical limits of his inquiry that Woolf seems understandably weak, and yet information from precisely those areas might have helped him the most.[142]

There is no need for Ando's commentary to remind us that Woolf's study has its geographical limits. It is superfluous to reiterate an obvious fact that Roman Gaul delimits empirical evidence that could contribute to a more comprehensive understanding of the so-called Romanization process, to which any regional study is subject. What Ando directs our attention to is that Roman Gaul is a geographical boundary not only in an empirical sense but also in an epistemological sense. Referring to and influenced by the French tradition of Gallo-Roman studies, Woolf's study of Roman Gaul inherits its premises and frameworks to posit a continuous and whole entity from Roman Gaul to modern France. Even though he is conscious of the legacy and its limits, as Ando observes, '[Woolf] nevertheless adopts [it] as his own'.[143] Despite his critical tone, Ando's critique brings Woolf's epistemological background into attention. Ando criticizes its drawback, but its advantage deserves to be appreciated at the same time. Although Woolf, as Ando critically notes, might possibly echo the limits of Gallo-Roman studies in French scholarship, he on the flip side introduces new premises and frameworks to the Anglo-American discourse on Romanization that can disrupt the Romanization model prevailing in Romano-British studies in Anglo-Saxon scholarship. In other words, Woolf's study on Roman Gaul potentially contributes to decentring the discourse grounded in Romano-British studies.

Ando explains the French tradition of Gallo-Roman studies which underlies Woolf's model, but he only gives an example of Braudelian *longue durée* and mentalité.[144] Indeed, the Annales school was prominent in French scholarship. They articulated enduring historical continuities that form over centuries and used them to project a primitive form of

---

[142] Ando 1999.
[143] Woolf attributes his learning of French Gallo-Roman studies to Christian Goudineau and Olivier Buchsenschutz: Woolf 1998: xii.
[144] Braudel 1949.

Becoming Roman: Power and Knowledge 137

nationhood to the past. Under the aegis of the Annales school, Roman Gaul came to be understood to first consolidate unique French spirit into one entity which would be later developed and realized into a form of modern France.[145] However, by the time of Woolf, the Annales school achieved international influence, and their ideas were hardly confined to French scholarship. Anglo-American scholarship has also witnessed kindred thoughts developing in Romanization studies. Romano-British scholarship, in its early stage, also used to project an idea of ancestral nationhood back to Roman Britain, and Finley and Harris most notably have coined a concept of Roman mentality thanks to the wide currency of the Annales school's thoughts. Woolf's approach to Roman Gaul as a unit to share a certain unique mentality and historical unity was no less Anglo-American than French. Yet, Ando's comment is not all in vain. Woolf's study has still become a conduit for French thought to travel to the Anglo-American discourse on Romanization – and despite it having slipped from many eyes – including that of Foucault.[146]

'Power is a slippery concept', thus Woolf broaches the subject of Roman imperial power.[147] He attempts to pin down the elusive nature of Roman power through the career path of a third-century Gallo-Roman elite, Titus Sennius Solemnis, as inscribed on a marble statue base.[148] Tracking Solemnis' rise to power via the network of patronage, Woolf makes the Roman imperial power tangible as a network of power relations infiltrating provinces. In the expanding Roman network of power configurations, Woolf argues that 'Gauls were not passive objects of Roman rule, but had been implicated by Rome in a new configuration of power, new complexes of domination'.[149] On the surface, Woolf seems to reproduce Millett's framework in a Gallo-Roman context. Woolf's promotion of Gallo-Romans from passive instruments to active agents in Romanization chimes with Millett's advancement of the Romano-British as negotiators in a trickle-down power structure. However, there stands a fundamental difference between Millett and Woolf. What Millett

---

[145] The tradition has been passed down from Camille Jullian and subsequently survived. See Jullian 1920; Demougeot et al. 1983. Yet, the way Woolf dealt with the Braudelian continuity between Roman Gaul and modern France appears to be less simplistic: '[r]egional diversity has in any case long been characteristic of France, a product in part of an environment that, without insulating populations, has permitted their circumscription into local communities and traditions. It is the brief convergence of Roman provincial cultures during the formative period that demands explanation.' Woolf 1998: 239.
[146] Timothy D. Barnes is one of the few who attributes Woolf's work to the influence of Foucault: Barnes 2000.
[147] Woolf 1998: 24.   [148] *CIL* XIII 3162.   [149] Woolf 1998: 24.

addresses is the power hierarchy between Romans and Britons. Shifting the axis of power closer to conquered Britons than the earlier models of Roman imperialism and Romanization, Millett restructures Roman imperialism and Romanization from unilateral control to dialectical hybrid that hinges on cultural brokers. Meanwhile, Woolf turns his attention to the concept of power itself. Although he appears to prefer not to discuss theories on power extensively, in one of his fine-print footnotes he drops a hint on his theoretical inspiration: 'dynamic conception of social power may also be related to Foucault's emphasis on the creative and productive aspects of power, and rejection of the notion of power as something that may be possessed and that acts primarily to prevent action'.[150] As discussed previously, Foucault made a singular contribution to deconstructing the conventional notion of dialectical power relations. Foucault renounces the traditional concept of power that is reduced to a single trajectory of being prohibitive, disciplinary, and punitive. Instead, he proposes a new concept, the network of power relations, that embraces multiple directions, forms, and effects of power, such as inter-dependence, complementarity, selective obstruction, subversion, and resistance. Using Foucauldian vocabulary to define imperialism as 'the expansion of configurations of power', Woolf strongly evokes Foucault's notion of the power network to re-conceptualize Roman imperialism and Romanization.[151]

Until Woolf introduced Foucault's power network to Roman imperialism and Romanization, the understanding of power relations underlying Roman imperialism and Romanization had been rather limited. The traditional model, most recently articulated by Brunt, posits Rome as a source of power emanating political and cultural influence to provinces in varying degrees, depending on their proximity to the centre of power.[152] In this model, Roman imperialism is conceptualized as a unilaterally dominant force, and Romanization is the unifying process. Later, the updated models, most notably brought by Millett, identify two points of power, Romans and natives, and conceive imperial culture as a product of the dialectical relationship between the two. In these models, whether natives either resist or emulate Romans, Romanization is a dialectical process between the two points of power.[153] Woolf then voices the need for 'a more nuanced picture of power in Roman Gaul'. He does not explicitly credit Foucault with his nuanced approach to Roman power, but his reference and vocabulary imply

---

[150] Woolf 1998: 24. [151] Woolf 1998: 26. [152] Brunt 1976.
[153] In Bénabou's model, natives are the second source of power in resisting Romanizing power. In Millett's model, natives are also the second source of power, but to emulate Romans and mediate Romanization.

that he applies Foucault's network of power relations to shed light on the complexity of Roman power. Like Foucault, Woolf attempts to put forward the wider network of power relations, which involves multiple points of power effecting in multiple directions – not just in dialectical directions, but disruptive, complementary, and/or interdependent. Instead of compartmentalizing natives' involvement into either resistance or emulation, he attempts to incorporate the complex power network into his model, 'one that admits the power of Nehalennia (a syncretized Gallo-Roman deity) and the dilemma of a mediating aristocracy in time of revolt'.[154] Furthermore, he argues that an understanding of the complex power network is vital, because 'there is no single or uniform experience of imperialism'.[155] To explain different fates resulting from imperial rule – some lost their tribal leadership while others gained new authority; some were dislocated from their land while others acquired new wealth; and some were integrated to the new imperial system and others were disintegrated from their old communities – Woolf expresses the necessity of deconstructing the power dialectics in Roman imperialism and Romanization and instead proposes Foucault's network of power configurations.

This, ergo, begs a question: how does Woolf deconstruct the power dialectics between Romans and natives in the discourse on Romanization? When Woolf mentions diverse experiences of imperialism, not just resistance or emulation but in-betweens, he leads us in a promising direction to deconstruct the colonial dialectics. Albeit from a distance, he somewhat echoes Bhabha's notion of ambivalence in colonial experience. Bhabha, earlier in 1987, had pinned down ambivalent desires of both the colonizers and the colonized entrenched in their complex network of power relations: the colonizers want the colonized to emulate them but still want to distinguish themselves, whereas the colonized want to mimic the colonizers but still want to overthrow and/or deride them. Significantly, Bhabha has proposed ambivalence as a key to deconstruct the dialectics between the colonizers and the colonized, since their internal contradictions between desire and fear, and between control and anxiety, create a complex web of power relations, rather than a dialectical relationship between the two.

However, the crucial link on how to deconstruct the colonial dialectics, as seen in Bhabha's works, unfortunately, remains wanting in Woolf's *Becoming Roman*. Perhaps that is why Ando regrets that '[w]hat is missing from Woolf's argument is power ... Woolf occasionally raises the problem of power: he observes, for example, that "the ideology of empire often leads

---

[154] Woolf 1998: 23.   [155] Woolf 1998: 26.

rulers to treat different subjects in different ways", but this complex assertion is, remarkably, the penultimate sentence in its section and receives no immediate elaboration of any kind'.[156] Indeed, towards the end of the chapter on Roman power, the complexity of the power network is left rather unresolved in relation to how complicatedly power relations were entangled and how the complex power network shaped an equally complex process of so-called Romanization:

> At that point the configuration of power that encompassed the Roman empire, imperial society and a new economy was transformed and expanded downwards *into* Gallic societies, upsetting the old order and forcing the creation of new mediating institutions through which the energies and resources of the Gauls were harnessed to new ends. The process might be compared to the demolition of street upon street of old houses, materials from which were used to create a towerblock to house the former inhabitants in a new style. Destructive and disruptive through this, some Gauls did well out of it. One group in particular stands out, a new aristocracy created out of the rubble of the old, but with greater authority, status, wealth and security than their grandfathers had ever had. That group was to take the lead in building Roman Gaul [emphasis in original].[157]

Without a strong proposition on how to deconstruct the power dialectics in the discourse on Roman imperialism and Romanization with the Foucauldian network of power relations, Woolf's Romanization model to some extent falls back into the dialectical relationship. To paraphrase Woolf's words, Romans expanded their power configurations *into* Gaul and absorbed colonized Gauls under their system, while Gauls were on the receiving end of the new Roman network of power configurations. Woolf refines how Roman power affected the colonized – not as a unilateral source of power, not as a superior power in competition with the dialectical inferior, but as a network of power relations transforming the colonized in multiple fronts and directions. Yet, the Foucauldian network of power configurations that holds the potential to destabilize the colonial dialectics was yet to be fully explored in Woolf's model. Leaving the question of colonial dialectics not fully answered, his model to a certain degree revises the colonial dialectics to a more nuanced version.

Nevertheless, Woolf's pivotal contribution to the discourse in Romanization also closely follows Foucauldian theories. Foucault stresses that one of the critical aspects in multifaceted and anti-Roman multi-directional power configurations is that power forms a 'régime of truth'.

---

[156] Ando 1999: 387. [157] Woolf 1998: 46–47.

Through a discourse which determines true and false in accordance with the values of a given society, a group of discursive knowledge – neither universally or permanently valid – is authorized, regulated, and circulated as truth. Truth, Foucault contends, is not a form of knowledge purified from political ideologies, but in itself is power. Crucially, Said takes this further and investigates the significance of Foucault's theory on power and knowledge/truth in colonial contexts. He explores how the modern Western colonizers have created a discourse concerning the Eastern colonized and have established it as a system of knowledge/truth to vindicate Western imperialism. It is accurate that Woolf does not allude to either Foucault's *Power-Knowledge* or Said's *Orientalism*. Their intellectual influence does not surface in the foreground. It is admittedly subtle, yet compelling. Woolf not only echoes Foucauldian and Said-esque vocabulary, such as power configurations, régime of values, cultural system, culture and imperialism, but also parallels their model of power and knowledge/truth with his own format of 'civilizing ethos'.[158] While many cultural historians have concentrated on tangible and traceable aspects of Romanization and have approached it as a change in material culture,[159] Woolf probes into the system of knowledge/truth behind Romanization. This approach evokes how Said has shown that Orientalism as a 'scientific' discipline was, in fact, discursive thoughts, imagination, and knowledge that the Western Self has gathered from geography, anthropology, philology, literature, and culture concerning the Eastern Other. In the same manner, Woolf draws to our attention the fact that the Roman Self has also created and circulated discursive knowledge about the colonized Other, in this case Gallo-Romans. Writings 'of earlier histories and ethnographies, of the propaganda of Roman generals, of administrative documents, itineraries ... of the accounts of soldiers, prisoners-of-war, exiles and traders' formed discursive knowledge about the Other, and Strabo's *Geography* and Pliny the Elder's *Natural History* effectively complied

---

[158] As to Woolf's mention of 'regime of values', see Woolf 1998: 178, 181, 184, 185. As to his mention of 'cultural system' and/or 'culture and imperialism', see Woolf 1998: 1–16, 56, 93, 193, 238–49. He mostly uses the term in the sense of the régime of aesthetic values and tastes to explain change in Gallo-Roman material culture. The wider significance in the Foucauldian and Said-esque sense, rather, parallels his explanation on civilizing ethos. For this idea, he accredits another French philosopher and sociologist, Pierre Bourdieu, who is closely connected to Foucault in the intellectual landscape for their studies on power. Compared with Foucault, Bourdieu concentrates on the symbolic power in the cultural sphere: see Bourdieu 1979.

[159] The theory of the Veblen effect, which explains the status-seeking consuming pattern, has been influential in archaeological studies to interpret material culture as a strategy of emulation. See Miller 1982. On the wider implications of material culture, see Hodder 1982. On the consuming pattern in the Roman Empire, see Wallace-Hadrill 2008.

discursive knowledge to codify the Romano-centric system of knowledge/truth:[160]

> This Romano-centrism is also evident in the natural rationales claimed for various Roman provincial boundaries, in the correlations between the extent of Roman knowledge and the extent of Roman power, and in the role accorded to Roman rule in civilizing the Gauls and in realizing their potential for prosperity.[161]

Like Said, Woolf identifies self-reflexive and self-serving Roman discourse where the Romano-centric régime of truth, or 'civilizing ethos', has been constructed to enable and sustain Roman military, economic, and cultural imperialism of the Other.

At the core of this Romano-centric discourse of 'civilizing ethos', according to Woolf, lies the concept of *humanitas*. Being an all-encompassing expression for various Roman virtues and codes of conduct, from *gravitas* to *mores*, *humanitas* is a difficult concept to pin down. It is not quite equivalent to Greek *paideia* either, which stands for a narrower definition of intellectual culture and cultivation. Rather, it embraces not only explicit lofty ideals of human virtues but also implicit connotations to grade people along the hierarchy of *humanitas* and to endorse or disapprove accordingly.[162]

> [I]t is clear that by the late first century BC *humanitas* had been formulated as a thoroughly Roman concept, embodying concepts of culture and conduct that were regarded by Romans as the hallmarks of the aristocracy in particular, yet also appropriate for mankind in general. *Humanitas* thus distinguished an elite as cultivated, enlightened, humane and so fitted to rule and lead by example, but it also encapsulated a set of ideals to which all men might aspire.[163]

Woolf describes how the concept of *humanitas* served as a cornerstone to uphold Roman imperialism. It was not simply a byword for Roman virtues but an ideological tool to legitimize the rule of the Roman elites. By placing themselves on the top echelon of *humanitas*, Roman elites saw their collective Self as optimal human beings, 'the fulfilment of the potential of the *genus humanum*' and, as one might expect, dehumanized the Other as lesser human beings, 'imperfect humans, part-way to

---

[160] Woolf 1998. As to ancient writings about the Other, see also Polybius, *Histories*; Caesar, *Gallic War*; Tacitus, *Germania*.
[161] Woolf 1998: 50.
[162] As to mentions of *humanitas* in Roman literature, see Cicero, *pro Caelio*; *de Officiis*; *ad Quintum fratrem*; Vitruvius, *de Architectura*; Pliny the Elder, *Naturalis Historia*, 3. 39; Virgil, *Aeneid*, 6. 851–53. Cf. Moritz 1962; Høgel 2015.
[163] Woolf 1998: 55.

beasts'.[164] Woolf argues that this implicit significance is integral to *humanitas*, since the concept of *humanitas* was critically forged as Romans came into contact with more foreigners during their expansion. This Roman system of power and knowledge/truth served its ideological end to distinguish the better Self from the lesser Other and to rationalize for the Self to colonize the Other. Thus Romans brought the Other into Roman learning, consciousness, mentality, and, ultimately, the Roman Empire.[165]

Woolf does not invoke a direct comparison with modern Western humanism, the similar role of which in legitimizing its colonialism has been most scathingly exposed by Fanon and further articulated and circulated by many postcolonial thinkers – that modern Western humanism categorized the Self as civilized and rational humans and dehumanized the Other as quasi-animals incapable of civilization and culture without help from the Self. They laid bare modern Western humanism sitting at the root of the colonialist epistemology. What Woolf argues about Roman *humanitas* corresponds to what postcolonial thinkers have revealed about modern Western humanism. A direct parallel may perhaps have been avoided because of the all-too-familiar caveat of making a comparison between the two: Roman *humanitas* was not anchored in ethnocentrism in the same way modern Western humanism was. Notwithstanding, Woolf underlines that *humanitas*, despite being available to foreigners in theory, in reality still functioned as an exclusive quality of the few to justify their imperialism – not to a certain ethnicity, but to the Roman elites.

Thus participating in poststructuralist and postcolonial tides led by Foucault and Said, Woolf approaches Roman imperialism and Romanization in a way radically different from his predecessors. Up until then, it had been largely understood that Roman imperialism wielded dialectical force against the Other and Romanization directed the Other either through persuasion or emulation to reach a set of rather homogenous ideals of Roman civilization. In these paradigms, provincial culture, which contains patchy elements of Roman civilization, was perceived as a diluted outcome of Romanization mediated by native elements, either by syncretism or resistance. In other words, the discourse at its root has implicated a dialectic relationship between the Roman and the Other, totalization of

---

[164] Woolf 1998: 59. On the perception and representation of the barbarian Other in Roman World, see Dauge 1981; Chauvot 2016; Ferris 2003. Yet, subversion of these ideas was also possible, most famously exemplified in Tacitus, *Agricola*. Cf. Wiedemann 1986.

[165] 'The Orient that appears in Orientalism, then, is a system of representations framed by a whole set of forces that brought the Orient into Western learning, Western consciousness, and later, Western empire.' Said 1978: 202–03.

Roman civilization and culture, and teleology of Romanization. By contrast, Woolf reconceptualizes Roman imperialism as the expansion of its network of power configurations that its imperialist régime of truth – formulated from imperial discourses – sustains. Consequently, Romanization becomes a process in which Gauls and the colonized Other partook in the discourse, the régime of truth, and the network of power configurations. As he describes, '[b]ecoming Roman was not a matter of acquiring a ready-made cultural package, then, so much as joining the insider's debate about what package did or ought to consist of at that particular time'.[166] It was a holistic process in which each participant at his or her differentiated position in the network of power relations responded to the Roman imperial discourse in his or her respective way. Hence, according to Woolf, the question of whether Romans civilized the Other or the Other emulated or resisted the Romans is heuristically misguided by supposing a dialectical relationship between the Romans and the Other:

> The motivations of individuals are always difficult to disentangle, and it is probably pointless to attempt to disentangle cultural action designed as a conscious strategy for self advancement from that prompted from a deep internalization of elite Roman values, but there is a clear convergence between the pragmatic interests of new Gallo-Roman aristocrats and the civilizing ethos of the empire's ruling classes. ... It is thus pointless to ask whether Rome civilized the Gauls or whether they civilized themselves [by emulating the Romans]. The educated elite of the empire joined together in the civilizing mission, sharing an identity that was Roman, humane and aristocratic.[167]

To demonstrate the process of how the Gauls gradually engaged with the Roman system of power and knowledge/truth, Woolf investigates various aspects such as epigraphy, urbanization, consumer goods, and religion. An increase in funerary inscriptions in Gaul suggests that the Gauls piecemeal picked up the Roman epigraphic habit of honouring a person and his or her deeds with an inscription;[168] an increase in gridded towns in Gaul implies that Gallic communities steadily engaged with the Roman mode of living *urbanitas*;[169] an increase in *amphorae* and Campanian ware indicates that

---

[166] Woolf 1998: 11.   [167] Woolf 1998: 74–75.
[168] Ramsay Macmullen introduced the concept of the 'epigraphic habit': MacMullen 1982. And Elizabeth Meyer connected the epigraphic habit with Romanization: Meyer 1990. Expanding the notion, Woolf interpreted the epigraphic habit as a symptom of the Roman social structure: Woolf 1996.
[169] On *urbanitas*, see Ramage 1973. The key to Roman *urbanitas*, according to Woolf, is not the celebration of urban life, but the notion of the city as a space in relation to the surrounding spaces from suburbs to countryside. The Roman perspective on settlement differentiation encapsulates *urbanitas*. On settlement differentiation, see Alcock 1995. Note that the urban anthropology is in many ways indebted to a French philosopher, Gaston Bachelard, who in turn has influenced Foucault and Bourdieu: Bachelard 1964 (originally published in French in 1958).

Becoming Roman: Power and Knowledge 145

the Gauls step by step tinkered with the Roman style of diet, aesthetics, and life;[170] and an increase in Gallo-Roman deities reflects that the Gauls gradually familiarized themselves with the Roman approach of *pietas* and *religio* to divinity.[171] It was a process drawn out over a long period in which the Gauls internalized the Roman code of conduct, cultural symbols, status differentiations, spatial poetics, etc., that is, the Roman system of power and knowledge/truth. 'By stages now difficult to measure, the styles and goods that had once symbolized Roman and not Gaulish, civilized and not barbarian came to mean rich and poor, and educated and not boorish'.[172] Eventually, it progressed into a phenomenon whereby the Gauls became involved in Roman discourse to create differences in form, dispersions in space, and discontinuities in time in the wider fabric of Roman imperial culture. Accordingly, Woolf asserts that it was by no means a process in which the Gauls were inevitably converging to the homogenized ideals of the Roman elites.[173] As he argues, to interpret the changing patterns in epigraphy, urbanization, consumer goods, and religion as an index of Romanization, and native elements as limits of Romanization, is a heuristic reduction to the dialectical model, hence limited as a means to explain the complex configuration of power and knowledge/truth. In his words, 'to attempt to measure the "*romanitas*", to debate whether Roman Gaul is more Gallic or more Roman, 'would be to debate ... whether the glass is half full or half empty'.[174] Rather, Gauls became Romans as they absorbed and navigated the Roman imperial system in both practice and theory, that is, not only Roman military, political, and economic control, but also the Roman régime of truth of *humanitas, urbanitas, religio,* and *pietas* in their own ways.

The difference in tone between Said and Woolf might at a first glance obscure the similarity in their approach to the imperial system of power and knowledge/truth. Said forthrightly takes a political position to expose Western colonialist epistemology, and in following Foucault, he contends that because knowledge in itself is power and political, claims to pure knowledge, including his own, are paradoxical. On the other hand, Woolf takes a different approach: '[u]nless the historian's aim is simply to condemn past imperialists by modern standards, understanding empire necessitates some considerations of these issues [among them notions of race and class, religion and sexuality, civility and nature, history and progress],

---

[170] Miller 1982; Wallace-Hadrill 2008.   [171] North 1979; Gordon 1990.   [172] Woolf 1998: 240.
[173] In fact, Woolf mentions convergence to describe Roman Gaul. He uses the term to explain convergence within Roman Gaul, convergence of Romano-Gallic communities, rather than convergence with Roman elites. Woolf 1998: 238–9.
[174] Woolf 1998: 208.

perhaps even some empathetic efforts'.[175] Compared with Said and other political thinkers, Woolf does not profess to take a political stance, and rather tries not to make his historical thesis on ancient Roman imperialism be politicized. Despite the difference in how they view their own research, inherently political or not, what Woolf reveals about Roman imperialism, in essence, agrees with what Said exposes about modern Western imperialism: imperial power, as a complex network of power configurations, exerts not only military, political, and economic domination, but also epistemic domination. Epistemic domination pivoting on the notion of Roman *humanitas*, as well as Western humanism, establishes an imperialist régime of knowledge/truth, enables imperial force, and vindicates imperialism. Woolf might not condemn Roman imperialists by modern standards, but he reveals the mechanism behind how Roman imperialism effected the so-called process of Romanization: the Roman system of power and knowledge/truth.

Appendix 3: History and Classics in Postwar France

> Today's French Classicists have a great deal to say about 'Western' thought. Unlike some of their Anglo-American counterparts, however, they tend to treat their subject more objectively as a living historical fact – not as some moribund fetish that needs to be propped up against the ever-fresh onslaughts of 'theory' or even barbarism. This book is lacking in grim exhortations that call upon Classicists to man the ramparts of crumbling empires. It is pervaded, rather, by a far more easy going atmosphere, one that fosters a general sense of intellectual optimism about 'Western' thought. The French Classicists' freedom from cultural insecurity – as Classicists – is palpable. ... In the long run, French Classicists view the term 'Western' in terms of historical contingency, not manifest destiny.[176]

This, quoted earlier in Appendix 1, yet again captures how French classicists and ancient historians perceive themselves, particularly in relation to their Anglo-Saxon peers in the postcolonial intellectual world. The pride of French classicists and ancient historians is not merely a hollow echo of the bygone glory of the nineteenth-century elitist Classics. On the contrary, it reflects a redefined prestige of the disciplines of history and Classics in the twentieth century. Compared with Anglo-American scholarship, which underwent radical changes

---

[175] Woolf 1998: 48.   [176] Nagy, Slatkin, and Loraux 2001: 2.

Appendix 3: History and Classics in Postwar France

within and outside the discipline – professionalization, marginalization, and democratization of the discipline; Marxism and multiculturalism across the intellectual world – French scholarship was yet to witness such a sweeping transformation in its immediate surroundings.

From the late nineteenth century, professionalization of academia and higher education has been established following the German model, which emphasizes disciplinary training and research in relation to the traditional public lecture.[177] The elitism tied to classical education has waned, but the significance of history and Classics has changed and endured. In particular, history became the focal point of intellectual culture in France. The ideological influence of history during the time of rivalry with Germany reinforced its significance and prestige, and the positivist climate of stressing methodological rigour offered it new direction and intellectual legitimacy in the new era of professional academics. Even after a hiatus caused by two World Wars, Revel explains, '[t]he postwar situation, which made the French feel both a part of history and a need to maintain their place, was also favourable to history in the professional sense. Indeed, the discipline proved very attractive to students who began their studies in the years immediately after the war. In their eyes history enjoyed the combined prestige of both intellectual commitment and ideological engagement'.[178] In the second half of the twentieth century, being a professional historian meant pursuing an admirable path of *intellectuel engagé*. It was not only in title or prestige. The number of academic positions and research centres in postwar France doubled; the number of academic works published has multiplied; the influence of the discipline in both academia and intellectual culture has expanded; and swelling public interest in history has added authority and significance to professional academic historians.

The presence of classicists in France did not dwindle either. Instead of aristocratic identification with the past, intellectual engagement with new thoughts promised to sustain the significance of Classics. Loraux, Nagy, and Slatkin describe the atmosphere: '[I]t is clear that these same French Classicists consider themselves leaders, not followers, in modern and "postmodern" thinking. More importantly, they have been acknowledged as leading thinkers by such non-Classicist counterparts as Foucault, Derrida, and Lévi-Strauss. French Classicists are in the forefront of contemporary

---

[177] Fritz K. Ringer's study of French academia in relation to its German counterpart provides lucid insight: Ringer 1992.
[178] Revel 1995: 15.

thinking on such vital topics as sexuality, *écriture*, and society itself'.[179] The social status, political position, and ideological role of the two disciplines, history and Classics, were distinct, but Roman historians as members of both disciplines, held in high regard, dodged marginalization on the scale of Anglo-American scholarship, which happened hand in hand with professionalization. Compared with the sharply marginalized position of Classics in Anglo-American scholarship, the disciplines of both history and Classics have enjoyed relatively high esteem and support in French scholarship until experiencing some gradual decline in the twenty-first century.

The underlying intellectual currents in Roman scholarship from the early twentieth century – the Annales school and positivism – continued to predominate in the second half of the twentieth century. The elision of Marxism might startle some at this point, as Marxism was unquestionably one of the hallmarks of postwar French intellectual thought and undoubtedly influenced French scholarship of history in general. Yet, French Marxism notoriously lacked attentive readers and theoretical foundations. It stirred many students into revolts and set the general mood of intellectuals, but failed to convert academics convincingly. The violent sweep of Marxism established the concept of the class system and Marxist economics as one of the quintessential factors to comprehend not only contemporary societies but also history, but failed to convince Roman historians that it is a master key. In the midst of the overflow of positivism and the Annales school, epistemological questions were raised by a Roman historian – and all-too-often overlooked. '[I]nspired by German historicism and fortified by British and American epistemological reflections, which seriously undermined the scientific pretensions of the new history,' Paul Veyne 'instead proposed looking at historical writing as the construction of narrative plots' in *Comment on écrit l'histoire : essai d'épistémologie*, published in 1971.[180] Veyne addressed the malaise of unreflective practices of positivist history, but his warning went unheeded. The fervour fed into the perverse positivism not infrequently encountered in French scholarship, where data and methodology appear to be bewildering rather than elucidating. It to a certain degree stifled questions on how to write history and quelled the philosophy of history in French scholarship. The decline of Marxism and the Annales school accentuated the epistemological vacuum. The epistemological questions which postcolonialism posed were overlooked by the majority of French historians who were trained in the positivist tradition without significant exposure to epistemological criticism.

[179] Nagy, Slatkin, and Loraux 2001: 2.   [180] Revel 1995: 41; Veyne 1971.

Appendix 3: History and Classics in Postwar France   149

However, it is false to conclude that French scholarship on Roman history did not yield any works written from anti-colonial or postcolonial perspectives. In the 1970s, Abdallah Laroui and Marcel Bénabou posed a challenge to Eurocentric and Romano-centric historiography in their respective controversial volumes: *L'histoire du Maghreb : un essai du synthèse*, published in 1970, and *La résistance africaine à la romanisation*, published in 1976.[181] Roman Africa became a contentious area of study where modern French and ancient Roman imperialism were interwoven in the scholarly discourse, whilst Roman Gaul was consolidated as a site of heritage memory to recover Gallic *patrimoine*.[182] The portrayal of the natives in Roman Africa betrayed double imperialist epistemologies. As David J. Mattingly observes, '[t]he role of indigenous people was relegated to one of being passive receptors of the fruit of civilization or characterized as anarchic barbarians, incapable of proper self-government or socio-economic advancement without outside (European) intervention. The contrast between French scholarship on Roman Gaul and Roman Africa could not be more marked in this respect'.[183] Laroui and Bénabou attempted to overturn the prevailing notion of Roman Africa, exposing the French paradox built in the historiography of Roman Africa, particularly, in relation to that of Roman Gaul.

Laroui argues that the natives were not barbarous rebels to recoil from the benefits of Roman civilization but organized resistance fighters to overthrow the colonial rule. Bénabou then extends that native resistance took place not only in the military sphere but also in the cultural sphere. Their perspectives and approaches are akin to those of Dyson to a certain extent. As Dyson flips his perspective from the Romans to the natives while resorting to the dialectical framework, Laroui and Bénabou also reorient their perspective to the rebelling natives while maintaining the dialectical framework. Although they did not make further steps to destabilize the colonial epistemology, they certainly question the Eurocentric and Romano-centric teleology and totalization that has governed the historiography of Roman Africa. There may be a shared anti-colonial sentiment of the time, but it may be far-fetched to connect the dots among the contemporary works of Dyson, Laroui, Bénabou, and poststructuralist thinkers when they do not refer to one another or share common reference points. It would be more accurate to regard Laroui and Bénabou as the Innovators in French scholarship, rather than the Early Adopters of travelling ideas. Besides, there is another reason that it would be inappropriate to

---

[181] Laroui 1970.   [182] For an overview on Roman Africa, see Shaw 1980.   [183] Mattingly 2011a: 43.

consider them as the Early Adopters who shaped the course of French scholarship. Their revolutionary theses indeed elicited heated responses and polarized the debate between French and Maghrebian scholars. While Maghrebian scholars welcomed their works as significant moments to crystallize national identity in history, French counterparts rejected their works mainly by keeping silent.[184] Even to this day, their works are rarely included in bibliographical listings or referenced by French scholars for studies on either Roman Africa or Roman imperialism. The collective amnesia about the imperialist epistemologies thereafter seems to haunt French scholarship. From Anglo-American scholarship, by contrast, they occasionally received sympathetic responses.[185] The seed of epistemological shift sprouted in French scholarship, but it did not take hold to diffuse further or to reorient discourse on Romanization. Postcolonial ideas that travelled across the Channel from the late twentieth century were yet to find the Early Adopters in the scholarship of Roman history, either.

---

[184] Some French historians argued against their works. On their counter-arguments, see Mattingly 2011a: 60–63.
[185] Mattingly 2011a: 60.

CHAPTER 4

Towards a Paradigm Shift in the Age of Globalization

After the dissolution of the Soviet Union in 1991, the bipolar world system of the Cold War effectively yielded to a new international system led by the United States as the sole superpower. By the turn of the twenty-first century, globalization became a byword for the post-Cold War world order. The Internet had started to connect more people across borders; McDonald's could be found from Tokyo to Delhi to Cairo; and supranational organizations, such as the European Union, the World Trade Organization, or the International Criminal Court, began to wield increasing power. In 1999, when the concept of globalization was arguably at its height, Thomas L. Friedman, *New York Times* columnist and author, published *The Lexus and the Olive Tree: Understanding Globalization*. He explicates the phenomenon using metaphors of the Lexus for global convergence on the surface and of the olive tree for local, cultural, and geopolitical factors beneath the surface:

> In the Cold War system, the most likely threat to your olive tree was from another olive tree. It was from your neighbor coming over, violently digging up your olive tree and planting his in its place. The threat has not been eliminated today, but, for the moment, it has been diminished in many parts of the world. The biggest threat today to your olive tree is likely to come from the Lexus – from all the anonymous, transnational, homogenizing, standardizing market forces and technologies that make up today's globalizing economic system. There are some things about this system that can make the Lexus so overpowering it can overrun and overwhelm every olive tree in sight – breaking down communities, steamrolling environments and crowding out traditions – and this can produce a real olive tree backlash. But there are other things about the system that empower even the smallest, weakest political community to actually use the new technologies and markets to preserve their olive tree, their culture and identity. Traveling the world in recent years, again and again I have come on this simultaneous wrestling match, tug-of-war, balancing act between the Lexus and the olive tree.[1]

---
[1] Friedman 1999: 34–5. He also wrote another bestselling book on globalization, Friedman 2005.

Writing with the insight of his hands-on experience as a widely-travelled investigative journalist, Friedman attests that '*[g]lobalization does not end geopolitics* [emphasis in original]'.[2] In short, he identifies two forces represented in the form of the Lexus and the olive tree, operating side by side to shape the new world order of globalization.

Joseph E. Stiglitz, a Noble laureate in economics, conveyed more or less the same sentiment in his academic tome on globalization, *Globalization and Its Discontents*, published in 2002.[3] In the same way that social, economic, or cultural globalizations do not converge to bring an end to local geopolitical cultures, identities, or conflicts, Stiglitz also argues that, contrary to the neo-liberal advocates of the Washington Consensus, global prosperity propelled by the United States does not trickle down to solve poverty in other corners of the world:[4]

> Part of the social contract entails 'fairness,' that the poor share in the gains of society as it grows, and that the rich share in the pains of society in times of crisis. The Washington Consensus policies paid little attention to issues of distribution of 'fairness.' If pressed, many of its proponents would argue that the best way to help the poor is to make the economy grow. They believe in trickle-down economics. *Eventually*, it is asserted, the benefits of the growth of *trickle down* even to the poor. Trickle-down economics was never much more than just a belief, an article of faith. Pauperism seemed to grow in nineteenth century England even though the country as a whole prospered. Growth in America in the 1980s provided the most recent dramatic example: while the economy grew, those at the bottom saw their real income decline.... [I]f this had not worked in the United States, why would it work in developing countries? While it is true that sustained reductions in poverty cannot be attained without robust economic growth, the converse is not true: growth need no benefit at all. It is not true that 'a rising tide lifts all boats.' Sometimes, a quickly rising tide, especially when accompanied by a storm, dashes weaker boats against the shore, smashing them to smithereens.[5]

Stiglitz asserts that the merits of trickle-down economics are a myth. Trickle-down economics failed on a national scale, and he contends that it inevitably fails on a global scale: benefits of global economic growth do *not* trickle down to the developing countries. Although Friedman and Stiglitz examine globalization from different perspectives, what both point out is that the top-down approach is not sufficient to grasp the

---

[2] Friedman 1999: 387.   [3] Stiglitz 2002.
[4] Coined by John Williamson, the term 'Washington Consensus' describes a set of economic policies, endorsed by Washington, DC-based American and international organizations, to support developing countries in the late twentieth century. See Williamson 1990.
[5] Stiglitz 2002: 78.

entirety of globalization. It is because globalization did not homogenize the world unilaterally, but rather has connected different parts of the world multilaterally. Despite the powerful forces of international organizations, multinational firms, and the Internet converging to establish a set of global standards from the top, local factors on the ground level continue to play a significant part to sketch out the various courses globalization can take. Despite what some have depicted as the overwhelmingly positive impact of globalization from the upper strata at the international level, there exists the lower strata at street level where growth does not trickle down, backlash against multinational corporate expands to a global platform, and localized versions of global culture infiltrate back into the global market. Indeed, Friedman and Stiglitz highlight that globalization requires attention from both top-down and bottom-up approaches.

Thereafter, the current discourse on globalization added another dimension to postcolonialism. In particular, apartheid in South Africa was abolished in 1991, and this signalled that the world was no longer compartmentalized into European and native sectors as in the times of Fanon. For some time, the Cold War compartmentalized the world into communist and capitalist blocs and seemed to have obscured any narrative of the colonial or imperial divide – except the sharp reawakening from the Vietnam War. Nevertheless, polarization brought by globalization was *en masse* reminiscent of the former divide between the colonizing West and the colonized non-West, except that it had been reformulated into a nebulous construct of neo-liberal globalization.[6] The discourse on globalization soon propagated new narratives in the form of neo-liberalism and neo-colonialism and kept postcolonialism pertinent. As (neo)colonialism in the globalized world became more complex, postcolonialism became proportionately more difficult to articulate. The words of Chandra Muzzaffar, the president of a Malaysian human rights organization called International Movement for a Just World, as quoted by Friedman, capture the very difficulty:

> I think that globalization is not just a rerun of colonialism. . . . People who argue that have got it wrong. It is more complex than that. Look around. As a result of globalization, there are elements of culture from the dominated peoples that are now penetrating the north. The favourite food of Brits eating out is not fish and chips today, but curry. It is no longer even exotic for them. But I am not just talking about curry. Even at the level of ideas there is a certain degree of interest in different religions now. So while you

[6] For the relationship between globalization and postcolonialism, see Krishna 2009.

have this dominant force [Americanization], you also have a subordinate flow the other way ... There are opportunities now for others to state their case through the Internet. Iran is highly linked to the Internet. They see it as a tool that they can use to get their point of view across. In Malaysia, Mahathir now gets some coverage [all over the world] through CNN. The campaign for banning land mines was launched through the Internet. This is what globalization does for marginalized groups. To argue that it is just a one-way street is not right and we should recognize its complexity. People operate at different levels. At one level they can be angry about injustices being done to their society from Americanization and then talk about it over McDonald's with their kids who are studying in the States.[7]

While we are not here to delve into the intricate relationship between different concepts of neo-liberalism, neo-colonialism, or globalization, Muzzaffar's remarks indicate that the discourse on globalization has encouraged a new generation of thinkers to develop a more nuanced understanding of colonialism and postcolonialism in the era of global connectivity. For example, among the postcolonial thinkers discussed in the previous chapters, Bhabha engages with the impact of globalization and refines the colonial dialectics between colonizing Europeans and colonized non-Europeans into ambivalence flowing both ways from top-down and bottom-up.

Yet again, whether these intellectual currents have broken into the scholarship of Roman history remains another question, because the scholarship, as illustrated earlier, in general tends to be slower in attuning to cutting-edge intellectual movements. Nonetheless, the works of the Early Adopters of the Foucauldian and Said-esque epistemological shift, from Finley and Harris to Millett and Woolf, have built up to a Tipping Point to shift the intellectual landscape of Romanization studies in the late twentieth century. Postcolonial questions on Romanization have started to catch on with the wider audience, if not with the Majority yet. The most marked milestones in this regard can be seen in two conferences, *Roman Imperialism: Post-colonial Perspectives* and *Dialogues in Roman Imperialism*, held at the University of Leicester in 1994 and at the University of Reading in 1995 respectively.[8] These conferences became a forum for the post-imperial generation of historians and archaeologists to introduce other postcolonial concepts to Romanization studies and to propose alternative

---

[7] Friedman 1999: 357–8.
[8] Webster and Cooper 1996; Mattingly and Alcock 1997. Also, for the wider discipline of Classics' engagement with postcolonial thought, see: Hingley 2001; Scott and Webster 2003; Goff 2005; Hardwick and Gillespie 2007.

paradigms. In addition, the Theoretical Roman Archaeology Conferences (TRAC), held since 1991, encouraged scholars to be more mindful of the issue of theories and epistemologies underlying Roman scholarship.[9]

The earlier waves of Marxism and multiculturalism in Roman history eased the introduction of postcolonialism into Roman history. The sceptical reservations towards the application of modern theories to ancient history still lingered, but the earlier studies inspired by Marxism and multiculturalism convinced many scholars that there was a merit in applying modern ideas. It helped Roman historians and archaeologists in their marginalized position to participate in the wider intellectual discourse and to take a step away from the elitist tradition. In a similar vein, the social, political, and historical realities of the late twentieth century attracted Roman scholars to postcolonialism. Not only did Said's *Orientalism* become an established tour de force to define the intellectual climate, but also the multi-ethnic and multi-cultural fabric of major cities in the postcolonial world became an increasingly palpable reality. Both factors inspired Roman scholars to investigate the multi-ethnic and multi-cultural fabric of ancient Roman societies from postcolonial perspectives. In the midst of the ongoing flourishing of social-cultural history, postcolonial thought travelled into the scholarship of Roman history and drew attention to a set of questions around identity in the Roman Empire:

> [S]cholars have been engaged in a lot of hard thinking about the rather astonishing cohesive capacity of an empire that was so thoroughly multi-ethnic, or multicultural, and that remained so over the long course of its political survival. It therefore seems urgent to ask: What did being Roman actually mean? How did one become a Roman? Why was it so attractive to be Roman? How did one display one's standing as a Roman? What happened to the many local cultures as they were subsumed by Roman (at least political) hegemony? In short, the matter of identity formation and its wide implication for the harmony of an extremely far-flung realm have recently been issues of paramount interest to historians working on what is, ultimately, the fabric of Roman society.[10]

In order to grapple with this issue, a number of scholars have found postcolonial thinking useful. Postcolonialism was already emerging as the next intellectual wave after the fall of Marxism in the Anglo-American intellectual world and slowly appeared attractive to a number of Roman

---

[9] On Roman imperialism and Romanization, to name a few, Freeman 1997b; Grahame 1998; Terrenato 1998.
[10] Peachin 2011: 12.

scholars – especially Jane Webster, David J. Mattingly, and Richard Hingley, all of whom are, in fact, primarily archaeologists.[11]

This also presented fresh possibilities for new history. Postcolonialism allowed Roman historians and archaeologists to reflect upon and break through the imperialist historiography of Roman history and to reach out to the intellectual discourse of the postcolonial age. For instance, a recent, albeit minor, exhibition at the British Museum showcased the change that postcolonial perspectives on Roman history could bring. *The Meroë Head of Augustus: Africa Defies Rome* (December 2014 – February 2015) was a small exhibition dedicated solely to a bronze head of Augustus excavated in the territory of the ancient kingdom of Kush in modern-day northern Sudan (see the image on the book cover).[12] The exhibition provided an unusually detailed explanation to contextualize the history of the artefact, that is, the history of resistance against the Roman Empire which led to the decapitation of Augustus' statute and the burial of its head below the Kushite victory temple for the passers-by to trample over the decapitated Augustus. As Bradley maintains, 'the British Museum's classical collections were expanded, enriched, rehoused, and rearranged across the course of its history, and the organic relationship between British identity and classical antiquity was constantly reformulated and rearranged alongside the development and collapse of the British Empire'.[13] The reformulation of narrative behind the Meroë head at the British Museum demonstrates how Roman history with postcolonial perspectives slowly leaves imperialist historiography behind and communicates with the postcolonial Anglo-American world.

Nonetheless, it is difficult to measure the extent to which Roman historians and archaeologists were inspired by or knowledgeable about postcolonial studies when adopting an epistemological shift in Romanization studies. On one hand, it appears that postcolonial studies and theories did not substantially infiltrate the scholarship of Roman history. Important issues of postcolonial discourse, such as Orientalism, subalternity, and hybridity, are often mentioned by Roman historians and

---

[11] From the time of Haverfield up to the twenty-first century, leading scholars in Romano-British studies have mostly been archaeologists. Hence, the trend in the wider discipline of archaeology would have played a part: for instance, post-processual archeology, which developed in tandem with poststructuralism to critique the assumption of cultural evolutionism in processual archaeology. Not familiar with the theoretical developments in archaeology, I did not delve into this aspect here. However, a further enquiry into this aspect would shed more interesting light onto the development of the discourse on Romanization.

[12] The Meroë head was also brought into public attention when it was listed in *A History of the World in 100 Objects*, a BBC Radio 4 series broadcast in 2010.

[13] Bradley 2010: 2.

Towards a Paradigm Shift in the Age of Globalization 157

archaeologists, but they still remain to be explored. It is more often the case that Roman scholars either cite popular anthologies of postcolonial studies, for example *Colonial Discourse and Post-colonial Theory: A Reader* and *Key Concepts in Post-colonial Studies*, or rely on the secondary sketches of postcolonial studies by other Roman scholars in *Roman Imperialism: Post-colonial Perspectives* and *Dialogues in Roman Imperialism: Power, Discourse, and Discrepant Experiences*.[14] With the exception of Said's *Orientalism* and *Cultural and Imperialism*, which became an intellectual phenomenon of the time, Roman historians and archaeologists rarely engage with the key primary texts of postcolonial studies by Fanon, Bhabha, or Spivak and do not critically examine the applicability or value of postcolonial theories. Most Roman historians touch on postcolonial thought somewhat tangentially. On the other hand, the three prominent scholars to reorient Romanization studies in the twenty-first century, Webster, Hingley, and Mattingly, all used vocabulary related to postcolonial thought, such as creolization, globalization, and discrepant experiences, for their alternative paradigms. Owing to their works, globalization and postcolonialism, although belatedly, took off in the discourse on Romanization. Their works became the channel for postcolonial thought to travel into Romanization studies.

At the risk of overgeneralizing, what distinguishes the new cohort of scholars from the earlier group is their sharpened sensitivity to postcolonial thought in the age of globalization and, ultimately, their postcolonial epistemological shift. They turned their attention to the lower strata of the colonial power structure, the colonized and silent Other outside the hegemonic system of power and knowledge/truth – that is, the subaltern, in the vocabulary of Gramsci and Spivak.[15] Roman historians and archaeologists thus far have primarily reflected on the problem of alterity by *othering* Romans from the modern Self and questioned the teleology and totalization predicated in the Roman historiography. Aside from Dyson, Roman historians and archaeologists discussed in the previous chapter, from Finley to Harris, Millett, and Woolf, have fundamentally taken a top-down perspective to understand the mechanism of Roman imperialism and Romanization, a mechanism which either promoted emulation of the colonized or absorbed the colonized into Roman power/knowledge configurations. In contrast, adopting the

---

[14] Chrisman and Williams 1993; Ashcroft, Griffiths, and Tiffin 1998; Webster and Cooper 1996; Mattingly and Alcock 1997.
[15] Gramsci 1975; Spivak 1988.

Foucauldian and Said-esque epistemological shift, a new generation of scholars aimed at exposing the Romano-centric and Eurocentric epistemologies underlying the paradigm of Romanization itself. Answering the postcolonial challenge, they used that very seed to bring the Romano-centric imperialist narrative, which had been in turn sustained by Eurocentric imperialism, into crisis.

Overall, the fundamental questions posed by postcolonial theorists to Western history still remain to be addressed in depth in the Anglo-American scholarship of Roman history: How can we challenge the Western epistemology in Roman history? How do we place the Self and the Other in relation to the overlapping history of colonialism in the recent past and the ancient past? How and in what direction can we push the epistemological boundaries in Roman history? These theoretical and fundamental issues of postcolonial studies are too often bypassed by many Roman historians and archaeologists. Without the colonized peripheries to push the epistemological boundaries, the discourse on Romanization hitherto has echoed the limits of poststructuralism in being self-reflective about its own imperialist epistemology underlying the colonial discourse. Webster, Hingley, and Mattingly pulled a trigger to transpose the same epistemological shift from poststructuralism to postcolonialism onto the discourse on Romanization. As postcolonial thinkers posed the question of alterity directly back to Western historiography to break away from the Eurocentric system of power and knowledge/truth, Webster, Hingley, and Mattingly posed more or less the same question directly back to Roman historiography. As Spivak turned her attention to the subaltern Other outside the hegemonic system of power and knowledge/truth to push epistemological boundaries, this new group of scholars looked towards the subaltern Other in the Roman Empire. Henceforth, they opened up the possibility of destabilizing Romano-centric epistemology in the Romanization discourse. Now, let us take a closer look at each alternative paradigm proposed by them.

Creolization: Webster

> It is a peculiar sensation, this double-consciousness, this sense of always looking at one's self through the eyes of the others, of measuring one's soul by the tape of the world that looks on in amused contempt and pity. One ever feels his twoness – an American, a Negro; two souls, two thoughts, two unreconciled strivings, two

warring ideals in one dark body, whose dogged strength alone keeps it from being torn asunder.

Such a double life, with double thoughts, double duties, and double social classes, must give rise to double words and double ideals, and tempt the mind to pretence or revolt, to hypocrisy or radicalism.[16]

As a matter of fact, Webster does not refer to W. E. B. Du Bois' 'double consciousness'. Instead, she cites the works of contemporary scholars in cultural studies and historical archaeology, such as Roger D. Abrahams, Anne E. Yentsch, and Leland Ferguson, to illustrate creolization.[17] To clarify its definition briefly, creolization originally described the linguistic process whereby creole languages emerge from multicultural contacts, especially between the Old World and the New World in colonial contexts and particularly in African diaspora cultures. More widely, creolization is used to represent the cultural change in unequal power dynamics, particularly in contrast with acculturation, which describes the process whereby people absorb the dominant culture. Yet, I dare say that Du Bois' notion of 'double consciousness' from *The Souls of Black Folk* makes a more apt introduction to Webster's alternative paradigm of creolization to replace Romanization than spelling out the definition of creolization. Ambiguity and ambivalence, concepts that sit at the crux of creolization, are poetically articulated by Du Bois. Besides, these interrelated concepts of ambivalence, ambiguity, and creolization in postcolonial studies also align with hybridity, a notion put forward by Bhabha, as discussed previously. Although Webster does not allude to ambivalence or hybridity as postcolonial terms per se, Webster was certainly the first Roman scholar of the new generation to forge a pathway for a group of aforementioned interrelated concepts to travel to the discourse on Romanization via her pioneering piece 'Creolizing the Roman Provinces', published in 2001.

Ambiguity, ambivalence, creolization, and hybridity, above all, attempt to disperse the polarity in colonial discourse and epistemology. It is not our purpose here to distinguish creolization from hybridity, but Richard C. Rath sums up the case for using the paradigm of creolization: '[h]istorians use linguistic models of creolization as a solution to what is known as the "Herskovitz-Frazier debate"'.[18] In a nutshell, Melville J. Herskovitz argues that African heritage survived in America to lay the foundation for African-American culture, whereas E. Franklin Franzier contends that slavery had effectively broken African heritage, leaving little vestige, and that new

---

[16] Du Bois 1996.   [17] Abrahams 1983; Yentsch 2003; Ferguson 1992.   [18] Rath 2000: 102.

African-American social circumstances conditioned their culture and identity.[19] According to Rath, creolization provides a possibility of resolving the dilemma between the unequal forces of acculturation and continuity underlying the hybrid culture. This appears to be the reason Webster opted for the paradigm of creolization: 'creole material culture represents not the gradual replacement of one way of life by another, but the blending of both, in a clearly nonegalitarian social context'.[20] To begin with, Webster identifies a debate in Romanization studies analogous to the Herskovitz-Frazier debate. She outlines the historiography of Romanization in Anglo-American scholarship, arguing that it likewise has oscillated between the two poles of acculturating to Roman civilization and continuing the native custom. As she sketches, alternating between the models emphasizing the influence of either Romans or natives from the times of Haverfield throughout the twentieth century, '[all] models of Romanization thus lead us to the same place: a polarized provincial world of Romans (or Romanized natives) and natives, with no gray areas in between'.[21] In the context of the discourse on Romanization with these two poles at each end, hybrid models, Webster underlines, were 'a balancing act, ... with the upper classes and the towns at one end of a sliding scale, and the lower classes and the villages at the other. Fusion is seen as a problem-free process at all levels of society ... taking placing beyond the politics of power'.[22] In other words, each model contended to shift the pendulum from one place to another within the same unilateral spectrum of acculturation: 'latent persistence of folk customs (Haverfield/Collingwood); overt resistance (the north African nativist model); Romanization as a veneer (the British nativist model); and preconquest regional differences (the 1990s approach typified by Millett and Haselgrove)'.[23]

Webster points out that the debate amongst various models, in essence, presupposed the linear acculturation and, henceforth, reduced natives as reactionaries to mitigate top-down influence – whether resistant or persistent. She further analyses that the historiographical tradition in one form or another has continued to overlook an alternative possibility: 'Equally important, continued faith in Haverfield's notion that anyone who could have Romanized would have when given the chance means that the failure to emulate must be explained, wherever encountered. Unfortunately, the point where the trickle-down effect tapered off is never examined in terms of *localized choices*'.[24] Leaving out the possibility of bottom-up influence to

---

[19] Herskovits 1941; Frazier 1957. [20] Webster 2001: 216. [21] Webster 2001.
[22] Webster 2001: 212. [23] Webster 2001: 216. [24] Webster 2001.

envisage bilateral or multilateral hybrids, these models, she demonstrates, operated within more or less the same parameter inherited from Haverfield:

> it ... suggests that without a push from the top (whether Roman or native), Romanization was not the unstoppable cultural force many assume it to have been ... In this scenario of elite indifference, non-elites simply become passive receptors of those random elements of Roman culture that trickle down to them. The unstated assumption here, is that these Roman influences were always welcomed.
>
> Elites and urban dwellers may have well been motivated by self-interest, as Millett has persuasively argued, but what did the rural poor have to gain by adopting the symbols of Romanitas? Without an element of self-interest, the only motor for change becomes the superiority of Roman culture, bringing us full circle to Haverfield's original (acculturative) conception of Romanization as the unstoppable march for civilization.[25]

Without question, the notion of Roman superiority has no longer remained valid since the mid-late twentieth century. The scholars discussed in the previous chapter have already exposed and rejected this. However, what Webster further deconstructs about the Romanization framework is that teleology of Romanization, totalization of Romanocentrism, and colonial dialectics have continued to epistemologically underpin the later models that vacillate within the spectrum of unilateral acculturation. She reveals that the discourse on Romanization has not yet pushed its epistemological boundaries to the colonized and silent Other. The discourse on Romanization thus far has lacked the presence of epistemological peripheries that could challenge the dominant epistemology, for example the counter- or subculture phenomenon of the lower class.

To effect a shift in epistemology, Webster proposes creolization as an alternative paradigm. Although terminology-wise Webster prefers creolization to hybridity, her paradigm evokes Bhabha's hybridity in postcolonial studies. Possibly, given the context of the discourse on Romanization – in which hyphenated hybrid cultures, such as Romano-British and Gallo-Roman, tend to suggest a midway in the unilateral spectrum of acculturation – creolization could present a clearer objective and a fresh orientation to 'move *beyond*' the two poles and to convey fluidity and ambiguity in a new culture.[26] Still, the core ideas that comprise Bhabha's hybridity and Webster's creolization chime with

---
[25] Webster 2001.
[26] Both Webster and Bhabha articulate their aim in the same phrase – to 'move beyond' Romanization and colonial historiography respectively.

each other: subversion/counterculture and ambivalence/ambiguity.[27] In the light of the limited capacity of a sixteen-page article to develop a fully -fledged paradigm, it should be acknowledged that the trace of travelling ideas from Bhabha's postcolonial hybridity might appear fragmentary. Nevertheless, the postcolonial influence on Webster's paradigm overall is unmistakable from her references to postcolonial thinkers such as Aimé Césaire, Fanon, Léopold S. Senghor, Said, Bhabha, and Young.[28] Let us, therefore, further consider counterculture and ambiguity in Webster's paradigm of creolization.

Counterculture of non-elites, a possibility that Webster raises, poses a fundamental challenge to the existing paradigms of Romanization. It betrays that the discourse on Romanization has thus far operated within the polarized and teleological framework of 'Romans and aspiring Romans'.[29] Non-elite culture has been ruled out as a reservoir of native persistence where the flow of trickle-down Romanization dried out. Webster indicates that this perspective surviving through different models of Romanization has continued to reduce non-elites to the position of passive agents with neither will nor power to have an impact. She repeatedly acknowledges the asymmetric power structure precluding non-elites from impressing their point of view under Roman rule, but emphasizes that they still expressed themselves mainly through material culture. 'In this sense, material culture encapsulates colonial experience', as Webster asserts.[30] She relates that, in contrast to the elite-driven culture of the colonizers from the top, non-elite counterculture of the colonized from the bottom slowly adapted to the new influence while maintaining its own traditions. In particular, religion, according to Webster, is a fertile ground to explore non-elite counterculture, since it is most resistant to elite-driven acculturation. From Romano-Celtic religion, she illustrates that the horse goddess *Epona* is a product of creolization with a strong element of non-elite counterculture. Earlier paradigms have characterized *Epona* as either: (i) 'a Celt among the Romans', that is, 'pure Celticity under a Roman veneer', because of her association with zoomorphic iconography and popularity in 'less Romanized' northern provinces, or (ii) a Romanized Celtic deity, because of her anthropomorphic representation.[31] Webster identifies that these interpretations posit a dialectical relationship between Roman and Celtic. For an alternative interpretation, she focuses on the

---

[27] The theoretical influence of Bhabha's hybridity appears to be more crucial, since Webster does not mention Édourd Glissant, who was a key figure in coining créolité, Cf. Glissant 1997.
[28] Webster 1996; Césaire 1995; Senghor 1970.   [29] Webster 2001: 217.   [30] Webster 2001: 218.
[31] Linduff 1979; Webster 2001: 221; Henig 1984.

power struggle between the two forces, the Roman tradition of anthropomorphic representation and the Celtic resistance to epigraphic name-pairing.[32] The subtle context underlying the images of *Epona* requires an understanding that is not bipolar but more nuanced, as Webster argues: 'Epona cannot be regarded as a Celtic deity or a Roman one. She is a product of the post-Roman negotiation between Roman and indigenous beliefs and iconographic traditions: she is thus a Romano-Celtic deity but not ... the product of a problem-free or spontaneous synthesis'.[33] In other words, *Epona* was a creole deity that encompasses not only the top-down Roman influence on the Celtic tradition, but also the bottom-up non-elite counterculture.

Non-elite counterculture does not conform to Roman imperialism and Romanization and remains outside the Roman system of power and knowledge/truth. By introducing it as a quintessential part of Roman provincial history, Webster pushes the epistemological boundaries of the discourse on Romanization to its peripheries, to the colonized and silent Other – and consequently disrupts the teleology of Romanization and contradicts the totalization of Romano-centrism. In fact, Webster is not the first to introduce the colonized Other to the discourse on Romanization. As discussed earlier, Dyson in his article 'Native Revolts in the Roman Empire', published in 1971, inverts the colonial dialectics to flip the colonized Other as the Self – rebelling natives who lie outside of the linear spectrum of Romans and aspiring Romans – to destabilize the teleology of Romanization and the totalization of Romano-centrism.[34] Yet, mirroring Fanon's anti-colonial writings, Dyson's inversion of Romano-centric history relies on the colonial dialectical framework that is, at the same time, a legacy of colonial epistemology.[35] Hence, despite his attempt to reorient Romano-centric historiography, his model of Romanization is unavoidably locked in colonial epistemology. His paradigm falls short of moving *beyond* the Romano-centric historiography.

On the other hand, Webster's paradigm of creolization heralds a fresh step forward to move *beyond* the Romano-centric historiography. She proposes the colonized subaltern's counterculture as a point at which the authority of Roman imperialism and Romanization is subverted. If both Romans and aspiring Romans operated within the Roman system of power and knowledge/truth, the subaltern Other operated on its peripheries. Webster's move to the epistemological peripheries resonates with Spivak's redrawing of the fault line in colonial discourse. Spivak refined

---

[32] See Aldhouse-Green 1989; Webster 1995a.   [33] Webster 2001: 221.   [34] Dyson 1971.
[35] Fanon 1965.

the fault line of colonial epistemology as being no longer the old colonial dialectics between the colonizing Self and the colonized Other but the hegemonic system of power and knowledge/truth, in other words, the elite Self within the system and the subaltern Other outside the system. Instead of variants of a linear acculturation model based on colonial dialectics, Webster proposes an alternative paradigm of creolization as a multilateral process which extends to the subaltern Other and disperses the colonial dialectics. In her attempt to move *beyond* the polarization embedded in colonial epistemology and to write alternative history, Webster's creolization echoes Bhabha's hybridity, even though the preferred terms differ. Bhabha emphasized that hybridity is not merely a euphemistic manoeuvre to resolve the tension between the colonizing Self and the colonized Other by bringing them together into a conflict-free fusion. Instead, it is a process in which the colonized Other's 'denied' system of power/knowledge – or, non-elite counterculture, in Webster's vocabulary – enters the dominant discourse, disturbs the colonial rules of approval, and subverts the colonial dialectics. In this way, Spivak's subaltern theory and Bhabha's theory of hybridity underpin the kernel of Webster's paradigm of creolization.

It is not only the overall paradigm of Bhabha's hybridity that has travelled to Webster's creolization. One of Bhabha's key concepts, ambivalence, has also found its way to Webster's paradigm as ambiguity. Again, Webster opts for a term different from Bhabha's perhaps due to contextual inapplicability. While Bhabha borrows the concept of ambivalence from psychoanalysis, most notably presented by Sigmund Freud, and applies it to the postcolonial context as a psychoanalytical term, Webster investigates the material culture in Roman provinces and its significance from postcolonial perspectives without stretching it to psychoanalytical aspects.[36] It may be that ambiguity is more appropriate to suggest plural elements in material cultural in relation to ambivalence that conveys contradictory feelings in human psychoanalysis. Nevertheless, their core messages resonate with each other. Bhabha adopts the concept of ambivalence to depict the oscillating identity between the colonizing Self and the colonized Other – between identification and alienation, between emulation and distinction, and between desire and fear. Webster's search for ambiguity in provincial material culture resembles this. She employs the notion of ambiguity to shed light on grey areas where the polarized compartmentalization of material culture into either Roman or native becomes blurred 'between acceptance and resistance'. For example, 'a few representations of

---

[36] Freud 1930.

Mercury from Roman Britain appear to have horns in place of the god's more usual winged hair or *petasos* ... [I]t is sometimes difficult for the modern observer to determine whether horns or wings were intended, but as [Green] points out, this may represent for Romano-Celtic observers a conscious flexibility or ambiguity, allowing the spectator to see what it was appropriate for him or her to see; the classical god or a horned indigenous deity'.[37] Fundamentally, both Webster and Bhabha direct their steps towards dismantling the colonial dialectics. As the two distinct systems of power and knowledge/truth of the colonizers and the colonized interact with each other, they do not remain unaffected in their distinction between the Self and the Other. Certainly, as both Bhabha and Webster repeatedly remind readers, there is an imbalance in power for one system of power and knowledge/truth to dominate over the other. Yet, it results in neither replacement of one system with another nor a halfway mixture. Rather, ambiguity and ambivalence with the existing systems of power and knowledge/truth indicate an on-going struggle to formulate a new system of power and knowledge/truth that is no longer anchored in the earlier colonial dialectics. In short, like Bhabha, Webster uses ambiguity to disperse the colonial dialectics and to move *beyond* colonial epistemology.

Let us briefly return to Du Bois' 'double consciousness' in the context of Webster's creolization. It is not merely a coincidence that the double consciousness of African-Americans to a certain extent chimes with the Romano-British experience. As mentioned earlier, Webster gives credit to creolization models developed from American and Caribbean studies, rather than by postcolonial thinkers. Certainly, creolization studies in New World archaeology provides a more appropriate lens to reinterpret material evidence from Roman provincial archaeology, where a historiographical study from an archaeological perspective might shed more interesting light. Yet, for our purpose, the epistemological shift that Webster introduces to the discourse on Romanization through her paradigm of creolization was a travelling idea with a much longer and more complex journey. Having discussed the epistemological shift that has travelled through interrelated concepts, from subaltern, counterculture, ambivalence, and ambiguity, it would not be too far-fetched to trace the travel of the epistemological shift back to Du Bois. In his day, Du Bois would have been an Innovator in coining the concept of 'double consciousness', but later it formed a theoretical basis for the Early Adopters to formulate postcolonial concepts, including ambivalence, hybridity, and creolization, which, in turn, travelled

---

[37] Webster 2001: 223; Aldhouse-Green 1997.

further across different disciplines. In the scholarship of Roman history, after the Tipping Point marked by Millett's *The Romanization of Britain* published in 1990, Webster is the first to achieve a significant milestone in engaging with postcolonial thoughts to propose an alternative paradigm. Although there is an immediate connection with creolization studies, the fundamental epistemological shift, which perhaps remains under the surface and between the lines in her article, has travelled through various postcolonial thinkers, from Du Bois to Spivak and Bhabha. Writing an alternative history based on the postcolonial thought that Spivak and Bhabha had refined in the wake of globalization, she extends the postcolonial epistemological shift to the discourse on Romanization. Next, let us move to Hingley's paradigm, which draws on contemporary globalization more explicitly.

Globalization: Hingley

> For me history is perpetually a fiction. Part of my work is thinking about systems of display as they relate to historical representation throughout culture. Much of my work is an attempt to manipulate these forms of presentation/representation.[38]

This remark by Adam Pendleton, an American conceptual artist, would be a wild statement, especially as an introduction to the work of a well-respected historian and archaeologist, Hingley's *Globalizing Roman Culture: Unity, Diversity and Empire*, published in 2005.[39] However, it would serve as a good, if not the most expected, opening to one of the few scholars who has used the term 'creativity' to describe history writing. Pendleton's thoughts on history, which were most notably expressed in his influential 'Black Dada' series, resonate with Hingley's ideas. Pendleton juxtaposes European Dadaist texts, which respond to the violence of World War I, with the works of African-American activists and writers, which respond to the violence of racism. In a nutshell, Black Dada is 'about "radical juxtaposition", i.e. bringing voices together in a way that disrupts easy logic and established history'.[40] The very process of writing history, according to Pendleton, is a creative as well as critical act: to question dominant discourses, to bring disparate elements together, and to open an alternative discourse. Hingley also expresses the same sentiment:

> What I take from the works that I have reviewed is that critical thought has an important role if we are to avoid total anachronism, but at the same time

---

[38] Pendleton 2009.   [39] Hingley 2005.   [40] Trouillot 2017.

there is a need to balance this with an emphasis upon the importance of imagination and creativity. Postmodernism has liberated us from the burden of arguing for the ultimate objectivity of any one idealized past that is an independent of context. As a result, we have been freed to explore any number of different accounts, but with an eye upon the reliability of the interpretations that we draw.[41]

Unsurprisingly, creativity has been one of the least anticipated terms to be associated with the modern way of history writing. Having moved away from ancient history as a literary activity since the nineteenth century, ancient history as a modern academic discipline remodelled itself as a quasi-scientific investigation based on facts, objectivity, and critical analysis. On the flip side, the conviction in modern positivist history has come at the cost of reflection on historical epistemologies. Hingley brings this element of history writing to the forefront of his project. Alluding to the postmodernist turn, he carefully proposes a new epistemological framework to write history – a critical yet creative intellectual activity – and to rewrite Romanization.

Befitting its aim 'to push interpretation in new directions that are both more original and more challenging', Hingley's *Globalizing Roman Culture* distinctively breathes an air of contemporaneity from its title – which was still far from popular practice in the scholarship of Roman history.[42] Globalization swept across the intellectual discourse on the cusp of the twenty-first century, and Hingley is not shy about making a direct connection with contemporary thought. To contextualize his choice, perhaps it is worthwhile reminding ourselves that the scholarship of Roman history in general has focused more on internal discourses than on wider intellectual trends. Certainly, the broader intellectual developments have inevitably influenced the course of Roman scholarship, but to a limited extent and at a limited pace. It is also worth stressing that the historians and archaeologists discussed here do not represent mainstream scholarship, but were the Innovators and the Early Adopters, in Gladwell's terminology. They were frontrunners to adopt the seeds of the epistemological shift from poststructuralism and postcolonialism to bring a paradigm shift into the discourse on Romanization.

Yet, even among the scholars open to contemporary thoughts, no one was more forthright about the influence of contemporary thought in Roman scholarship or the inextricable relationship between the present and the past than Hingley. In his earlier monograph *Roman Officers and*

---

[41] Hingley 2005: 12.   [42] Hingley 2005: 13.

English Gentlemen: The Imperial Origins of Roman Archaeology, published in 2000, Hingley particularly examines how Romano-British scholarship from the late Victorian period up to the modern era has, without fully acknowledging it or reflecting upon it, been shaped in tandem with contemporary British imperial politics.[43] Later, in *Globalizing Roman Culture*, he moves on to focus on the historiography of Roman identity and culture in modern Western (primarily British) scholarship.[44] He contends that the Eurocentric notion of civilization and humanism and the modernist notion of progress through Romanization have underpinned the undercurrents of the discourse on Romanization. As Hingley asserts, even though the subject of the discourse is the Roman past, the epistemology underlying the discourse is anchored in the present: '[p]resent concerns influence the pictures of the past that we drive from the evidence. At the same time ... the past is constantly drawn upon to inform the present and this makes the inter-relationship of past and present highly complex.' Thus, the question ultimately comes down to: 'If we cannot avoid imposing the present upon the past, how should we proceed?'.[45] His answer is to '[acknowledge] the old truth that "each generation writes its own history"', and to harness the epistemology rooted in the present as a critical yet creative source to write history alternative to dominant discourses.[46] Hence, in order to understand Hingley's paradigm, it is vital to take into account the pertinent contemporary intellectual currents.

Therefore, prior to applying contemporary thoughts to formulate an alternative paradigm, Hingley devotes a substantial portion of his book to tracing epistemologies underlying the dominant discourses in Romanization studies from Haverfield to Woolf. As a matter of fact, the structure of Hingley's *Globalizing Roman Culture* somewhat parallels that of Webster's 'Creolizing the Roman Provinces' in preceding his alternative paradigm with the historiography of Romanization, which highlights his (as well as her) epistemological shift away from previous paradigms. While maintaining more or less the same narrative strategy, Hingley expands the scope and depth of his historiographical analysis in his extended format. In fact, Jonathan R. W. Prag, in his review of Hingley's book, expresses his

---

[43] Hingley 2000.
[44] Jonathan R. W. Prag, in his review of Hingley's *Globalizing Roman Culture*, points out that the work is narrowly focused on British scholarship: 'The almost total absence of other European voices from this debate is striking: this is a remarkably British, post-colonial debate, and the opening quotation from Mattingly is almost unbearably apt (it scarcely needs pointing out that voices from beyond Europe can rarely even be adduced as missing).' Prag 2006: 215.
[45] Hingley 2005: 12.   [46] Mouritsen 1998: 174. As quoted in Hingley 2005: 12.

impression of the imbalance: '[t]his is not, *prima facie*, a book about globalization ... this is a review of the primarily anglophone debate of the last ten years, focused almost exclusively upon the North-Western provinces ... it is extremely difficult at times to extricate [Hingley]'s voice from the summary of others'.[47] His criticism that Hingley's new paradigm of globalization is lopsided compared to the historiographical survey and is pushed to the very end rings true. Extensive historiographical discussion and a comprehensive list of references left relatively little space for him to sufficiently develop his synthesis and alternative paradigm. Indeed, it would be more accurate to understand Hingley's alternative paradigm as one of many attempts to explore *beyond* the Romano-centric epistemology and historiography rather than as a fully - fledged model to firmly imprint a paradigm shift. Yet, what escapes Prag's attention is that Hingley does not simply sketch the development of the discourse on Romanization, but illustrates that epistemologies underlying the discourse have been rooted in each contemporary intellectual current. The words of Andrew Gardner more aptly describe Hingley's contribution: 'His latest book attempts to go beyond critique, and to develop an alternative approach to understanding the Roman past, inspired by a different set of modern discourses: those surrounding the phenomenon of globalisation. The explicit recognition of the complex relationship between past and present is one of the book's many strengths'.[48] In other words, acknowledging and demonstrating historians' susceptibility to their contemporary surroundings through his own historiographical study forms a part of Hingley's strategy to support his own alternative paradigm. He not only acknowledges but also actively uses the influence of contemporary intellectual current as a critical and creative source of epistemological shift to move the discourse on Romanization forward. That being said, before delving into Hingley's model of globalization, his historiographical study demands consideration.

As a matter of fact, the overarching epistemological shift that underpins Hingley's historiographical study is not postcolonialism per se. Instead, he uses the framework of modernism and postmodernism to comprehend the development of modern discourse on Romanization. Although a group of 'post-isms' developed in the late twentieth century, including postmodernism, poststructuralism, and postcolonialism, and share more or less the same orientation to destabilize totalization and the teleology of the old grand narratives, Hingley's choice of lens, postmodernism, for his alternative

[47] Prag 2006. [48] Gardner 2007: 389.

paradigm draws attention. He took part in the conferences *Roman Imperialism: Post-colonial Perspectives* in 1994 and *Dialogues in Roman Imperialism* in 1995, which explicitly posited postcolonialism as a way to move the discourse on Romanization forward.[49] But for his own monograph, he instead opts to attribute the shift of the discourse on Romanization to postmodernism:

> The idea of a move from modernist to postmodern conceptions provides a very simple account of the development of the theory of Romanization, itself based upon the type of binary abstractions that postmodernism often claims to set itself against. It does, however, capture a general change in the views of those who have studied the empire, focusing upon the years between 1960 and the present day. In fairly broad terms, over time, Roman specialists have come to question the initial focus of Romanization theory upon the centrality, or coherence, of Roman identity. This questioning has occurred as a result of a situation in which many people in both western Europe and the USA have become less supportive of some of the ideas that were used to justify imperialism during the nineteenth and earlier twentieth centuries.[50]

According to Hingley, the discourse on Romanization has taken a postmodernist turn to be self-reflective about the absoluteness of a Romano-centric vision of progress, to be self-conscious about its own historical relativity as a discourse shaped and supported by modern imperialism, and to emancipate the discourse from universalism to seek heterogeneity. Within this broad trend, historians who take up postcolonial perspectives to critique the Romanization framework become a part of a self-reflexive discourse, rather than a critique of self-reflexive discourse or a further attempt to push epistemological boundaries.[51] It might have been correct to interpret the overall development of the discourse along the modernist-postmodernist shift at the time Hingley was writing, when the postcolonial approaches were yet to push the epistemological boundaries to the subaltern Other. Nevertheless, the crucial distinction, the postcolonial epistemological shift, is absent in Hingley's paradigm.

Although explained earlier, elucidation from Helen Tiffin, a postcolonial theorist, would facilitate our understanding of the difference at this point. 'The application of such labels [postmodernism and postcolonialism] is thus

---

[49] Hingley 1996, 1997. *Roman Imperialisms: Post-colonial Perspectives* was a symposium held at the University of Leicester in 1994. *Dialogues in Roman Imperialism* comes from the first Roman Archaeology conference held at the University of Reading in 1995. Also, for the wider discipline of Classics' engagement with postcolonial thought, see: Hingley 2001; Scott and Webster 2003; Hardwick and Gillespie 2007.

[50] Hingley 2005: 30–31.

[51] Some of the works mentioned in Hingley's reference include: Alcock 1977; Barrett 1997a; Freeman 1997b; Woolf 1998; Laurence 2001.

Globalization: Hingley 171

not a minor a quibble about influence or timing', she argues, 'but involves questions of a survival strategy against the reinscription of non-European realities into a dominant European system'.[52] She notes that while postmodernism and poststructuralism revolve around the 'crisis of European authority', postcolonialism attempts to reinscribe alternative systems of power and knowledge/truth to the mainstream narrative:

> It is a very different project and it produces very different results, whatever the superficial similarities. To question one's own authoritative bases as European post-modernism perceives itself as doing is different from, on the one hand, opposing another fully-fledged system on equal terms to that of Europe, and on the other, interrogating that authority with a view to erecting a systematic alternative to define a denied or outlawed self. But the crisis in European authority has ironically resulted in the hegemonic appropriation of 'the other' into a European system where it can comfortably represent the titillating *possibility* of an ontological fracture which can and will never occur while it is so firmly bound within the European episteme.[53]

Accepting that the postcolonial epistemological shift, in essence, was yet to take hold in the discourse on Romanization, it becomes clear that what Hingley identifies as a postmodernist turn is a crisis of Roman authority in history, that is, the crisis of the Romano-centric epistemology and historiography. Simultaneously, Hingley's own historiographical study reflects the self-reflexive nature of postmodernism; he treats the discourse on Romanization as a self-contained discourse that becomes self-conscious about its own historical relativity due to changing concerns of the present *sans* the epistemological Other. Nonetheless, he further makes a singular contribution to this postmodernist self-reflection. By explicitly acknowledging the relationship between the intertwined epistemologies of the past and the present, that is, Romano-centrism and Eurocentrism, he suggests that the crisis of Roman authority in history implicates a crisis of Western authority as an investigator of Roman history.

In a nutshell, Hingley shows that the paradigm of Romanization is a legacy not only of ancient Roman imperialism but also of modern Western imperialism. It is as much a part of the ancient Roman colonial discourse as a part of the modern Western colonial discourse. Probing into the studies of the last few decades, he forthrightly exposes the unstated assumptions that have been guiding the discourse on Romanization. While Woolf has revealed the system of power and knowledge/truth underlying

[52] Tiffin 1988: 171.   [53] Tiffin 1988: 171–2.

the Roman imperial discourse of the past, Hingley demonstrates that there are two interrelated systems of power and knowledge/truth, one of the past and another of the present, to sustain the discourse up to the scholarship of the present day. A Romano-centric régime of truth – notions like civilizing ethos and *humanitas* in particular – that has upheld the Roman imperial discourse has formed the cornerstone of the Eurocentric régime of truth, composed of mirroring concepts of civilizing mission and Western humanism, which in turn vindicated the Western colonial discourse. He shows that the so-called classical inheritance in Western Europe is, in fact, an appropriation of the ancient Greek and Roman past to continue and realize the teleology of the colonial discourse:

> Eurocentrism focuses upon the idea of a classical inheritance. ... 'Civilization' and Western origin are, effectively, used as an excuse and justification for the imperial domination that Western powers exercise over others. The Eurocentric perspective suggests that civilization was successively displaced in time and space from the ancient Near East through 'Western' (and democratic) classical Greece and then to Rome. Rome acted as the link to the Christian Middle Ages and then civilization passed through the western European Renaissance and to the modern European imperial powers, finally to form the inheritance of the countries of contemporary Europe and of the USA. In these terms, Eurocentric discourse renders history as a sequence of empires: *Pax Romana, Pax Hispanica, Pax Britannica* and *Pax Americana*. In all cases western Europeans, or their descendants, are seen to provide the 'motor', or impetus for historical change ... Writers in the West appropriated ancient cultures for their own interests in terms of teleology in which the significance of the past lay primarily in its relevance to the imperial present.[54]

In the context of Eurocentric historiography, Hingley measures the significance of the Romanization framework. It fundamentally developed as one of the currents of modern imperial discourse to trace and link Western identity with Roman imperialism. The result was that the discursive Roman identity as an imperial authority became anchored onto the modern Western identity as its predecessor. Against the backdrop of the Eurocentric historiography of Romanization, as Hingley observes, a new wave of postmodernist scholarship aimed to de-territorialize and de-centre Roman identity.

Subsequently, Hingley moves on to bring recent studies into a synthesis. Even though he portrays the recent development in the discourse on

[54] Hingley 2005: 21–2.

Romanization as a postmodernist turn, what he achieves through his own synthesis seems closer to postcolonial rewritings of Roman imperialism and Romanization. Recent studies that Hingley gathers for synthesis reflect, to a certain extent, the late twentieth-century intellectual climate of post-isms to question the grand narratives, but in general were not necessarily produced with sharp awareness about the epistemological shifts introduced by post-isms. On the other hand, Hingley's synthesis and recasting of Roman culture and identity based on these recent studies, executed with more consciousness about the core ideas of recent theories, comes closer to taking a step towards a postcolonial epistemological shift. After questioning the Eurocentric and Romano-centric authority in history, he attempts to write an alternative history – via an alternative paradigm of globalization, which encompasses not just the Lexus top-down but also the olive tree bottom-up. This signals a further step from postmodernist or post-structuralist self-reflection about the Western or Roman authority in history towards postcolonial action to reinscribe an alternative narrative. Furthermore, integrating the bottom-up perspective into his model, he pushes the epistemological boundaries to the subaltern Other in his alternative history of Romanization. On the whole, he reads recent studies of the last few decades through the postmodernist lens of de-centring and channels them into his alternative paradigm – which amounts to implementing a postcolonial epistemological shift.

Even at a glance, the postcolonial vocabularies used to build his synthesis, such as Eurocentrism, colonial discourse, and power and knowledge, manifest his postcolonial undertone. We still cannot completely eliminate the possibility that the term Hingley uses to describe his alternative paradigm, globalization, was a conscious choice to distinguish his approach from postcolonialism; and Gardner, in fact, categorizes revisionist approaches to Roman imperialism into the two distinct strands: postcolonialism and globalization.[55] However, Gardner's analysis focuses on developments into different models, instead of their epistemological background. He looks into the different models current in the discourse on Romanization that essentially originated from the same postcolonial epistemological shift. Both the changing realities and the theory of globalization certainly provided Hingley with a fresh label for his alternative paradigm to replace the old paradigm of Romanization. Still, just as the postcolonial epistemological shift continued to shed light on how the Eurocentric system of power and knowledge/truth in the globalized

[55] Gardner 2013.

world operates in more complex ways, e.g. Spivak and Bhabha, it provided a theoretical basis of postcolonialism for Hingley's alternative paradigm of globalization.

To put it briefly, Hingley's globalization model brings top-down elite perspectives and bottom-up non-elite counterparts together. He argues that simply replacing the top-down perspective with the bottom-up one, for example the negotiation model that emphasizes native agency, is still locked in the colonial epistemology, as '[t]he adoption of such a supposedly "bottom-up", rather than "top-down" process in the contemporary world could be seen as exonerating Western powers from any blame for their imperial actions. It resulted from postcolonial guilt derived from the recent imperial history of Britain and the West'.[56] While Webster has raised the criticism that the negotiation model simply shifts the pendulum while maintaining the same framework of linear acculturation, Hingley adds that it may be too simplistic a solution for Western scholars to avoid addressing postcolonial thought while overlooking their scholarly traditions shaped by colonial, as well as classical, inheritances. According to Hingley, as well as Webster, a negotiation model which shifts the agency to natives is a mirror reflection of the old Romanization model and does not push the epistemological boundaries to write an alternative history. Hingley recapitulates the dilemma of a Western historian:

> There is a certain irony in these arguments, since we have seen that Millett developed his interpretation of Romanization as a direct and explicit attempt to escape from the imperial notions of progress inherent in earlier theories. The less interventionist school of thought that has developed as a result of the perspective that he outlined is now subject to criticism on the grounds of its relationship to a post-imperial guilt. ... it would appear that one is 'damned if one does and damned if one doesn't'.

Yet, he suggests a move to forward the discourse:

> One solution to this apparent *impasse* is to adopt an approach to the issue of imperial control and native response that combines aspects of two positions that are often developed in the form of opposites. We need to focus upon the commonplace imposition of order, social norms and new culture practices in the Roman empire, but to balance this against negotiation and cultural interaction. As Dick Whittaker has argued, the two positions of an interventionist Roman state and a responsive native elite need not act in opposition; direct intervention and innovation could occur alongside one another.

---

[56] Hingley 2005: 46.

Like Webster, Hingley proposes to bring top-down and bottom-up forces together as a way to introduce an epistemological shift to the discourse on Roman imperialism and Romanization. By contrast, how Hingley perceives the end product differs from the way Webster does. Whilst Webster argues that elite culture and non-elite counterculture interacted with each other to produce creole culture and identity, Hingley maintains that the fact that these two occupy different strata results in fragmented identities in a globalized culture.

In light of his emphasis on postmodernist thought, fragmentation, which rejects any emergence of a coherent system of power and knowledge/truth, chimes with Hingley's focal point. Evoking discrepant experiences in the age of globalization, he insists that the colonizing and the colonized people in the Roman Empire built a complex web of power configurations in which they negotiated their status, culture, and identity in both imperial and local contexts. Adopting Woolf's model of power and knowledge in *Becoming Roman* as a theoretical foundation, Hingley quotes Woolf in order to illustrate a dynamic and heterogeneous system of power and knowledge/truth: 'a new, highly differentiated social formation incorporating a new cultural logic and a new configuration of power ... The process might be compared to the growth of an organism that metabolizes other matter and is itself transformed by what it feeds on'.[57] Hingley does not spell out in detail how his model of globalization differs from Woolf's model of 'becoming Roman', but he provides a glimpse into his understanding of the contemporary discourse on Romanization and the place of Woolf's and his own models in it:

> These approaches have been created both through the general idea of 'becoming Roman' and also by the less Romano-centric approaches to fragmented identities. The developing consensus appears to be that the deconstruction of coherent concepts that have dominated studies, such as the myth of the unity of Graeco-Roman culture, is, in itself, a liberating exercise. Works that focus upon the variability of response within the empire, however, may develop alongside unquestioned assumptions that broadly comparable forces of regional 'emancipation' within the current world system are a force for good across the globe.[58]

In other words, Hingley, to a certain extent, agrees with Woolf that becoming Roman is not a process of converging to a homogenous set of ideals but of partaking in the imperial discourse to create differences, dispersions, and discontinuities in the system of power and knowledge/

[57] Woolf 1997: 347.   [58] Hingley 2005: 119.

truth – whether emulating or resisting. The fact that Hingley positions his model and Woolf's model on the same trajectory within the Romanization discourse reflects that. Yet, he points out that the imperial connectivity by which the colonized subjects could engage with the imperial discourse was limited to the elite strata. Even though Woolf attempts to move away from the Romano-centric epistemology and historiography by rejecting the colonial dialectics between Romans and the Other as meaningless, Hingley suggests that there is still a further step to be taken to push the epistemological boundaries away from Romano-centrism: 'The idea of Roman identity is useful as a concept of cultural unity that allows the exploration of power relations, but we need to accept that it is only a partial picture of the connections through which the empire was brought into being and maintained. It is an image that focuses upon the elite, while providing a very limited understanding of others'.[59]

Hingley contends that access to the imperial discourse to reconfigure the system of power and knowledge/truth either by emulating or resisting was limited to the upper class. With the advent of the Augustan imperial system, the group empowered to lay down the foundation of the imperial system of power and knowledge/truth shifted from the hereditary Roman elites to the specialist groups in charge of government, the military, and religion across the Empire.[60] Then, 'Roman identity [came to be] articulated as an international culture'.[61] The emerging class of the imperial elites in Rome and the provinces joined the imperial discourse to create, negotiate, modify, perpetuate, and circulate the system of power and knowledge/truth across 'literary, intellectual, aesthetic, artistic and architectural styles', which came to be known as the Augustan revolution.[62] Thus far, Hingley overall adopts Woolf's 'becoming Roman' approach in that Romans expanded their régime of truth to their provinces. However, Hingley decidedly departs from Woolf's approach to make 'empathetic efforts' to understand Roman imperial strategy.[63] In other words, while accepting the theoretical model of Woolf, Hingley switches his position in relation to Romans and, henceforth, reorients his paradigm. In a distinctively different tone, he explicitly proclaims that Romanization was the elite discourse, centring on colonizing the subaltern Other. The Roman civilizing ethos de facto was 'a discourse of the dominant ... [and] an instrument of

---

[59] Hingley 2005: 93. It is worth nothing here that Hingley alludes to Simon James and Webster in his notes: James 2001; Webster 2001.
[60] E.g. Galinsky 1996; Schiesaro and Habinek 1998; Wallace-Hadrill 2008.   [61] Hingley 2005: 57.
[62] E.g. Syme 1939; Zanker 1988; Habinek 1998; Taplin 2000.   [63] Woolf 1998: 48.

Globalization: Hingley 177

imperialism'.[64] For instance, Latin literature, epitomized by Virgil (despite ambivalence), became a medium to inculcate aristocratic standards and authority and to construct, uphold, and disseminate the imperialistic narrative.[65] Also, urban architecture visually imprinted the imperial imagery in order to 'civilize' and 'control' the provincial landscape and manipulate the social order around its space.[66] Hingley does not neglect the local elites' response to the imperial discourse, their recasting of Roman influence in native traditions in which numerous local variations manifest, such as urban planning, architecture, and religion. According to the needs of each province, local elites adapted the imperial discourse, which John C. Barrett calls 'deviant readings'.[67] Diversity of local deviant readings across the Roman Empire does not necessarily indicate local resistance against Roman imperialism. Instead, Hingley underlines, it indicates the power of Roman imperialism to establish a common discourse across the imperial elite class in spite of their differences: 'The requirement for this local version of the culture to be recognizable (and acceptable) to elite groups based elsewhere within the locality, province and empire will have regulated the degree to which such local cultures diverged from broader concepts of what it was to be Roman'.[68]

Nevertheless, this accounts for only one side of the social, economic, and cultural change, Hingley insists. The modern phenomenon of globalization provides a cue, or a critical yet creative lens. As global connectivity has provided opportunities and environment for a new group of global elites to emerge, the social, economic, and cultural gap between the global elites and the poor has widened. While the global elites joined the new global discourse to maintain their social, economic, and cultural power, the majority of the poor was cut off from global connectivity, did not benefit from increasing global wealth, and continued to be a part of the local discourse of cultures and identities. The overall picture may not diverge widely from what was happening in the Roman Empire, as Hingley suggests, when we bring the elite-oriented studies and the non-elite-oriented studies side by side.

> On one side of the argument (Haley), Roman imperialism is seen as providing considerable opportunities for economic expansion. This liberated a substantial group of innovative native people from their inherited positions of subservience within an elite-focused social system that was broken down, at least to a degree, by the economic forces of Roman

[64] Hingley 2005. [65] Stahl 1997. [66] E.g. Macdonald 1986.
[67] Barrett 1997b. See also Potter 1999. [68] Hingley 2005: 71.

imperialism. On the other side (Downs), Rome had a relatively limited impact across many of the provinces, as indigenous elites continued to dominate their communities under the new circumstances of Roman control, integrating themselves into the economic system to varying degrees, but with a substantial degree of continuity from the pre-Roman pattern.[69]

Hingley fundamentally questions whether the Roman Empire connected its colonized subjects into the imperial discourse and its systems of power and knowledge/truth. The non-elites were under Roman power and influence, but their epistemology and their discourse were not fully integrated into the imperial discourse. As modern Western scholarship had overlooked the presence of the non-elite alternative epistemology and historiography, Hingley alerts us to the fact that Roman historiography has, unsurprisingly, paralleled its orientation: Romano-centric, elite-driven, and at times imperialistic.

> The approaches to globalizing Roman culture continue, on the whole, to place a fairly positive spin upon the effects of Roman imperialism. The Roman elite is considered to have been involved in a series of connected political actions that enabled members of various native societies to define their identities in new and original ways. This was accomplished through the use of surplus and widespread contacts, including service in the Roman army, or involvement in industry, trade and agriculture.[70]

Like Webster, Hingley considers the non-elite epistemological peripheries as a key to break away from Romano-centric and Eurocentric historiography. Although he does not make a case based on the non-elite counterculture like Webster, he suggests that non-elites operated within their own separate discourse and régime of truth. According to Hingley, the prevailing view that non-elites emulated local elites who in turn emulated Romans to engage with the imperial discourse at a lower level is a reflection of a Romano-centric perspective. Non-elites' adoption of Roman practices, such as writing Latin and using *terra sigillata* (a type of fine red ancient Roman pottery), does not automatically betray their will to emulate Roman elites or represent their vulgar imitation of the elite culture: 'these people were not necessarily seeking their own regionally distinctive local way of "becoming Roman", but were retaining the core of their cultural identity, with the addition of certain powerful innovations which assisted them to live in new ways under changing conditions'.[71] In other words, adopting Roman practices does not indicate that non-elites

---

[69] Hingley 2005: 115; Haley 2003; Downs 2000.   [70] Hingley 2005: 119.
[71] Hingley 2005: 99. See Cooley and Burnet 2002; Adams 2003.

adopted the Roman imperial system of power and knowledge/truth. Rather than the imperial discourse imposing its system of power and knowledge/truth onto non-elites, non-elites pulled some elements of the imperial discourse into their own system of power and knowledge/truth to suit their own needs and contexts. It was the Romano-centric (as well as Eurocentric) epistemology that inclined us to assume that its system of power and knowledge/truth subsumed the subaltern Other.

Furthermore, being a Romano-British archaeologist himself, Hingley perceives that the archaeological evidence is also exposed to the influence of Romano-centrism. Romano-centrism has not only coloured the interpretation of archaeological data, but also governed the process of collecting archaeological data. '[A] determined search for the progressive value of Roman innovation' often dictated the objective and direction of the collection of archaeological data and construing their historical significance.[72] For instance, in provincial studies, urban planning and architecture and suburban villas sidelined small towns and rural farmsteads, and *terra sigillata* eclipsed indigenous types of pottery. The Romano-centric perspective overshadowed the epistemological peripheries where the subaltern Other has operated their own régime of truth in Roman scholarship. Hingley's postmodernist initiative to destabilize the homogenous notion of Roman culture and identity by introducing the subaltern Other into Roman historiography effectively led to the postcolonial epistemological shift.[73]

In his conclusion, Hingley proposes discrepant experiences in the globalized Roman Empire as a paradigm to explain the intricate power relations between the imperial discourse and regional discourses.[74] Depending on where each individual is situated in the structure of differences, whether urban or rural, elite or non-elite, male or female, negotiating or conflicting, each occupied a differentiated position to undergo discrepant experiences within the Roman Empire. As mentioned earlier, while Webster proposes creolization as a process in which asymmetric interaction between elite and non-elite discourses generates a new system of power and knowledge/truth that plays with ambiguity, Hingley assumes a postmodernist approach to formulate his alternative paradigm. Instead of arguing for an alternative

---

[72] Hingley 2005: 116.
[73] Post-processual archaeology, influenced by postmodernism, has developed since the 1980s in reaction to positivist processual archaeology in order to introduce subjectivity in archaeological interpretations. See Hodder 1982.
[74] Hingley acknowledges that the concept of 'discrepant experiences', put forward by Said in *Culture and Imperialism*, was first introduced to Roman scholarship by Mattingly: Said 1994; Mattingly and Alcock 1997. Later, based on the very notion of discrepant experiences, Mattingly expands his views in his other works. Mattingly 2006, 2011b.

180   Towards a Paradigm Shift in the Age of Globalization

coherent system of power and knowledge/truth, he attempts to disperse any hegemonic view on Roman imperialism and Romanization: 'I have provided an account that reacts against the idea that one coherent interpretation *could* provide an adequate explanation for the complex evidence'.[75] According to Hingley, postmodernism has the potential to emancipate Roman scholarship from its own scholarly traditions and to move it forward by opening its doors to contemporary epistemological questions, that is, a critical yet creative practice. If postmodernism has inspired his project, poststructuralist and postcolonial epistemological shifts, nonetheless, underpin his paradigm. Challenging teleology and totalization and advocating dispersion, difference, and discontinuity, Hingley puts a poststructuralist epistemological shift at the heart of his paradigm. His historiographical study lays this foundation. He does not simply outline recent works on Roman imperialism and Romanization but illustrates that Romano-centric and Eurocentric epistemologies have driven the discourse into the teleological and totalizing framework. Then, pushing the epistemological boundaries to the subaltern Other to destabilize Romano-centric epistemology and historiography, he adopts the postmodern as well as postcolonial epistemological shifts and writes an alternative history in the paradigm of discrepant experiences under globalization. Although he ends by opening up more questions and possibilities for future scholarship, rather than providing a conventional closure to the discourse on Romanization, he also moves the discourse a step closer towards a paradigm shift.

Imperial Possession: Mattingly

> Legate, I had the news last night – my cohort ordered home
> By ships to Portus Itius and thence by road to Rome.
> I've marched the companies abroad, the arms stowed below:
> Now let another take my sword. Command me not to go!⁷⁶

Thus spoke Rudyard Kipling's Roman officer when ordered to leave Britain. Kipling composed the poem *The Roman Centurion's Song* more than a century ago in 1911, at the height of the British Empire, unequivocally projecting the British imperialist vision onto Roman Britain. Nevertheless, Mattingly questions whether the imperialist epistemology woven into Roman historiography has, in fact, been cleared, enabling us to reframe our understanding of Roman Britain in the postcolonial age. Crucially, Mattingly asks '[c]an we reconstruct a British perspective on

[75] Hingley 2005: 120.   [76] Kipling 1911.

these events?', a question that evokes Spivak's pivotal work 'Can the Subaltern Speak?' from 1988.[77]

As discussed earlier, there have been undercurrents about the subaltern Other in the discourse on Romanization stirred by Webster and Hingley, but Mattingly makes another milestone achievement to broach the postcolonial perspective to the wider audience, in other words, for the Majority to catch on to the postcolonial epistemological shift. Among his other works written with a related objective, *An Imperial Possession: Britain in the Roman Empire, 54 BC – AD 409*, published in 2006, heralds another threshold point in the discourse, possibly another Tipping Point.[78] Since Mattingly's *An Imperial Possession* was published more than a decade ago, it would certainly be arguable to compare the impact that it has had with that Millett's *The Romanization of Britain* incurred three decades ago, and to ask whether it has tipped a worldview or shifted a paradigm beyond its immediate reach. Regardless, given the scope and the target audience of Mattingly's project, he certainly aims at tipping a paradigm shift in the discourse on Roman imperialism and Romanization.

As previously discussed in this chapter, Webster in 2001 and Hingley in 2005 propose alternative paradigms to replace the framework of Romanization. After arguing that the European imperial past has formulated the Romano-centric historiography of Roman imperialism and Romanization, both suggest alternative paradigms which posit the subaltern Other in the Roman Empire as the breakthrough point to bring an epistemological shift. Introducing the postcolonial epistemological shift, they present alternative theoretical frameworks and open up possibilities of expanding them into alternative historical narratives. Subsequently, Mattingly's *An Imperial Possession* brings the postcolonial epistemological shift onto the next step, as he develops it to write an alternative narrative. As Mattingly declares in his preface, from the beginning his project was conceived for the very purpose of taking advantage of the platform offered by The Penguin Histories of England to reach a wider audience and to write an alternative history that could tip a paradigm shift:

> As I sit typing the final words of my own book, I am very conscious of the fact that Ian Richmond's *Roman Britain* was published in 1955, exactly fifty years ago, and, with revisions, has remained in print ever since. ... Consequently, and like other writers in this new series, I have felt humbled and daunted by the task of writing an account for the twenty-first century.

[77] Mattingly 2006; Spivak 1988.
[78] For other works of Mattingly, see Mattingly 2002, 2004, 2011b.

In short, I have tried to write a controversial book, but one that will be accessible to a wide audience, a book that will make people think for themselves about issues, and that does not always have clear answers to difficult questions. In the process I have tried to dispense with a series of sacred cows – most notably the intellectually lazy recourse to the concept of Romanization (which ultimately means everything and nothing).[79]

To this purpose, he chooses not to synthesize recent works of history and archaeology into a format most congenial to the academic audience, with meticulous references, or with a focus on social and economic analyses as is common in Romano-British studies.[80] On the contrary, he weaves elements of conventional history writing in the narrative format with those of contemporary academic convention propelled by archaeological data to compose an alternative historical narrative. Overall, Mattingly arrives at an unconventional historical narrative that might catch his readers off guard, especially those who were expecting an updated volume on Roman Britain written in a traditional vein after Penguin's earlier version by Richmond. Notwithstanding the less than enthusiastic reception in the academic readership immediately after its publication, Tom Holland's review, published in *The Spectator* in 2006, implies that Mattingly's work was appropriately balanced to trigger a Tipping Point to change the public understanding of Roman imperialism and Romanization. Holland dubs it 'the invention of tradition', that is, 'the portrait of a Roman Britain that was neither a Good Thing, nor necessarily, by the much crueller standards of the time, a Bad Thing – just different, immeasurably and unnervingly different'.[81]

Holland's article in a reputable British magazine indicates that Mattingly contributed to making the postcolonial epistemological shift on the discourse on Romanization more widely accessible, but his comment should be read with caution. It would be misleading to accept his understanding of Mattingly's work at face value. Rather than arguing that Roman imperialism was simply a remote past alien to modern perception, Mattingly asserts that Roman imperialism had inflicted substantial damages on the colonized population: '[t]he point here is that the Roman state could be a ruthless military power, inflicting major damage on its enemies ... This "beneficent" imperialism is an important aspect of the

---

[79] Mattingly 2006: xi-xii.
[80] Reviewers have shared their frustration concerning the absence of footnotes. They have suggested that the Bibliographical Essay at the end proved to be not particularly helpful in navigating and crosschecking Mattingly's argument. See Watts 2007; Ireland 2007.
[81] Holland 2006. Cf. Hobsbawm and Ranger 1983.

Imperial Possession: Mattingly 183

Roman case, but can be overstated if we want to assess the broader impacts on society as a whole'.[82] He does not deny that some, particularly cooperative local elites, benefited from Roman imperialism to augment their own power and wealth under Roman patronage, but he maintains that this led to an unbalanced understanding of Roman Britain for decades. He states that his aim is to address 'a too ready and uncritical approbation of the Roman empire ... [that had drawn] attention from the exploitative and repressive aspects of imperial rule':[83]

> This book seeks to explore the nature of life under Roman domination from a variety of perspectives. It offers a critical and sceptical view of the nature of imperial systems. An empire is in general interested in its own maintenance, with regional development a secondary consideration, in itself underscored with self-interest. Wherever economic development did take place, there the state could extract more revenue. Where social institutions took root, there the state could govern more effectively and often more economically.[84]

By flipping the perspective on Roman imperialism from that of many earlier works on Roman Britain, Mattingly attempts to effect a paradigm shift in the Romano-British historiography. As a matter of fact, almost three decades ago, Harris had already brought a paradigm shift with regards to Roman imperialism. Amidst the swirl of Vietnam Syndrome, Harris introduced the poststructuralist epistemological shift of reflecting upon the historical relativity of power and knowledge/truth to Roman scholarship and contended that Romans, celebrating war and expansion, aimed at extending their *imperium* aggressively. The paradigm shift that Mattingly seeks, on the other hand, rests on the very perspective of the receiving end of Roman aggressive imperialism, that is, the colonized subaltern Other. Pushing the epistemological boundaries to write alternative history, he attempts a postcolonial history of Roman aggressive imperialism from the perspective of the colonized subaltern Other.

To write such a history, Mattingly departs from the approaches and/or perspectives taken by previous works on Roman Britain. First, he questions the positivist methodologies deployed thus far and advises epistemological reflection on sources and methodologies. He urges readers to take both literary and archaeological sources with a pinch of salt, as the contexts in which each type of evidence was produced are too often overlooked. As Mattingly warns, it should be noted that literary sources rooted in Romano-centrism repeatedly mythologized Britons as half-naked warlike

---

[82] Mattingly 2006: 6–7.   [83] Mattingly 2006: 11.   [84] Mattingly 2006: 13.

savages, and archaeological evidence driven by academic agendas preordained the representation of the Romano-British landscape to be seen as an island which benefited from Roman towns, roads, and facilities. Second, he shifts the guiding epistemology from colonial to postcolonial to re-interpret the sources. He explains that colonial and Anglo-centric régimes of truth have governed the discourse on Roman imperialism and Romanization. The nostalgia for both *Pax Britannica* and Roman heritage in national mythology has come to equate Roman rule with development and civilization, instead of exploitation and subjugation.[85] Postcolonialism, Mattingly maintains, provides an epistemological shift to change the paradigm. Third, he proposes an alternative paradigm. While maintaining the overall format of narrative history, he does not write a traditional chronological narrative but a modern thematic narrative. He divides Roman Britain into three distinct communities of the army, the urban population, and the rural population, which underwent discrepant experiences of Roman imperialism, and composes 'three parallel social histories'.[86] If Webster's and Hingley's alternative paradigms focus on shifting epistemologies, Mattingly attempts to channel the postcolonial epistemological shift into an alternative historical narrative. Let us enquire into each step Mattingly takes to write his alternative history.

First, Mattingly underlines the epistemological context of primary sources. Limited literary sources survived to portray *Britannia* as the furthest outpost of Roman *imperium*. Britain was mythologized as the wildest and remotest island that lies outside of the familiar circuit of the Mediterranean, *mare nostrum*, separated by the untamed Channel, *Oceanus*, that eventually came under Roman civilizing and military power. Geographical and historical knowledge about Britain was recorded and transmitted by the '*alien elite[s]*, whose lives were closely bound to the maintenance of the Roman Empire [my emphasis]'[87] to reflect their understanding of Britain brought to order by Romans. Mattingly cites a passage from Procopius, a sixth-century Byzantine historian, to illustrate how a persisting narrative tradition conjured up an image of Britons as the barbarian Other:

> [i]n this island of *Britta* the men of old built a long wall, cutting off a large part of it, and the air and the soil and everything else is different on the two sides of it. For to the east of the wall there is healthy air ... and many men dwell there ... and the crops flourish ... But on the other side everything is the opposite of this ... innumerable snakes and all kinds of wild beasts

---

[85] Hingley 2000.   [86] Mattingly 2006: 18.   [87] Mattingly 2006.

occupy the place as their own ... and the natives say that if a man crosses the wall and goes to the other side he forthwith dies, unable to bear the pestilential nature of the air.[88]

Although scholars strive to sift through 'the victor's perspective' to acquire 'meagre crumbs of information', Romano-centric historiography has often slipped through the modern parallel Eurocentric epistemology to sustain colonial historiography.[89] While the pitfalls of the literary sources have been better recognized, Mattingly, also a Romano-British archaeologist himself, warns that archaeological sources likewise bear the same epistemological issue – contrary to popular belief. Archaeological sources, especially in the context of Romano-British scholarship, promised a future to move the scholarship forward, not only to fill the gap in literary sources but also to offset their biases. They held the potential to counterbalance the elite-oriented and Romano-centric literary sources. For that reason, Romano-British archaeology has not only attracted many talents to lead Romano-British scholarship, from Haverfield to Millett, Webster, Hingley and Mattingly, but also increased its breadth and depth of research, from urban to rural and from military to civilian archaeology, which makes any attempt to synthesize them a daunting challenge. However, Mattingly reveals that Romano-British archaeology as a discipline has systematically favoured tracing Roman influences: 'in 1921–25 military sites/major towns/villas comprised 75 per cent of the total. In 1991–95, these three types still comprised 68 per cent, although non-villa rural settlements had risen from 7 to 23 per cent of excavations'.[90] Mattingly reasons that academic agendas driven by Romano-centrism have predisposed the archaeological finds and have thus skewed the current understanding of Roman Britain. Because Romano-centrism is incorporated into the production of not only literary but also archaeological sources, re-interpreting them to dislodge it would require a fundamental shift in perspectives.

Consequently, Mattingly uniquely pronounces his postcolonial epistemological shift to counterbalance the Romano-centric narrative. Although all three – Webster, Hingley, and Mattingly – participated in the aforementioned two conferences in 1994 and 1995 that drew on postcolonial perspectives to the scholarship of Roman Britain, Mattingly alone explicitly gives credit to postcolonial theories in his individual

---

[88] Procopius, *de Bellis*. In Mattingly 2006: 36.
[89] Mattingly 2006: 25–6. On the literary constructions of Britain, see Stewart 1995; Clarke 2001.
[90] Mattingly 2006. On recent reflection on the academic agendas driving Romano-British archaeology, see James and Millett 2001.

work.[91] He attributes the key concept of his work – discrepant experiences – to Said's *Culture and Imperialism*, published in 1994. The words of Said are borrowed here to facilitate our understanding of the travelling ideas:

> The notion of 'discrepant experiences' is not intended to circumvent the problem of ideology. On the contrary, no experience that is interpreted or reflected on can be characterized as immediate, just as no critic or interpreter can be entirely believed if he or she claims to have achieved an Archimedean perspective that is subject neither to history nor to social setting. In juxtaposing experiences with each another, in letting them play off each other, it is my interpretative political aim (in the broader sense) to make concurrent those views and experiences that are ideologically and culturally closed to each other and that attempt to distance and suppress other views and experiences. Far from seeking to reduce the significance of ideology, the exposure and dramatization of discrepancy highlights its cultural importance; this enables us to appreciate its power and understand its continuing influence.[92]

As Said explains, the concept of 'discrepant experiences' foregrounds the asymmetry that colonialism inherently builds into the involved parties. The asymmetrical power structure of colonial rule not only produces discrepant experiences, cultures, and identities with immediate effect, but also shapes discrepant historical narratives as its extended consequence. It appears that the emphasis on asymmetry is the reason Mattingly considers Said's concept of 'discrepant experiences' more appropriate to bring a paradigm shift, instead of the globalization paradigm argued by Hingley. As a matter of fact, Hingley also alludes to discrepant experiences and pivots on the concept to argue that the globalization paradigm explains the fragmentation due to the separate elite global culture and non-elite local cultures. Yet, Mattingly maintains that the paradigm shift from postcolonial perspectives should be more explicit in exposing and integrating the brutal nature of colonial power and its consequences into historical narratives. He voices his concern that globalization may slip into becoming another term to gloss over the very overlooked asymmetrical power structure of Roman imperialism: '[h]owever, as with Romanization, globalization will prove no better a concept in seeking to understanding Britain under Roman rule, if we use it to emphasize conformity rather than investigate diversity. If anything, globalization highlights the unintentional and random impacts of Roman culture on provincial societies'.[93]

---

[91] Webster and Cooper 1996; Mattingly and Alcock 1997.   [92] Said 1994: 32–3.
[93] Mattingly 2006: 17.

Imperial Possession: Mattingly 187

Said has articulated a similar concern about the globalization model and its episteme:

> [T]he tendency in anthropology, history, and cultural studies in Europe and the United States is to treat the whole of world history as viewable by a kind of Western super-subject, whose historicizing and disciplinary rigor either takes away or, in the post-colonial period, restores history to people and cultures 'without' history. Few full-scale critical studies have focused on the relationship between modern Western imperialism and its culture, the occlusion of that deeply symbiotic relationship being a result of the relationship itself.[94]

Globalization propelled by Western (neo)colonialism could subsume alternative epistemologies through its power structure and, therefore, subdue or disperse the re-inscription of historical realities of the subaltern colonized Other into a so-called globalized historical narrative. Although it would be another political and economic challenge to redress the asymmetrical power structure between dominant and subaltern epistemologies, as Said contends, a paradigm that does not take into account the asymmetry between two types of epistemologies is fundamentally blind to the fact that historical narratives are influenced by a power asymmetry that has not only political and economic but also epistemological dimensions. Hence, Said contends that knowledge, including historical knowledge, in itself is power and political. Without conscious intellectual efforts to get closer to epistemological equilibrium, particularly in the context of continuing political and economic disparity, any claim to pure or objective knowledge about colonial and imperial history is short-sighted, according to Said. In the discourse on Romanization, Mattingly is alone in expressing sympathy with Said in acknowledging that knowledge in itself is power and political, not only in ancient Roman but also in contemporary contexts, and, furthermore, in asserting his political position on historical knowledge. While most historians and archaeologists continue to claim that their work consists of objective historical writing about the Roman imperial past, Mattingly does not make any claim to objective historical knowledge but attempts to contribute to a balanced understanding of Roman imperialism from his own political stance on historical knowledge. In that sense, Mattingly's project tallies closest with postcolonial thinkers by, first, acknowledging the power asymmetry between dominant and subaltern epistemologies and, second, attempting to redress it by writing an

---

[94] Said 1994: 35.

alternative history that pushes the epistemological boundaries onto the subaltern Other.

Henceforth, Mattingly's alternative history rests on discrepant experiences across the unequal power structure – from a ruling military community to hybrid urban civilian communities to subaltern rural civilian communities. As he writes, 'what distinguishes [his paradigm] is the starting premise that these broad communities did not share a single common culture, but there were significant differences between them (and indeed further levels of divergence within each of these major communities)'.[95] First, the military community.[96] Contrary to the widespread view that the Roman military served as a conduit to bring order and to spread *romanitas* across the provinces after the initial conquest, Mattingly insists that they were agents of Roman imperialism who organized oppression and expedited exploitation. To argue that the damage of military conquest was compensated for by order and efficiency, he challenges, reflects a Romano-centric perspective on the colonial rule. From the perspective of the colonized, '[I]n the aftermath of defeat and occupation of territory, a further series of impacts might be felt over a period of years: arrests and execution of suspected troublemakers, enslavement of elements of the population, forcible disarmament, seizure of property (especially portable wealth, crops and livestock), confiscation of lands'.[97] The military maintained its exclusive power, culture, and identity that only spilled over to those closely linked by marriage or trade. Evidence of the Latin epigraphic habit, Roman artistic iconographies of war and conquest, and martial Roman deities were largely restricted to the military community. Soldiers and veterans did not propagate the so-called civilizing *romanitas*, but used their exclusive access to literacy, artistic iconography, and religion to express Roman military might and to demonstrate their dominance over and difference from the colonized population. The *romanitas* that the military community communicated to the colonized population was a Roman celebration of war and conquest so that 'their whole society became structured around the idea of war, and focused on the sacrifices, training and organization necessary to win'.[98] For instance, Mattingly illustrates that the act of *interpretatio*, most frequently implemented with Mars (comprising more than half of the cases of name-pairing), 'was more of a monologue than a dialogue' to convey that Roman deities subjugated local deities.[99] Resorting to the framework of *interpretatio* and/or

---

[95] Mattingly 2006.   [96] On the Roman army, see Le Bohec 1994; Goldsworthy 2000.
[97] Mattingly 2006: 92.   [98] Mattingly 2006: 87.
[99] Mattingly 2006: 216. *Interpretatio* is a religious practice, usually in polytheistic systems, to adopt foreign deities by translating them into/merging with existing deities.

syncretism would be to use convenient bywords to un-problematize the colonialism and power asymmetry built into provincial religious practices.[100] Furthermore, military culture and identity was not a uniform or static system to preserve the same exclusive so-called 'Roman' signifiers throughout, but fluid and able to absorb diverse elements, such as Germanic cults and Christianity, especially in the third and fourth centuries, and to refashion itself. What bound the military community was a flexible but shared system of power and knowledge/truth to differentiate itself from the colonized. Hence, Mattingly contends that the military community did not impart a specific Roman system of power and knowledge/truth to the colonized population – from the perspective of the colonized. Instead, remaining separate from the civilians in its position of power, the military exercised its own exclusive system of power and knowledge/truth, that is, to uphold the asymmetrical colonial power structure in Britain.[101]

Mattingly then examines the two distinct civilian communities, the urban and the rural. Surveying towns and villas to small settlements and rural countryside in Britain, he attempts to portray the imperial landscape of Britain from the perspective of the colonized, that is, the majority of the people in Roman Britain. A broad picture of Britain emerges in which the rural countryside served as an arena to be exploited for crops, mineral resources, labour, etc. and where the urban centres and road networks were built as infrastructure to connect focal points in order to facilitate access to resources. In the debate between Roman military and administrative intervention and native agency in shaping the imperial landscape, Mattingly argues that the actual picture would have been closer to treading a subtle line between the two conflicting forces.[102] The conflict between the two forces often resulted in hybrid forms of (sub)urban structures, religious practices, and language usages. One of the striking phenomena to demonstrate their complex nature – unique to civilian communities – is the so-called curse tablets, *defixiones*. Using Latin cursive script, the literate people in the lower strata, who had access to relatively simple Latin but no access to petition against wrongdoings, sought justice by recording spells on thin sheets of lead. The overwhelming majority of the curse tablets found across Britain seek revenge against theft. Although the curse tablets are found across the provinces, Mattingly highlights a British peculiarity: 'in fact the overwhelming emphasis in Britain on issues relating to theft is quite unlike the pattern elsewhere, where curses relating to litigation, to

---

[100] See Webster 1995a, 1995b, 1997.   [101] Blagg and King 1984.
[102] Grew and Hobley 1985; Millett 1990.

competition, to commercial enterprises and to erotic or amatory adventures are also common. Curse tablets occur at a wide range of British sites, both urban and rural, but – with a single exception – not on military sites'.[103] For example, one curse tablet from Bath records that:

> The person who has lifted my bronze vessel is utterly accursed. I give (him) to the temple of Sulis, whether man or woman, whether slave or free, whether boy or girl, and let him who has done this spill his own blood into the vessel itself.[104]

Mattingly understands that '[t]he curse tablets can be read as a transcript about the workings of Roman imperialism – with divine help being recruited to help subjects address some of its shortcomings'.[105] Using the curse tablets as an example, he maintains that the hybrid forms of Romano-British practices do not necessarily indicate that the colonized population developed a hybrid identity. Rather, he points out that the subaltern Other, despite supposedly Roman practices on the surface, kept their own epistemology; the curse tablets hint that, from the perspective of subaltern epistemology, Romans were exploitative colonialists – a perspective inaccessible from Romano-centric epistemology. From the perspective of the colonized, exploitation was not isolated events sporadically committed by some abusers but a natural state of colonization. Undergoing their own discrepant experiences of Roman imperialism, the subaltern colonized Other were Romans in their own separate regional way without 'becoming Romans' – that is, without partaking in the Roman system of power and knowledge/truth.

Holland concludes that Mattingly's work is '[f]rom brothel to procurators, then, from the very lowest to the highest, all are here in a magnificent work of resurrectionism'.[106] Indeed, Mattingly resurrects wide-ranging sources from the perspective of the subaltern Other into an alternative historical narrative. Certainly his project still bears its own epistemological weakness, as pointed out by Stanley Ireland: '[I]n many respects, however, overtly anti-imperialist viewpoints are in danger of merely replacing one blinkered approach with another'.[107] Nonetheless, borrowing Said's concept of discrepant experiences, Mattingly resurrects an understanding of Roman Britain that is more refined and subtler that an anti-imperialist narrative. Each community, from military to urban and rural civilian, underwent discrepant experiences within the power asymmetry of

---

[103] Mattingly 2006: 310–11. See Tomlin 2002. [104] Tomlin 1988. [105] Mattingly 2006: 315.
[106] Holland 2006. [107] Ireland 2007: 364.

Roman imperialism and accordingly formulated a different narrative of Roman imperialism. Apart from the well-documented Romano-centric narrative, he contends that there existed other epistemologies and histories that cannot be epistemologically subsumed under a Romano-centric perspective. As his work is one of the earliest attempts to bring a postcolonial epistemological shift to an alternative history in Roman scholarship, there remain various aspects to refine and improve on. For example, how to measure the silence in the literary and archaeological sources to retrieve the muted subaltern Other into postcolonial history, the very question which Spivak delved into. Furthermore, does resurrecting ancient Britons into the colonized contribute to pulling the discourse on Romanization away from the Eurocentric colonial system of power and knowledge/truth? Perhaps, could postcolonial concepts of hybridity, ambivalence, and creolization, used in Webster's and Hingley's alternative paradigms, prove to be more useful to explain complexities of power asymmetry, linked through ancient and modern imperialism, into alternative history in the future? Having said that, writing an alternative history, Mattingly introduces to the Majority the postcolonial epistemological shift that is currently tipping the historiography on Roman imperialism and Romanization.

The Lexus and the Olive Tree, or the *Terra Sigillata* and the *Epona*

Let us turn back to Friedman's *The Lexus and the Olive Tree*. His symbols of globalization that embody the two forces of the upper global and the lower local strata resonate with the works of Webster, Hingley, and Mattingly, published in the early twenty-first century, particularly when compared with the works of scholars of the earlier generation, from Finley to Harris, Millett, Dyson, and Woolf, in the second half of the twentieth century. The earlier scholars as the first postcolonial generation served as the Early Adopters of the seeds of poststructuralist and postcolonial thought, but in general the colonized and silent Other of the Roman Empire continued to remain invisible and silent. These scholars centred on reorienting how to understand the ruling Roman elites' régime of truth – not as a parallel past of the modern Western Self, but as the alien Other. Their shift in position with regards to ancient Romans, which is rooted in the travelling ideas of the Innovators of the time, of the Cold War and the decolonization era, that is, Fanon, Foucault, and Said, unsurprisingly inherited the scope, perspective, and limit of their adopted thoughts.

It was only after globalization became a palpable phenomenon across the world that not only many scholars but also the general public felt the need for more sophisticated postcolonial thought that could explain a complex web of neo-liberal and neo-colonial systems of power and knowledge/truth. The challenge was most notably dealt with by Spivak and Bhabha. Primarily, they both pitched towards pushing the epistemological boundaries to explore the colonized and silent Other in order to destabilize the (neo-)colonial epistemology. Becoming the Early Adopters of Spivak's and Bhabha's refined set of postcolonial thought, Webster, Hingley, and Mattingly marked a second wave of the postcolonial generation of scholars. The works of these three Roman scholars (all of whom are Romano-British archaeologists), hence, all pivot on the epistemological divide between the global elite and the local non-elite, as Friedman's does.[108] In this sense, it would not be too far-fetched to substitute Friedman's symbols of modern globalization with those of the Roman equivalent – perhaps, the *terra sigillata* and the *Epona* – in order to capture their new paradigms. In tandem with the postcolonial discourse in the age of globalization, they attempt to reinstitute an independent epistemology and historiography of the colonized and silent Other to the mainstream historical narrative of the Roman Empire.

The models that Webster, Hingley, and Mattingly respectively propose, of course, differ from each other, from creolization to globalization to imperial possession. Webster argues that the elite and non-elite discourses interacted with each other in the asymmetric power structure to result in a creole culture; Hingley stresses that the two separate epistemologies operated at different levels to constitute the globalized Roman empire; and Mattingly focuses on the discrepant experiences of the colonized population which the elite-oriented discourse has overlooked. Nevertheless, in the broader sense, they all aim at writing an alternative history. If we are to make a comparison with the works of the earlier

---

[108] Of course, this should not be mistaken as stating that most works on Roman imperialism produced during the time shared the same postcolonial thought in recognizing the silent Other as a source of epistemology. For example, one of the influential works on Roman imperialism of the time, Arthur Eckstein's *Mediterranean Anarchy, Interstate War, and the Rise of Rome*, published in 2006, was a product of the era of globalization, focusing on the supranational structure governing nation-states' behaviour. He argues that the system of anarchy which conditioned each state's decision-making process had driven the Roman Republic to pursue its *imperium*, like any other of her neighbouring powers. The success of Rome, according to Eckstein, lies not in its military conquests but in its Romanizing strategy, which enabled it to gather human and natural resources to continue war and expansion successfully. Paying attention solely to the upper strata in the globalized Mediterranean, Eckstein takes a contrasting position to the above-mentioned Romano-British historians/archaeologists. Eckstein 2006.

historians to make the difference easier to understand, the earlier works would be better understood as revisionist history, that is recasting the significance of *terra sigillata* in light of poststructuralist and postcolonial thought on the colonial perspective and narrative. The subsequent scholars, on the other hand, were not only more explicit about the epistemological reflection but also more proactive in moving towards a new epistemology and historiography. They attempt to reinscribe the resistance, adaptation, ambivalence, and hybridity of the colonized and silent Other under the colonial system of power and knowledge/truth into their alternative histories. In other words, they incorporate not only the impact of *terra sigillata* but also the significance of *Epona* into the historical narratives.

Do they signal a paradigm shift in the Romanization discourse? The poststructuralist and postcolonial epistemological shift certainly travelled into the Anglo-American scholarship of Roman history through a number of the Early Adopter scholars and reached the Tipping Point at Millett's *The Romanization of Britain* in 1990, inspiring more scholars to delve into the issue. Since then, postcolonialism has entered into the list of staple concepts to discuss in the discourse on Romanization and has resulted in alternative models. It is worth noting that scholars who have put forward new paradigms have their backgrounds in Romano-British archaeology. Certainly, Romano-British archaeologists were not alone in engaging with travelling ideas of postcolonialism, and ancient historians and classicists also produced many works that are in step with the postcolonial epistemological shift.[109] However, this may suggest that: first, the discourse on Romanization is still chiefly a preserve for a cohort of scholars trained in Romano-British archaeology, and second, the discourse may benefit from collaboration among classicists, historians, and archaeologists working on various themes, such as slavery and gender, from postcolonial perspectives. The current discourse is far from reaching a consensus that one particular paradigm provides an answer sufficient to decisively replace the paradigm of Romanization. However, aided by the intellectual currents of twenty-first century globalization, the general orientation – to move *beyond* the existing epistemology and historiography, to push the epistemological boundaries to the subaltern Other, and to write an alternative history – may hope to gather momentum from various corners of the scholarship.

---

[109] For instance, Goff 2005; Hardwick and Gillespie 2007; Vasunia 2013.

Appendix 4: Separate or Franglais?

Did postcolonial thought travel to unfold in French discourse on Romanization in the twenty-first century? Was the postcolonial shift in the discourse on Romanization restricted to Anglo-American scholarship or was it a franglais phenomenon? The point of departure was a franglais phenomenon of postcolonialism. Often, poststructuralism is labelled as a French intellectual movement, and postcolonialism as an Anglo-Saxon equivalent. Yet, at least for the purpose of tracing back the travelling ideas, the strand of postcolonialism of interest here is an intellectual development that spans across the Channel for the following two reasons: first, postcolonialism in its primary sense is rooted in French poststructuralism, and second, in its secondary sense of travelling ideas in the context of Roman scholarship, it is also closely related to French poststructuralist ideas. The significance of French poststructuralism, Foucault's epistemological shift in particular, is not always highlighted but cannot be overstated, not only in postcolonial studies but also in Romanization studies. This is certainly not the place to discuss Foucault's wide-ranging legacy in its entirety. Rather, here we focus on his theory on history, power, and knowledge among others that set off ripple effects to postcolonial and Romanization studies, triggering paradigm shifts.

Thus far, we traced the journey of travelling ideas from the point of departure to the point of arrival and examined how postcolonialism diffused into and shifted the discourse on Romanization almost exclusively in the Anglo-American scholarship. Now, it begs a question: why is the discussion on another point of arrival, French scholarship, rather meagre? As mentioned earlier, because the postcolonialism of interest here is a franglais intellectual phenomenon, its immediate reach, both Anglo-American and French scholarship, would form a natural scope to trace the journey of travelling ideas and to compare the two points of arrival. François Dumasy provides a quick answer to the question:

> ... le silence de la recherche francophone dans le débat sur l'écriture d'une histoire de la colonisation, demanderai[en]t à être expliqué[s]. Il est tentant d'y voir la persistance d'une inégalité intériorisée, tant chez les anciens colonisateurs que chez les ex-colonisés, le signe finalement d'une « décolonisation » inachevée de la pensée historique.[110]

---

[110] '... the silence of Francophone research on the debate about how to write a history of colonization demands an explanation. It is tempting to see there the persistence of internalized inequality, both among the former colonizers and among ex-colonised, the ultimate sign of an unfinished "decolonization" of historical thought. Dumasy 2005 (translation by the present author).

Appendix 4: Separate or Franglais?

While Anglo-American scholarship underwent an intellectual epidemic of postcolonialism, of which an epidemic curve can be traced via the works of the Early Adopters, French scholarship did not experience the same postcolonial phenomenon. In short, French scholarship on Roman history, as well as in general, regards postcolonialism as an Anglo-Saxon phenomenon. Postcolonial discourse in French scholarship on Roman history is largely limited to reporting recent developments in the Anglo-Saxon scholarship.[111] This, indeed, begs a further question – why French scholarship, which used to be an intellectual powerhouse and produced many pioneering historians who questioned epistemologies in knowledge and history, did not welcome postcolonial thought. In Roman scholarship during the 1970s, there were some notable historians who posed epistemological questions to imperialist historiography, such as Paul Veyne, Marcel Bénabou, and Yvon Thébert.[112] Since then, however, these questions have disappeared from French scholarship. There could be a variety of factors that hindered the travel of postcolonial thought, for instance, the conflict with French universalist republicanism, but one of the significant factors could be attributed to 'a phase of epistemological anarchy' in French scholarship after a period of confidence and certitude.[113] Without any shared platform to discuss, lead, or challenge epistemologies, postcolonialism is yet to gather enough Early Adopters to diffuse the epistemological shift and to trigger a paradigm shift in French scholarship. Dismissing revolutionary vocabulary from the postcolonial epistemological shift, the French scholarship of Roman history on the whole operates within the continuing tradition.

Therefore, is the travel of postcolonialism to the discourse on Romanization a separate or franglais phenomenon? The two points of arrival, Anglo-Saxon and French scholarship, significantly diverged. Postcolonialism travelled to Anglo-Saxon scholarship, tipped the epistemological shift through the Early Adopters, and is continuously moving the discourse on Romanization towards a paradigm shift, whereas it was lost amidst the epistemological anarchy in French scholarship. As postcolonialism took different positions across the Channel, it travelled to the Romanization studies of each branch of scholarship through different routes and resulted in different discourses. Although the response of each branch of scholarship differed according to their respective political, historical, and intellectual circumstances, the travel of the postcolonial epistemological shift may still be regarded as a franglais phenomenon, which could further benefit

---

[111] e.g. Le Roux 2004. [112] Veyne 1975; Bénabou 1978; Thébert 1978. [113] Revel and Hunt 1995.

from an in-depth comparative study. A comparative study of the discourse on Romanization, which I have ventured in a series of appendixes in brief, attempts to explore how the travelling ideas of postcolonialism not only offer new ways of understanding Roman imperialism and Romanization but also shed light on the relationship between the past and the present, and the relationship between history and epistemology – in a way that is not predetermined or static but dynamic and varied.

Historical Intervention

> Classics needs to change. We need to change. We are part of a field that has proven to be very resistant to change and those of who are not willing to move forward are wholly complicit in the weaponisation of the classical world against BAME, women, working class scholars, people with disabilities, the list goes on. In its current form, Classics is a vehicle for white supremacy. There are people who actively use the classical world and western civilisation as ammunition against us, and if it becomes clear that Classics cannot distance itself from its ties with white supremacy then it is a discipline that deserves to die. I will kill Classics with my bare hands and walk out of this room with my head held high if we cannot change. But there is still time and I feel hope. I don't know if you all feel it but I feel that something big is coming in Classics, we are on a knife's edge and whichever side we fall on is dependent on what we do when we leave this room and go back to work tomorrow.[1]

Listening to these words of Hardeep Singh Dhindsa at a workshop on 'Classics and Race' held at St Andrews University in 2019, I could feel the tension in the room. His words might sound as provocative as those of Gilley in the Introduction. However, in contrast to Gilley's article, it was not the content but the tone that struck the audience as provocative in Dhinsa's words. His frustration with classical scholarship, as witnessed from his own personal experiences, that seeped through his calmly uttered words made the audience face the fact that the postcolonial change in the discipline of Classics and ancient history – which some might have regarded as enough, pacing, or calibrated – is far from enough. His urgent call to confront the question of colonial epistemology underlying the discipline reverberated in the room for a while.

Romanization studies, which owes its own inception to modern Western imperialism, could probably more deeply contemplate the words of Dhindsa.

---

[1] Dhindsa 2019.

There certainly has been a movement to shift the discourse on Romanization from poststructural and postcolonial perspectives over decades, powered by the works of the Early Adopters from Dyson to Mattingly. Each work of the Early Adopters is recognized as a significant work in the discipline to garner ongoing interests and stimulate the discourse. Most recently, Emma Dench's work *Empire and Political Cultures in the Roman World*, published in 2018, made a notable contribution to the discourse. Bringing together a vast number of studies on Roman imperialism and Romanization in her nuanced reading, she rejects the totalizing conversion model of 'becoming Roman' and resurrects the 'messiness' of life under the Roman empire. For example, '[w]e might extend this "backs against the wall" self-motivation to a more everyday self-determination reflected in the examples we have seen of self-aggrandizement, group reinforcement through the imperial experience, and distinctly idiosyncratic articulation of efficacious rituals and formulas, all of which arguably contribute to the dynamism of warfare and enforcement in the Roman empire'.[2] Nevertheless, Romanization as a term and a framework is still current, and the postcolonial turn is yet to 'infect' the Majority. We are still not yet at the moment where we can decisively pronounce that the moment of paradigm shift has happened in the discourse on Romanization. A stream of new research tends to add *up* to the discourse on Romanization, but rather fewer voices have emerged to add *to* disrupt the discourse, to borrow the words of Bhabha. Why has the discourse on Romanization remained more or less static in the last decade after Webster, Hingley, and Mattingly proposed alternative models? Here I believe that the words of Dhindsa may also speak to frustration about the fact that the Romanization framework is still in place despite decades-long efforts, either due to the lack of a satisfactory model or to hesitancy to move the discourse forward.

Postcolonialism has been facing more or less the same predicament, appearing to reach a plateau and see-sawing between the sense of hope and frustration. Social and political turmoil from the 2010s seems to harbour the vacillating mood – the Arab Spring led by the younger generation to rise against corruption and to seek more political and economic equity, starting in the early 2010s, and the subsequent power vacuum, military interventions, and civil wars in the region; the EU migrant crisis ignited by the Syrian civil war from the mid-2010s and the rise of (far-)right nationalist movements in Europe, headed by Nigel Farage in Britain, Marine Le Pen in France, and Matteo Salvini in Italy; the 2016 UK referendum to leave the European Union and the era of the Trump presidency in the

---

[2] Dench 2018: 130.

United States from 2017 to 2021; the #MeToo movement surging with the Harvey Weinstein scandal in 2017 and its backlash afterwards; the COVID-19 pandemic and increasing instances of xenophobia as well as solidarity; escalation of the Black Lives Matter (BLM) movement following the murder of George Floyd in 2020 and its ripple across the globe, including the statue of Edward Colston (a seventeenth/eighteenth-century merchant, slave trader, and philanthropist) in Bristol being toppled; to name a few. The overall impression from this list of events is very much Western metropole focused, as affairs outside the Western world are deemed relevant and important when their ripples hit 'home' in the form of the influx of refugees and consequent political, economic, and social unrest. Otherwise, lots of other unmentioned events often remain regional affairs. However, the increasing level of connectivity only a decade from the turn of the century made it clear that the Lexus and the olive tree do not remain separate; IKEA, Starbucks, and Netflix have developed regionally differentiated products and marketing tactics, while kaftans, sushi, and K-pop have entered the global mainstream market. As the boundary between global elite culture and local culture has become more and more porous, confusion prevailed. Cultural authority, in Bhabha's terminology, as a stable system of reference, tradition, truth, and community was so vehemently contested in various corners that terms such as culture war and identity politics became buzzwords to capture the atmosphere of the time. In the midst of turbulent waves, some strove to redress the legacy of an unjust past, while others yearned for a simpler 'originary Past'.

Increasing connectivity, interestingly, played a rather counterintuitive role in this development. Many social media platforms, from older giants like Facebook, Twitter (now renamed X Corp.), and YouTube to newer key players such as Instagram, TikTok, and Reddit, certainly connected geographically distanced people but more often drove politically, religiously, and socio-economically distanced people further apart. Online networks which once harboured a hope of providing a space to bring diverse perspectives together and to build community through shared conversation became, to a disturbing extent, a platform for sociopolitical propaganda and a vehicle for social division. Facebook-Cambridge Analytica data misuse, which was exposed in 2018, exemplified the case.[3] Cambridge Analytica's political advertising scheme based on personal data gathered through Facebook did not aim to convert people's

---

[3] In 2018, Christopher Wylie, an ex-employee of Cambridge Analytica, exposed via *The Guardian* and *The New York Times* that Facebook and Cambridge Analytica colluded to feed certain types of data to

perspectives but to confirm their predispositions into firmer political action, which crystallized into social and political polarization. It successfully was party to the rise of extremist politics during campaigns across the world, from India and Kenya to Britain and the United States. In one of his interviews exposing the data misuse, Christopher Wylie reveals that: 'Cambridge Analytica was supposed to be the arsenal of weapons to fight that culture war'. It was not the scale of data breach that appalled people; rather, the exploitation of data to manipulate people's behaviour deeply unsettled people, especially when it arrived at the Western metropoles. Questions such as whether online content that one is exposed to has been corrupted and how and where to find reliable and unbiased sources of information, if there are any, became unavoidable. Another term frequently used since the mid-2010s, 'fake news', also speaks about more or less the same phenomenon. Of course, there is unquestionably false and incorrect information flooding the web, but how facts can be woven into both faithful and deceptive reports, reliable and misleading content, and impartial and prejudiced histories mostly confounded people. The framework of fake news (or histories, for that matter) became an easy recourse that besmirches the opposing side and that elides the fundamental question about epistemologies and the order of knowledge to define truth. The further polarization of social and political perspectives, with the help of online platforms, in the last decade attests to the fact that the cultural authority to define knowledge/truth is far from being stable and is being vigorously fought over with every means.

The enclave of classical scholarship was not immune from the so-called culture war. What came to be referred to as 'the incident' at the 2019 Society for Classical Studies conference in San Diego crystallized the rough shape of the culture war in the field of Classics and brought it to the fore. During a question-and-answer session at a panel on the future of Classics, Mary Frances Williams argued for defending Classics' intrinsic value of providing the foundation of Western civilization and then addressed one of the panellists, Dan-el Padilla Peralta: 'You may have got your job because you are black, but I would prefer to think you got your job because of merit.' To which Peralta responded:

> You are right, I was only hired because I am black ... I did not interrupt you once, so you are going to let me talk. You are going to let someone who has been historically marginalized from the production of knowledge in Classics

political campaigners for the purpose of advertising. See Cadwalladr and Graham-Harrison 2018; Rosenberg, Confessore, and Cadwalladr 2018.

talk. And here is what I have to say about the vision of Classics that you have outlined. If that is in fact a vision that affirms you in your white supremacy, I want nothing to do with it. I hope the field dies, that you have outlined, and that it dies as swiftly as possible. And I hope, I fervently hope that those of you in the room will take stock and consideration of what has happened here.

Soon Williams was escorted out of the room.[4] In the following days and weeks, reports and reflections were published not only by Peralta and Williams but also by other panellists, participants, and others.[5]

The overtly racist comment at the conference setting alarmed many, but I doubt the main contention did. In fact, the question about the value of Classics and ancient history has been plaguing the field for a while and was not restricted to the traditional academic sphere. Classicists and ancient historians, not only Mary Beard but Joshua Katz and Peralta himself, published their views via mainstream newspapers and magazines,[6] and *Eidolon*, an online journal founded by Donna Zuckerberg, provided a new type of platform where classicists and ancient historians expressed their views, 'a home for scholarly writing about Classics that isn't formal scholarship', according to Zuckerberg.[7] Beside professionals and aficionados publishing across various platforms, the recent decade also witnessed the rise of the alt-right's appropriation of Greek and Roman references and symbols.[8] Views polarized across academics and the public about the role of Classics in the contemporary world, the relationship between Classics and Western civilization, and ways to move the discipline forward. In short, '[o]n top of the problems facing the humanities as a whole – vanishing class sizes caused by disinvestment, declining prominence and student debt – classics was also experiencing a crisis of identity'.[9] Though Poser here describes Classics scholarship in the USA, the situation was not far different across the Atlantic.[10] The cultural authority that Classics used to hold was no longer upheld and was being contested in various corners. Some yearned to restore the old glory of Classics in its originary Past, whereas others looked to acknowledge the disciplinary knowledge formation of the past and to redefine Classics and rewrite ancient history. While

---

[4] Unedited full video recording is available on the YouTube channel of the Society for Classical Studies: www.youtube.com/watch?v=lcJZCVemn-4
[5] Sarah Bond, one of the panellists, compiled a list of publications about the incident on the blog of Society for Classical Studies. Bond 2019.
[6] For example, see Gold 2017; Gold and Peralta 2017; Katz 2020; Poser 2021.
[7] Zuckerberg 2015.   [8] Zuckerberg 2018.   [9] Poser 2021.
[10] Mathura Umachandra gives her insight into the difference between British and American perspectives in the current scholarship. See Umachandran 2019.

the discipline is going through its soul-searching, the mood oscillates between hope and frustration. Where do we go from here then?

Postclassicisms, authored by a group of nine senior scholars in the United States and Britain, addresses this very question:[11]

> [H]ow can we reconcile our commitment to a past that is not just the product of our fantasies or a disparate heap of unrelated events and artifacts with our own situatedness and capacity to tell compelling stories about antiquity by marshalling a range of epistemic techniques (methodological, linguistic, philosophical, and so on)?[12]

In the midst of confusion, when the value of Classics is no longer enshrined and the role of Classicists and ancient historians seems superfluous, the Collective seeks to redefine the value of Classics and to explore new ways of doing Classics – in a way that matters to the contemporary world.

> We therefore make the acknowledgment of our own situatedness part of what it means to engage antiquity responsibly.
> Responsibility here is not just about recognizing the limits of knowledge. It's about being accountable for the epistemic positions we do take up (and the positions we ignore or reject). That is, situatedness doesn't just point to our entrapment in given historical, cultural, and biographical conditions. It also recognizes our responsibility to use both disciplinary and extradisciplinary resources to create new ways of seeing, valuing, and therefore engaging with antiquity.[13]

The Collective argues that postclassicists can make 'intellectual and moral interventions' that '*renew* [emphasis in original] the past with each new present'.[14] Acknowledging the knowledge formation in place, postclassicists can not only break (away from) the hegemony of a régime of knowledge/truth but also channel intellectual currents to shed new light on the ancient past and to find the value of the antiquity as a productive resource for contemporary intellectual discourse. *Postclassicisms* does not provide a detailed blueprint for the discipline, but theorizes how to rethink the ancient past around key themes and how to redefine the cultural authority of Classics.

However, in practical terms with regard to the history of Roman Empire, how can we rewrite it? How do we use postcolonial thought to

---

[11] The Postclassicisms Collective comprises: Alastair Blanshard, Simon Goldhill, Constanze Güthenke, Brooke Holmes, Miriam Leonard, Glenn Most, James Porter, Phiroze Vasunia, and Tim Whitmarsh.
[12] Postclassicisms Collective 2019: 42. [13] Postclassicisms Collective 2019: 43.
[14] Postclassicisms Collective 2019: 38, 39.

rewrite the narrative of Roman imperialism and to reframe Romanization? And what value does it hold? Does it matter to the contemporary audience? Can it make intellectual and moral interventions, and if so, what kind of interventions?

To ponder over these questions, let us bring ourselves back to Bhabha from the beginning. Thus far, we have traced how the ideas of poststructuralism and postcolonialism travelled and diffused into the discourse on Romanization to trigger a paradigm shift. However, the postcolonial shift called for from the discourse on Romanization is more than a paradigm shift to replace Romanization, but historical intervention using Bhabha's terminology: historical intervention which destabilizes the originary Past as a collective mythic memory that connects ancient Romans with modern Europeans as imagined communities living continuously from the past to the present and, instead, inserts repressed histories of migrants, exiles, and refugees through displacement and diaspora under Roman imperialism in a way that demonstrates fluctuating cultural authorities under Roman imperialism and resist the totalization of Romanization. Historical intervention that can revise the sense of belonging – particularly through the discourse on Romanization, which has played a significant role in sustaining the parallel myth between ancient Romans and modern Europeans – has been wanting. Yet, either willingly or not (perhaps, in accordance with empiricist tradition or not), revisionist histories written thus far which explore various responses to Roman imperialism, either resistance or negotiation, and investigate provincial cultures, either creolized or fragmented, fell short of realizing historical intervention that interrupts the present. When revisionist studies appear to depict local variants to fill the Roman Empire as a more diverse place, the recent discourse tends to revert back by resorting to the framework of Romanization.[15] Hence, frustration as well as hope.

To make historical interventions on Romanization, to write projective pasts of Roman imperialism, and to narrate repressed histories of the colonized and migrants can interrupt the present and negotiate a different future, I believe. Since postcolonial thought began to travel into the discipline of Classics and ancient history, scepticism has lingered about anachronistic application. To the sceptics, Webster distinguishes comparing colonial discourses from comparing colonialisms.[16] As she clarifies, postcolonial theories do not provide a point of reference to understand Roman imperialism in relation to modern Western imperialism, but an epistemological shift

[15] See Woolf 2014.   [16] Webster 1996.

in how to understand the imperial system of power and knowledge/truth. The purpose of using the postcolonial lens is, she argues, to deconstruct colonial epistemologies of the past and the present underlying the modern discourse on Romanization. Yet, this could, or should, be more than empirical studies to dislodge biased perspectives and to better understand lives under the Roman Empire. In fact, if the discourse continues to focus on collecting empirical data to illustrate cultural diversity across different provinces and classes and fails to investigate cultural difference underlying empirical data, the paradigm of Romanization will inevitably continue to haunt the scholarship. The postcolonial shift is not only to adopt contemporary thoughts to better understand the ancient past, but also to recover the repressed past to intervene in the contemporary notion of a homogenous community with linear progress, which continues to link ancient Romans with modern Europeans as successful imperialists.

Bhabha argues that the project of historical intervention, that is, to write a projective past, aims at revising our myths of belonging, the sense of belonging to a particular historically homogenous community. Likewise, historical intervention on Roman imperialism can revise the current sense of ownership of the classical antiquity, to start with. At the level of student bodies and academic communities, this will attract people who previously felt the subject irrelevant or the discipline uninviting. As Dwight Lewis, an American classicist, says in his interview with *Eidolon*, newly attracted student and scholars, for example, brown and black students, shall 'create epistemology, which will give us more innovation'.[17] For instance, the study of Caribbean and African diaspora literature on Classics has been gaining interest as an area of study which can draw attention to the migrant perspectives and de-centre the discipline.[18] Gender studies, which is often related to the subaltern perspective through intersectionality, but which I unfortunately was not able to delve into here, is also being explored as an avenue to deconstruct the framework of Romanization, to destabilize androcentric understanding of the ancient past, and, furthermore, to shape a new perspective in classical scholarship.[19] At the FIEC/CA 2019 conference (15th Congress of the Fédération internationals des associations d'études classiques and the Classical Association annual conference 2019) held in London, some of the themes reverberated, as shown by sessions such as 'Who "Owns" Classics? Redefining Participation and Ownership of the Field', 'Global Classics', and 'Caribbean Classicisms: Refractions of Homer in the Nineteenth and Twentieth Centuries'.

[17] Chae 2020. [18] See McConnell 2013. [19] See Revell 2010.

Therefore, ambitious or optimistic minds can surely envision that the historical invention will alter the deep-seated notion of our historical belonging. The history of migration and diaspora across different systems of reference, truth, tradition, and value within and outside the Roman Empire, if embraced by school curriculums and popular culture, will provide further hope for the project. For the less optimistic audience, Bhabha's words send the sense of hope as well as necessity:

> In the figure of the witness of a postcolonial modernity we have another wisdom: it comes from those who have seen the nightmare of racism and oppression in the banal daylight of the everyday. They represent an idea of action and agency more complex than either the nihilism of despair or the Utopia of progress. They speak of the reality of survival and negotiation that constitutes the moment of resistance, its sorrow and its salvation, but is rarely spoken in the heroisms or the horrors of history.[20]

The idea of historical intervention, which sits at odds with the long-standing and almost impregnable tradition of empiricist history, may sound too activist, not scholarly, or even uncomfortable. It challenges implicit epistemologies underlying the process of gathering, processing, and interpreting empirical data and has explicit objectives to write a projective past and to interrupt the present. Yet, it is neither fabricating history nor adding another narrative to rainbow histories, but exercising the right to narrate in order to revise our sense of place in history. Historical fiction has often become a creative outlet to narrate repressed pasts and unregistered histories and to empower the historically oppressed.[21] In comparison, historical intervention on Roman imperialism and Romanization can provide a better and wider structural lens on how to connect histories of the western and eastern provinces of the Roman Empire, on how to understand frontier histories of the Roman Empire, and on how to link the ancient past with the present.

---

[20] Bhabha 2004h: 365.
[21] Some of works from my own reading include: Conrad 1902; Ellison 1952; Achebe 1958; Márquez 1967; Rushdie 1981; Morrison 1987; Lee 1995; Adichie 2006; Lee 2017; Mengiste 2019.

References

Abrahams, Roger D. 1983. *The Man-of-Words in the West Indies: Performance and the Emergence of Creole Culture* (Johns Hopkins University Press: Baltimore).
Achebe, Chinua. 1958. *Things Fall Apart* (Heinemann: London).
Acheraïou, Amar. 2008. *Rethinking Postcolonialism: Colonialist Discourse in Modern Literatures and the Legacy of Classical Writers* (Palgrave Macmillan: Basingstoke).
Adams, James Noel. 2003. *Bilingualism and the Latin Language* (Cambridge University Press: Cambridge).
Adichie, Chimamanda Ngozi. 2006. *Half of a Yellow Sun* (4th Estate: New York).
Ageron, Charles-Robert. 2005. 'L'Exposition coloniale de 1931: mythe républicain ou mythe impérial?' In *De ' l'Algérie française' à l'Algérie algérienne*, 369–86. (Éditions Bouchène: Saint-Denis).
Alcock, Susan. 1977. 'The problem of Romanization, the power of Athens'. In *The Romanization of Athens: Proceedings of an International Conference Held at Lincoln, Nebraska (April 1996)*, edited by Michael C. Hoff and Susan I. Rotroff, 1–7. (Oxbow Books: Oxford).
　1995. *Graecia capta: The Landscapes of Roman Greece* (Cambridge University Press: Cambridge).
Aldhouse-Green, Miranda J. 1989. *Symbol and Image in Celtic Religious Art* (Routledge: London).
　1997. 'Images in opposition: polarity, ambivalence and liminality in cult representation', *Antiquity*, 71: 898–911.
Alston, Richard. 1995. *Soldier and Society in Roman Egypt: A Social History* (Routledge: London).
　1996. 'Conquest by text: Juvenal and Plutarch on Egypt'. In *Roman Imperialism: Post-colonial Perspectives; Proceedings of a Symposium Held at Leicester University in November 1994*, edited by Jane Webster and Nicholas J. Cooper, 99–109. (School of Archaeological Studies, University of Leicester: Leicester).
　2001. *The City in Roman and Byzantine Egypt* (Routledge: London).
Amin, Samir. 1989. *Eurocentrism* (Zed Books: London).
Anderson, Benedict R. O'G. 1991. *Imagined Communities: Reflections on the Origin and Spread of Nationalism* (Verso: London).
Ando, Clifford. 1999. Review of Becoming Roman: The Origins of Provincial Civilization in Gaul by Greg Woolf. *Phoenix*, 53: 386–8.

Ashcroft, Bill, Gareth Griffiths, and Helen Tiffin. 1998. *Key Concepts in Postcolonial Studies* (Routledge: London).
Ashcroft, Bill, Gareth Griffiths, and Helen Tiffin (eds.). 1994. *Post-colonial Studies Reader* (Routledge: London).
Bachelard, Gaston. 1964 (originally published in French in 1958). *The Poetics of Space* (Orion Press: New York).
Badian, Ernst. 1958. *Foreign clientelae (264–70BC)* (Clarendon Press: Oxford).
    1968. *Roman Imperialism in the Late Republic* (Blackwell: Oxford).
Balfour, Arthur James. 1908. *Decadence: Henry Sidgwick Memorial Lecture* (Cambridge University Press: Cambridge).
Bancel, Nicholas, and Pascal Blanchard. 2009. 'From colonial to postcolonial: reflections on the colonial debate in France'. In Charles Forsdick and David Murphy (eds.), *Postcolonial Thought in the French-Speaking World*, 295–305. (Liverpool University Press: Liverpool).
Barnes, Timothy D. 2000. 'Roman Gaul', *The Classical Review*, 50: 202–4.
Barrett, John C. 1997a. 'Romanization: a critical comment'. In David J. Mattingly and Susan Alcock (eds.) *Dialogues in Roman Imperialism: Power, Discourse, and Discrepant Experiences* (*Journal of Roman Archaeology*): 51–64.
    1997b. 'Theorising Roman Archaeology', *Theoretical Roman Archaeology Journal 1996*: 1–7.
Bayart, Jean-François. 2011. 'Les études postcoloniales: un carnaval académique', *Politique étrangère*, Winter: 912–18.
Beard, Mary, and John Henderson. 1995. *Classics: A Very Short Introduction* (Oxford University Press: Oxford).
Bénabou, Marcel. 1976. *La résistance africaine à la romanisation* (F. Maspero: Paris).
    1978. 'Les Romains ont-ils conquis l'Afrique?', *Annales. Economies, sociétés, civilisations* 33(1): 83–8.
Bernal, Martin. 1987. *Black Athena: The Afroasiatic Roots of Classical Civilization* (Rutgers University Press: New Brunswick, NJ).
Bhabha, Homi K. 2004a. 'The commitment to theory'. In *The Location of Culture*, 28–59. (Routledge: London).
    2004b. 'DissemiNation'. In *The Location of Culture*, 199–204.(Routledge: London).
    2004c. 'Interrogating identity: Frantz Fanon and the postcolonial prerogative'. In *The Location of Culture*, 57–93. (Routledge: London).
    2004d. *The Location of Culture* (Routledge: London).
    2004e. 'Of mimicry and man: the ambivalence of colonial discourse'. In *The Location of Culture*, 121–31. (Routledge: London).
    2004f. 'The other question: stereotype, discrimination and the discourse of colonialism'. In *The Location of Culture*, 94–120. (Routledge: London).
    2004g. 'Signs taken for wonders: questions of ambivalence and authority under a tree outside Delhi, May 1817'. In *The Location of Culture*, 145–74. (Routledge: London).
    2004h. 'Conclusion'. In *The Location of Culture*, 338–67. (Routledge: London).

Biel, Robert. 2015. *Eurocentrism and the Communist Movement* (Kersplebedeb: Montreal).

Blagg, Thomas F. C., and Anthony C. King (eds.). 1984. *Military and Civilian in Roman Britain: Cultural Relationships in a Frontier Province* (B.A.R.: Oxford).

Blagg, Thomas F. C., and Martin Millett (eds.). 1990. *The Early Roman Empire in the West* (Oxbow Books: Oxford).

Blanchard, Pascal, Nicolas Bancel, and Sandrine Lemaire (eds.). 2005. *La fracture coloniale: la société française au prisme de l'héritage colonial* (Découverte: Paris).

Blanchard, Pascal, and Sandrine Lemaire (eds.). 2003. *Culture coloniale: la France conquise par son empire, 1871–1931* (Autrement: Paris).

(eds.). 2004. *Culture impériale 1931–1961: les colonies au coeur de la République* (Autrement: Paris).

(eds.). 2006. *Culture post-coloniale, 1961–2006: traces et mémoires coloniales en France* (Autrement: Paris).

Boatwright, Mary Taliaferro. 1987. *Hadrian and the City of Rome* (Princeton University Press: Princeton, NJ).

Bond, Sarah. 2019. 'Blog: A Roundup of Reports, Reactions, and Reflections After the SCS Annual Meeting.'

Bourdieu, Pierre. 1979. *La distinction: critique sociale du jugement* (Les Éditions de Minuit: Paris).

Bowersock, G. W. 1974. '"The Social and Economic History of the Roman Empire" by Michael Ivanovitch Rostovtzeff', *Daedalus*, 103: 15–23.

Bowler, Peter J. 1984. *Evolution: The History of an Idea* (University of California: Berkeley).

Bradley, Keith R. 1984. *Slaves and Masters in the Roman Empire: A Study in Social Control* (Latomus: Bruxelles).

1994. *Slavery and Society at Rome* (Cambridge University Press: Cambridge).

Bradley, Mark. 2010. 'Introduction: approaches to Classics and imperialism'. In Mark Bradley (ed.), *Classics & Imperialism in the British Empire*, 1–26. (Oxford University Press: Oxford).

Braudel, Fernand. 1949. *la Méditerranée et le monde méditerranéen à l'époque de Philippe II* (Librairie Armand Colin: Paris).

1998. *Les mémoires de la Méditerranée: préhistoire et antiquité* (Editions de Fallois: Paris).

Braund, David. 1996. *Ruling Roman Britain: Kings, Queens, Governors and Emperors from Julius Caesar to Agricola* (Routledge: London).

Broughton, T. Robert S. 1951. *The Magistrates of the Roman Republic* (American Philological Association: New York).

Brunt, Peter A. 1976. 'The Romanization of local ruling classes in the Roman Empire'. In Dionisie M. Pippidi (ed.), *Assimilation et résistance à la culture gréco-romaine dans le monde ancien. Travaux du VIe Congrès international d'études classiques* (Editura Academiei: Bucharest).

Bryce, James. 1914. *The Ancient Roman Empire and the British Empire in India: The Diffusion of Roman and English Law throughout the World; Two Historical Studies* (Oxford University Press: London).
Cadwalladr, Carole, and Emma Graham-Harrison. 2018. 'Revealed: 50 million Facebook profiles harvested for Cambridge Analytica in major data breach', *The Guardian*, 17 March.
Césaire, Aimé. 1939. *Cahier d'un retour au pays natal* (Présence Africaine: Paris).
 1995. *Discours sur le colonialisme* (Présence Africaine: Paris).
Chae, Yung In. 2020. 'The first African to have attended a European university.' *Eidolon*. Available at https://eidolon.pub/the-first-african-to-have-attended-a-european-university-b4ef9b7f8c8a
Chakrabarty, Dipesh. 2000. *Provincializing Europe: Postcolonial Thought and Historical Difference* (Princeton University Press: Princeton, NJ).
Champion, Timothy C. 1996. 'Three nations or one? Britain and the national use of the past'. In Timothy C. Champion and Margarita Díaz-Andreu García (eds.), *Nationalism and Archaeology in Europe*, 119–45. (UCL Press: London).
Champion, Timothy C., and Margarita Díaz-Andreu García. 1996. *Nationalism and Archaeology in Europe* (UCL Press: London).
Chauvot, Alain. 2016. *Les barbares des Romains: représentations et confrontations* (Centre de recherche universitaire lorrain d'histoire: Metz).
Chrisman, Laura, and Patrick Williams (eds.). 1993. *Colonial Discourse and Post-colonial Theory: A Reader* (Harvester Wheatsheaf: New York).
Clarke, Katherine. 2001. 'An island nation: re-reading Tacitus' "Agricola"', *The Journal of Roman Studies*, 91: 94–112.
Clifford, James. 1989. 'Notes on travel and theory', *Inscriptions*, 5: 177–88.
Collingwood, Robin G. 1930. *The Archaeology of Roman Britain* (Methuen: London).
 1932. *Roman Britain* (Clarendon Press: Oxford).
 1936. *Roman Britain and the English Settlements* (Clarendon Press: Oxford).
 1946. *The Idea of History* (Clarendon Press: Oxford).
 1982. *An Autobiography* (Clarendon Press: Oxford).
 2005. *An Essay on Philosophical Method* (Clarendon Press:Oxford).
Conrad, Joseph. 1902. *Heart of Darkness* (Blackwood's Magazine: London).
Cooley, Alison E., and Andrew Burnet (eds.). 2002. *Becoming Roman, Writing Latin? Literacy and Epigraphy in the Roman West* (Journal of Roman Archaeology: Portsmouth, RI).
Cope, Zak. 2012. *Divided World, Divided Class: Global Political Economy and the Stratification of Labour under Capitalism* (Kersplebedeb: Montreal).
Coulanges, Fustel de. 1877. *The Ancient City: A Study on the Religion, Laws and Institutions of Greece and Rome* (Lee and Shepard; Charles T. Dillingham: Massachusetts).
Cowley, Jason. 2008. 'Stating the obvious, but oh so cleverly', *The Observer*, 23 November.
Cromer, Evelyn Baring. 1910. *Ancient and Modern Imperialism* (John Murray: London).

Cunliffe, Barry W. 1974. *Iron Age Communities in Britain: An Account of England, Scotland and Wales from the Seventh century BC until the Roman Conquest* (Routledge: London).

Curzon, George Nathaniel. 1907. *Frontiers: [lecture] Delivered in the Sheldonian Theatre*, Oxford, 2 November, 1907 (Clarendon Press: Oxford).

Dal Lago, Enrico, and Constantina Katsari. 2008. 'The study of ancient and modern slave systems: setting an agenda for comparison'. In Enrico Dal Lago and Constantina Katsari (eds.), *Slave Systems: Ancient and Modern* (Cambridge University Press: Cambridge).

Dauge, Yves Albert. 1981. *Le Barbare: recherches sur la conception romaine de la barbarie et de la civilisation* (Latomus: Bruxelles).

De Ste. Croix, Geoffrey E. M. 1981. *The Class Struggle in the Ancient Greek World: From the Archaic Age to the Arab Conquests* (Duckworth: London).

Demougeot, Emilienne, Paul-Albert Février, René Rebuffat, Robert Turcan, Christian Goudineau, Jean-Jacques Hatt, Gilbert-Charles Picard, Jean Rougé, and Pierre Grimal. 1983. *La patrie gauloise d'Agrippa au VIème siècle: actes du colloque (Lyon 1981)* (L'Hermes: Lyon).

Dench, Emma. 2018. *Empire and Political Cultures in the Roman World* (Cambridge University Press: Cambridge).

Derrida, Jacques. 1976. *Of Grammatology* (Johns Hopkins University Press: Baltimore).

Dhindsa, Hardeep Singh. 2019. 'What studying Classics taught me about my relationship with Western civilization.' In Classics and Race (workshop) University of St Andrews.

Dietler, Michael. 1994. '"Our ancestors the Gauls": archaeology, ethnic nationalism, and the manipulation of Celtic identity in modern Europe', *American Anthropologist*, 96: 584–605.

2010. *Archaeologies of Colonialism: Consumption, Entanglement, and Violence in Ancient Mediterranean France* (University of California Press: Berkeley).

Dirlik, Arif. 1999. 'Is there history after Eurocentrism?: globalism, postcolonialism, and the disavowal of history', *Cultural Critique* 42: 1–34.

Downs, Mary. 2000. 'Refiguring colonial categories on the Roman frontier in southern Spain'. In Elizabeth W. B. Fentress and Susan Alcock (eds.), *Romanization and the City: Creation, Transformations, and Failures, Proceedings of a Conference Held at the American Academy in Rome to Celebrate the 50th Anniversary of the Excavations at Cosa, 14–16 May, 1998* (Journal of Roman Archaeology: Portsmouth, RI).

Drinkwater, John F. 1983. *Roman Gaul: the Three Provinces, 58 BC–AD 260* (Croom Helm: London).

Du Bois, W. E. B. 1996. *The Souls of Black Folk* (Penguin: London).

Dumasy, François. 2005. 'L'impérialisme, un débat manqué de l'histoire contemporaine française? Pour une relecture des travaux d'Yvon Thébert dans la perspective de la colonisation', *Afrique & histoire*, 3: 57–69.

Dyson, Stephen L. 1971. 'Native revolts in the Roman Empire', *Historia: Zeitschrift für Alte Geschichte*, 20: 239–74.

2006. *In Pursuit of Ancient Pasts: A History of Classical Archaeology in the Nineteenth and Twentieth Centuries* (Yale University Press: New Haven).
Eckstein, Arthur M. 2006. *Mediterranean Anarchy, Interstate War, and the Rise of Rome* (University of California Press: Berkeley).
Ellison, Ralph. 1952. *Invisible Man* (Random House: New York).
Fanon, Frantz. 1965. *The Wretched of the Earth* (MacGibbon & Kee: London).
  1986. *Black Skin, White Masks* (Pluto: London).
Fentress, Elizabeth W. B., and Susan Alcock (eds.). 2000. *Romanization and the City: Creation, Transformations, and Failures, Proceedings of a Conference Held at the American Academy in Rome to Celebrate the 50th Anniversary of the Excavations at Cosa*, 14–16 May, 1998 (Journal of Roman Archaeology: Portsmouth, RI).
Ferguson, Leland G. 1992. *Uncommon Ground: Archaeology and Early African America, 1650–1800* (Smithsonian Institution Press: Washington).
Ferris, Iain M. 2003. *Enemies of Rome: Barbarians through Roman Eyes* (Sutton: Stroud).
Ferro, Marc. 2005. 'La colonisation française: une histoire inaudible'. In Pascal Blanchard, Nicolas Bancel and Sandrine Lemaire (eds.), *La fracture coloniale: la société française au prisme de l'héritage colonial* (Découverte: Paris).
Finley, Moses I. 1960. *Slavery in Classical Antiquity: Views and Controversies* (Heffer: Cambridge).
  1967. 'Class struggles', *The Listener*, 78: 201–02.
  1973. *The Ancient Economy* (Chatto and Windus: London).
  1983. *Ancient Slavery and Modern Ideology* (Penguin Books: New York).
  1985. *Ancient History: Evidence and Models* (Chatto & Windus: London).
Fleming, Andrew, and Richard Hingley (eds.). 2007. *Prehistoric and Roman Landscapes* (Windgather Press: Macclesfield).
Fogel, Robert William. 1974. *Time on the Cross: The Economics of American Negro Slavery* (Wildwood House: London).
Forsdick, Charles, and David Murphy. 2009. 'Introduction: situating Francophone postcolonial thought'. In Charles Forsdick and David Murphy (eds.), *Postcolonial Thought in the French-speaking World*, 1–28. (Liverpool University Press: Liverpool).
Foucault, Michel. 1972. *The Archaeology of Knowledge* (Tavistock Publications: London).
  1977. *Discipline and Punish: The Birth of the Prison* (Allen Lane: London).
  1979. *The History of Sexuality* (Allen Lane: London).
  1980. *Power-knowledge: Selected Interviews and Other Writings, 1972–1977* (Harvester Press: Brighton).
Frank, Tenney. 1914. *Roman Imperialism* (Macmillan: New York).
  1920. *An Economic History of Rome to the End of the Republic* (The Johns Hopkins Press: Maryland).
Frazier, E. Franklin. 1957. *Black Bourgeoisie* (The Free Press: New York).
Frederiksen, Martin W. 1975. 'Theory, evidence and the ancient economy', *The Journal of Roman Studies*, 65: 164–71.

Freeman, Philip W. M. 1993. "'Romanisation' and Roman material culture', *Journal of Roman Archaeology*, 6: 438–45.
　1997a. 'Mommsen through Haverfield: the origins of Romanization studies in late 19th-c. Britain'. In David J. Mattingly and Susan Alcock (eds.) *Dialogues in Roman Imperialism: Power, Discourse, and Discrepant Experiences* (*Journal of Roman Archaeology*).
　1997b. '"Romanization – Imperialism": what are we talking about?', *Theoretical Roman Archaeology Journal* 1996: 8–16.
Frere, Sheppard. 1967. *Britannia: A History of Roman Britain* (Routledge & Kegan Paul: London).
Freud, Sigmund. 1930. *Civilization and its Discontents* (Leonard & Virginia Woolf at the Hogarth Press: London).
Frézouls, Edmond. 1983. 'Sur l'historiographie de l'impérialisme romain', *Ktèma* 8: 141–61.
Friedman, Thomas L. 1999. *The Lexus and the Olive Tree* (Farrar, Straus and Giroux: New York).
　2005. *The World is Flat: A Brief History of The Globalized World in the Twenty-First Century* (Allen Lane: London).
Galinsky, Karl. 1996. *Augustan Culture: An Interpretive Introduction* (Princeton University Press: Princeton, NJ).
Gandhi, Leela. 1998. *Postcolonial Theory: A Critical Introduction* (Edinburgh University Press: Edinburgh).
Gardner, Andrew. 2007. Reviewed Work: Globalizing Roman Culture: Unity, Diversity and Empire by R. Hingley, *Britannia*, 38: 389–90.
　2013. 'Thinking about Roman imperialism: postcolonialism, globalisation and beyond?', *Britannia*, 44: 1–25.
Garlan, Yvon. 1975. *War in the Ancient World: A Social History* (Chatto and Windus: London).
Garnsey, Peter, and Richard P. Saller. 1987. *The Roman Empire: Economy, Society and Culture* (Duckworth: London).
Garnsey, Peter, and C. R. Whittaker (eds.). 1978. *Imperialism in the Ancient World* (Cambridge University Press: Cambridge).
Gelzer, Matthias. 1912. *Die Nobilität der römanischen Republik* (B.G. Teubner: Leipzig).
George the Poet. 2019. 'Listen closer.' In *Have You Heard George's Podcast?* BBC. Available at www.bbc.co.uk/programmes/p07915kd/episodes/downloads.
Gibbon, Edward. 1776. *The History of the Decline and Fall of the Roman Empire* (Strahan & Cadell: London).
Gilley, Bruce. 2017. 'The case for colonialism', *Third World Quarterly*: 1–17. Now withdrawn.
Gladwell, Malcolm. 2000. *The Tipping Point: How Little Things Can Make a Big Difference* (Little, Brown: London).
Glissant, Édouard. 1997. *Poetics of Relation* (The University of Michigan Press: Ann Arbor).
Goff, Barbara E. (ed.). 2005. *Classics and Colonialism* (Duckworth: London).

Gold, Solveig Lucia. 2017. "The colorblind bard." In *The New Criterion*. Available at https://newcriterion.com/blogs/dispatch/the-colorblind-bard-8761.
Gold, Solveig Lucia, and Dan-el Padilla Peralta. 2017. "The colorblind bard: An exchange." In *The New Criterion*. Available at https://newcriterion.com/blogs/dispatch/colorblind-bard-exchange.
Goldsworthy, Adrian Keith. 2000. *Roman Warfare* (Cassell: London).
Gordon, Richard. 1990. 'Religion in the Roman Empire: the civic compromise and its limits'. In Mary Beard and John North (eds.), 233–55. *Pagan Priests: Religion and Power in the Ancient World* (Duckworth: London).
Grahame, Mark. 1998. 'Redefining Romanization: material culture and the question of social continuity in Roman Britain', *Theoretical Roman Archaeology Journal* 1997: 1–10.
Gramsci, Antonio. 1975. 'Ai margini della storia (storia dei gruppi sociali subalterni)'. In *Quaderni del carcere*, Quaderno 25 (G. Einaudi: Torino).
Grant, Michael. 1991. *A Short History of Classical Civilization* (Weidenfeld and Nicolson: London).
Graves-Brown, Paul, Siân Jones, and Clive Gamble (eds.). 1996. *Cultural Identity and Archaeology: The Construction of European Communities* (Routledge: London).
Grew, Francis, and Brian Hobley (eds.). 1985. *Roman Urban Topography in Britain and the Western Empire: Proceedings of the Third Conference on Urban Archaeology Organized Jointly by the CBA and the Department of Urban Archaeology of the Museum of London* (Council for British Archaeology: London).
Griffin, Jasper. 1986. 'Introduction'. In John Boardman, Jasper Griffin and Oswyn Murray (eds.), *The Oxford History of the Classical World*, 11–21. (Oxford University Press: Oxford).
Gruen, Erich S. 1984. *The Hellenistic World and the Coming of Rome* (University of California Press: Berkeley).
Guha, Ranajit. 1983. *Elementary Aspects of Peasant Insurgency in Colonial India* (Oxford University Press: Delhi).
Guha, Ranajit, and Gayatri Chakravorty Spivak (eds.). 1989. *Selected Subaltern Studies* (Oxford University Press: Oxford).
Habinek, Thomas N. 1998. *The Politics of Latin Literature: Writing, Identity, and Empire in Ancient Rome* (Princeton University Press: Princeton, NJ).
Haley, Evan W. 2003. *Baetica Felix: People and Prosperity in Southern Spain from Caesar to Septimius Severus* (University of Texas Press: Austin, TX).
Hanson, William S. 1994. 'Dealing with barbarians: the Romanization of Britain'. In Blaise E. Vyner (ed.), *Building on the Past: Papers Celebrating 150 Years of the Royal Archaeological Institute*, 149–63. (Royal Archaeological Institute: London).
Hardwick, Lorna, and Carol Gillespie (eds.). 2007. *Classics in Post-Colonial Worlds* (Oxford University Press: Oxford).
Harris, William V. 1979. *War and Imperialism in Republican Rome, 327–70 B.C* (Clarendon Press: Oxford).

2011. *Rome's Imperial Economy: Twelve Essays* (Oxford University Press: Oxford).

2013a. 'A brief introduction'. In William V. Harris (ed.), *Moses Finley and Politics*, 1–4. (Brill: Leiden).

(ed.). 2013b. *Moses Finley and Politics* (Brill: Leiden).

2013c. 'Politics in the ancient world and politics'. In William V. Harris (ed.), *Moses Finley and Politics*, 107–22. (Brill: Leiden).

Haselgrove, Colin C. 1982. 'Wealth, prestige and power: the dynamics of late Iron Age political centralization in South East England'. In Colin Renfrew and Stephen Shennan (eds.), *Ranking, Resource and Exchange: Aspects of the Archaeology of Early European Society*, 79–88. (Cambridge University Press: Cambridge).

1984. 'Romanization before the conquest: Gaulish precedents and British consequences'. In Thomas F. C. Blagg and Anthony C. King (eds.), *Military and Civilian in Roman Britain: Cultural Relationships in a Frontier Province*, 5–63. (B.A.R.: Oxford).

1987. *Iron Age Coinage in South-East England: The Archaeological Context* (B.A.R.: Oxford).

1990. 'The Romanization of Belgic Gaul: some archaeological perspectives'. In Thomas F. C. Blagg and Martin Millett (eds.), *The Early Roman Empire in the West*, 47–71. (Oxbow Books: Oxford).

Haverfield, Francis J. 1911. 'An inaugural address delivered before the first annual general meeting of the society, 11th May, 1911', *The Journal of Roman Studies*, 1: xi–xx.

1913. *Ancient Town-Planning* (Clarendon Press: Oxford).

1923. *The Romanization of Roman Britain* (Clarendon Press: Oxford).

1924. *The Roman Occupation of Britain: Being Six Ford Lectures* (Clarendon Press: Oxford).

Henig, Martin. 1984. *Religion in Roman Britain* (Batsford: London).

Herskovits, Melville J. 1941. *The Myth of the Negro Past* (Harper: New York).

Hess, Gary R. 2009. *Vietnam: Explaining America's Lost War* (Blackwell: Oxford).

Hingley, Richard. 1982. 'Roman Britain: the structure of Roman imperialism and the consequences of imperialism on the development of a peripheral province'. In David Miles (ed.), *The Romano-British Countryside: Studies in Rural Settlement and Economy*, 17–52.(B.A.R.: Oxford).

1996. 'The legacy of Rome: the rise, decline and fall of the theory of Romanization'. In Jane Webster and Nicholas Cooper (eds.), *Roman Imperialism: Post-Colonial Perspectives*, 35–48. (School of Archaeological Studies, University of Leicester: Leicester).

1997. 'Resistance and domination: social change in Roman Britain'. In David J. Mattingly and Susan Alcock (eds.), *Dialogues in Roman Imperialism: Power, Discourse, and Discrepant Experience in the Roman Empire*, 81–102. (Journal of Roman Archaeology: Portsmouth, RI).

2000. *Roman Officers and English Gentlemen: The Imperial Origins of Roman archaeology* (Routledge: New York).

2001. *Images of Rome: Perceptions of Ancient Rome in Europe and the United States in the Modern Age* (Journal of Roman Archaeology: Portsmouth, RI).

2005. *Globalizing Roman Culture: Unity, Diversity and Empire* (Routledge: London).

2008. *The Recovery of Roman Britain 1586–1906: A Colony so Fertile* (Oxford University Press: Oxford).

Hobsbawm, Eric J. 1964. 'Introduction'. In E. J. Hobsbawm (ed.), Jack Cohen (trans.), *Pre-capitalist Economic Formations, by Karl Marx*, 9–65. (Lawrence & Wishart: London).

Hobsbawm, Eric J., and Terence O. Ranger. 1983. *The Invention of Tradition* (Cambridge University Press: Cambridge).

Hobson, Matthew S. 2018. 'A historiography of the study of the Roman economy: economic growth, development, and neoliberalism', *Theoretical Roman Archaeology Journal 2013*: 11–26.

Hodder, Ian R. 1982. *Symbols in Action: Ethnoarchaeological Studies of Material Culture* (Cambridge University Press: Cambridge).

Høgel, Christian. 2015. *The Human and the Humane: Humanity as Argument from Cicero to Erasmus* (V&R Academic: Göttingen).

Holland, Tom. 2006. 'Victims and /or beneficiaries.' In *The Spectator*, 8 July.

Holleaux, Maurice. 1921. *Rome, la Grèce et les monarchies hellénistiques au IIIe siècle avant J. C.* (273–205) (E. de Boccard: Paris).

Holmes, Christopher. 2013. 'Ignorance, denial, internalisation, and transcendence: a post-structural perspective on Polanyi's double movement', *Review of International Studies*, 39: 273–90.

Hopkins, Keith. 1978. *Conquerors and Slaves: Sociological Studies in Roman History* (Cambridge University Press: Cambridge).

1983. 'Introduction'. In Peter Garnsey, Keith Hopkins and C. R. Whittaker (eds.), *Trade in the Ancient Economy*, ix–xxiv. (Chatto & Windus: London).

Humphreys, Sarah C. 1969. 'History, economics, and anthropology: the work of Karl Polanyi', *History and Theory*, 8: 165–212.

Ireland, Stanley. 2007. 'Reviewed work: an imperial possession: Britain in the Roman Empire, 54 BC–AD 409 by D. Mattingly'. *The Journal of Roman Studies*, 97: 364–66.

James, Simon. 2001. '"Romanization" and the peoples of Britain'. In Simon J. Keay and Nicola Terrenato (eds.), *Italy and the West: Comparative Issues in Romanization*, 187–209. (Oxbow Books: Oxford).

James, Simon, and Martin Millett (eds.). 2001. *Britons and Romans: Advancing an Archaeological Agenda* (Council for British Archaeology: York).

Jenkyns, Richard. 1980. *The Victorians and Ancient Greece* (Blackwell: Oxford).

Jew, Daniel, Robin Osborne, and Michael Scott (eds.). 2016. *M. I. Finley: An Ancient Historian and his Impact* (Cambridge University Press: Cambridge).

Johnston, David. 1999. *Roman Law in Context* (Cambridge University Press: Cambridge).

Jones, G. D. Barri. 1997. 'From Brittunculi to Wounded Knee: a study in the development of ideas'. In David J. Mattingly and Susan Alcock (eds.),

Dialogues in Roman Imperialism: Power, Discourse, and Discrepant Experience in the Roman Empire (Journal of Roman Archaeology: Portsmouth, R.I).

Jones, Richard F. J. 1991. 'Cultural change in Roman Britain'. In Richard F. J. Jones (ed.), *Britain in the Roman Period: Recent Trends*, 115–20. (J.R. Collis: Sheffield).

Jullian, Camille. 1920. *Histoire de la Gaule* (Librairie Hachette: Paris).

Katz, Joshua. 2020. 'I survived cancellation at Princeton', *The Wall Street Journal*, 26 July.

Keay, Simon J., and Nicola Terrenato. 2001. *Italy and the West: Comparative Issues in Romanization* (Oxbow Books: Oxford).

Kipling, Rudyard. 1911. 'The Roman Centurion's Song (alternatively, The Roman Centurion Speaks, or The Roman Occupation of Britain – A.D. 300.)'. In *Three Poems* (n. pub: Oxford).

Kolko, Gabriel. 1985. *Anatomy of a War: Vietnam, the United States, and the Modern Historical Experience* (Pantheon Books: New York).

Krishna, Sankaran. 2009. *Globalization and Postcolonialism: Hegemony and Resistance in the Twenty-First Century* (Rowman & Littlefield Pub.: Lanham, MD).

Kuhn, Thomas S. 1962. *The Structure of Scientific Revolutions* (Chicago University Press: Chicago).

Laroui, Abdallah. 1970. *L'histoire du Maghreb: un essai de synthèse* (F. Maspero: Paris).

Laurence, Ray. 2001. 'Roman narratives: the writing of archeaological discourse – a view from Britain?', *Archaeological Dialogues*, 8: 90–101.

Le Bohec, Yann. 1994. *The Imperial Roman Army* (Batsford: London).

Le Roux, Patrick. 2004. 'La romanisation en question', *Annales. Histoire, Sciences Sociales*, 59: 287–311.

Lee, Chang-Rae. 1995. *Native Speaker* (Berkley Books: New York).

Lee, Min Jin. 2017. *Pachinko* (Grand Central Publishing: New York).

Linduff, Katheryn M. 1979. 'Epona: a Celt among the Romans', *Latomus*, 38: 817–37.

Livingstone, Richard Winn. 1916. *A Defence of Classical Education* (MacMillan: London).

Lucas, Charles Prestwood. 1912. *Greater Rome and Greater Britain* (Clarendon Press: Oxford).

Lyotard, Jean-François. 1984. *The Postmodern Condition: A Report on Knowledge* (Manchester University Press: Manchester).

Macdonald, William L. 1986. 'Empire imagery in Augustan architecture'. In Rolf Winkes (ed.), *The Age of Augustus: Interdisciplinary Conference held at Brown University, April 30–May 2, 1982*, 137–48. (Center for Old World Archaeology and Art, Brown University: Providence, RI).

Mackail, J. W. 1925. *Classical Studies* (J. Murray: London).

MacMullen, Ramsay. 1966. *Enemies of the Roman Order Treason, Unrest, and Alienation in the Empire* (Harvard University Press: Cambridge, MA).

1982. 'The epigraphic habit in the Roman Empire', *The American Journal of Philology*, 103: 233–46.
Majumdar, Margaret A. 2007. *Postcoloniality: The French Dimension* (Berghahn Books: New York).
Márquez, Gabriel García. 1967. *One Hundred Years of Solitude* (Editorial Sudamericana: Buenos Aires).
Mattingly, David J. 2002. '"Romanization", or time for a paradigm shift?', *Journal of Roman Archaeology*, 15: 536–40.
2004. 'Being Roman: expressing identity in a provincial setting', *Journal of Roman Archaeology*, 17: 5–25.
2006. *An Imperial Possession: Britain in the Roman Empire, 54 BC–AD 409* (Allen Lane: London).
2011a. 'From one colonialism to another: imperialism and the Maghreb'. In *Imperialism, Power, and Identity: Experiencing the Roman Empire*, 43–72. (Princeton University Press: Princeton, NJ).
2011b. *Imperialism, Power, and Identity: Experiencing the Roman Empire* (Princeton University Press: Princeton, NJ).
Mattingly, David J., and Susan Alcock (eds.). 1997. *Dialogues in Roman Imperialism: Power, Discourse, and Discrepant Experience in the Roman Empire* (Journal of Roman Archaeology: Portsmouth, RI).
McConnell, Justine. 2013. *Black Odysseys: The Homeric Odyssey in the African Diaspora since 1939* (Oxford University Press: Oxford).
Mead, Rebecca. 2020. 'George the Poet's undefinably good podcast.' In *The New Yorker*, 8 March.
Mengiste, Maaza. 2019. *The Shadow King* (W. W. Norton & Company: New York).
Meyer, Elizabeth A. 1990. 'Explaining the epigraphic habit in the Roman Empire: the evidence of epitaphs', *The Journal of Roman Studies*, 80: 74–96.
Meyer, John R., and Alfred H. Conrad. 1957. 'Economic theory, statistical inference, and economic history', *The Journal of Economic History*, 17: 524–44.
Miles, David, and Barry Cunliffe (eds.). 1984. *Aspects of the Iron Age in Central Southern Britain* (Oxford University Committee for Archaeology: Oxford).
Miller, Danny. 1982. 'Structures and stratagems: an aspect of the relationship between social hierarchy and cultural change'. In Ian R. Hodder (ed.), *Symbolic and Structural Archaeology*, 89–98. (Cambridge University Press: Cambridge).
Millett, Martin. 1990. *The Romanization of Britain: An Essay in Archaeological Interpretation* (Cambridge University Press: Cambridge).
Mills, Elliott Evans. 1905. *The Decline and Fall of the British Empire a Brief Account of those Causes which Resulted in the Destruction of our Late Ally, Together with a Comparison between the British and Roman Empires*. (Simpkin, Marshall, Hamilton, Kent & Co.: Oxford).
Mitra Das, Srijana. 2014. 'If classics become static objects of reverence, they're dead: Mary Beard', *The Times of India*, 17 February.

Momigliano, Arnaldo. 1966. *Studies in Historiography* (Weidenfeld and Nicolson: London).
Mommsen, Theodor. 1909. *The Provinces of the Roman Empire: From Caesar to Diocletian* (Macmillan: London).
1911. *The History of Rome* (J. M. Dent & Sons, Ltd: London).
Moritz, L. A. 1962. *Humanitas: An Inaugural Lecture Delivered at University College, Cardiff, 8th March, 1962* (University of Wales Press: Cardiff).
Morley, Neville. 2004. *Theories, Models and Concepts in Ancient History* (Routledge: London).
2006. 'Narrative economy'. In Peter F. Bang, Mamoru Ikeguchi and Hartmut G. Ziche (eds.), *Ancient Economies, Modern Methodologies: Archaeology, Comparative History, Models and Institutions*, 27–47. (Edipuglia: Bari).
Morris, Ian. 1999. 'Foreword'. In *The Ancient Economy, by Moses I. Finley, Updated Edition with a Foreword by Ian Morris*, ix–xxxvi. (University of California Press: Berkeley).
Morrison, Toni. 1987. *Beloved* (Alfred A. Knopf Inc.: New York).
Moura, Jean-Marc. 2008. 'The evolving context of postcolonial studies in France: new horizons or new limits?', *Journal of Postcolonial Writing*, 44: 263–74.
Mouritsen, Henrik. 1998. *Italian Unification: A Study of Ancient and Modern historiography* (Institute of Classical Studies: London).
2009. 'Modern nations and ancient models: Italy and Greece compared'. In Roderick Beaton and David Ricks (eds.), *The Making of Modern Greece: Nationalism, Romanticism, & the Uses of the Past (1797–1896)*, 43–49. (Ashgate: Farnham).
Murray, Oswyn. 1990. 'Cities of reason'. In Oswyn Murray and Simon R. F. Price (eds.), *The Greek City: From Homer to Alexander*, 1–25. (Clarendon Press: Oxford).
2020. 'The reception of Vernant in the English-speaking world', *History of Classical Scholarship*, 2: 131–57.
Nafissi, Mohammad. 2005. *Ancient Athens & Modern Ideology: Value, Theory & Evidence in Historical Sciences: Max Weber, Karl Polanyi & Moses Finley* (Institute of Classical Studies, School of Advanced Study, University of London: London).
Nagy, Gregory, Laura M. Slatkin, and Nicole Loraux. 2001. 'Introduction'. In Gregory Nagy, Laura M. Slatkin and Nicole Loraux (eds.), *Antiquities* (New Press: New York).
Nora, Pierre. 1984. *Les lieux de mémoire* (Gallimard: Paris).
North, Douglass C. 1990. *Institutions, Institutional Change and Economic Performance* (Cambridge University Press: Cambridge).
North, John A. 1979. 'Religious toleration in republican Rome', *Proceedings of the Cambridge Philological Society* 25: 85–103.
1981. 'The development of Roman imperialism', *The Journal of Roman Studies*, 71: 1–9.

O'Hanlon, Rosalind, and David Washbrook. 1992. 'After Orientalism: culture, criticism, and politics in the Third World', *Comparative Studies in Society and History*, 34: 141–67.
Patterson, John R. 1992. 'The city of Rome: from republic to empire', *The Journal of Roman Studies*, 82: 186–215.
Peachin, Michael. 2011. 'Introduction'. In Michael Peachin (ed.), *The Oxford Handbook of Social Relations in the Roman World*, 3–36. (Oxford University Press: Oxford).
Pendleton, Adam. 2009. *Adam Pendleton: EL T D K* [published on the occasion of the exhibition held at Haunch of Venison, Berlin, 28 February – 25 April 2009] (Haunch of Venison: Berlin).
Polanyi, Karl. 1944. *Great Transformation: The Political and Economic Origins of Our Time* (Beacon Press: Boston).
———. 1957. *Trade and Market in the Early Empires: Economies in History and Theory* (Free Press: New York).
Poser, Rachel. 2021. 'He wants to save Classics from whiteness. Can the field survive?' In *The New York Times*, 15 June.
Postclassicisms Collective. 2019. *Postclassicisms* (University of Chicago Press: Chicago).
Potter, David S. 1999. *Literary Texts and the Roman Historian* (Routledge: London).
———. 2006. 'The shape of Roman history: the fate of the governing class'. In David S. Potter (ed.), *A Companion to the Roman Empire*, 1–19. (Blackwell Pub.: Malden, MA).
Prag, Jonathan R. W. 2006. 'Reviewed work: Globalizing Roman Culture: Unity, Diversity and Empire, R. Hingley', *The Journal of Roman Studies*, 96: 214–16.
Prakash, Gyan. 1990. 'Writing post-orientalist histories of the Third World: perspectives from Indian historiography', *Comparative Studies in Society and History*, 32: 383–408.
Price, Simon R. F. 1984. *Rituals and Power: The Roman Imperial Cult in Asia Minor* (Cambridge University Press: Cambridge).
Raaflaub, Kurt A. 1996. 'Born to be wolves? Origins of Roman imperialism'. In Robert W. Wallace and Edward M. Harris (eds.), *Transitions to Empire: Essays in Greco-Roman history, 360–146 B.C. in Honor of E. Badian* (University of Oklahoma Press: London)
Ramage, Edwin S. 1973. *Urbanitas: Ancient Sophistication and Refinement* (University of Oklahoma Press for the University of Cincinnati: Norman, OK).
Rath, Richard Cullen. 2000. 'Drums and power: ways of creolizing music in coastal South Carolina and Georgia, 1730–1790'. In Steven G. Reinhardt and David Buisseret (eds.), 99–130. *Creolization in the Americas* (Texas A&M University: College Station).
Reagan, Ronald W. 1980. 'Address to the Veterans of Foreign Wars Convention in Chicago.'
Reinhold, Meyer. 1946. 'Historian of the Classic world: a critique of Rostovtzeff', *Science & Society*, 10: 361–91.

Revel, Jacques. 1995. 'Introduction'. In Jacques Revel and Lynn Avery Hunt (eds.), *Histories: French Constructions of the Past*, 1–63. (New Press: New York).

Revel, Jacques, and Lynn Avery Hunt (eds.). 1995. *Histories: French Constructions of the Past* (New Press: New York).

Revell, Louise. 2010. 'Romanization: a feminist critique', *Theoretical Roman Archaeology Journal 2009*: 1–10.

Rich, John, and Graham Shipley (eds.). 1993. *War and Society in the Roman World* (Routledge: London).

Richmond, Ian A. 1947. *Roman Britain* (Collins: London).

Ringer, Fritz K. 1992. *Fields of Knowledge: French Academic Culture in Comparative Perspective, 1890–1920* (Cambridge University Press: Cambridge).

Roelofs, Portia, and Max Gallien. 2017. 'Clickbait and impact: how academia has been hacked.' In *The LSE Impact Blog*. Available at https://blogs.lse.ac.uk/impactofsocialsciences/2017/09/19/clickbait-and-impact-how-academia-has-been-hacked/.

Rosenberg, Matthew, Nicholas Confessore, and Carole Cadwalladr. 2018. 'How Trump consultants exploited the Facebook data of millions', *The New York Times*, 29 March.

Rostovtzeff, Michael I. 1926. *The Social and Economic History of the Roman Empire* (Clarendon Press: Oxford).

Rousso, Henry. 1991. *The Vichy Syndrome: History and Memory in France since 1944* (Harvard University Press: Cambridge, MA).

Rushdie, Salman. 1988. *The Satanic Verses* (Viking: London).

Said, Edward W. 1978. *Orientalism* (Routledge and Kegan Paul: London).

  1983. *The World, the Text, and the Critic* (Harvard University Press: Cambridge, MA).

  1994. *Culture & Imperialism* (Vintage: London).

  2012. 'Traveling theory reconsidered'. In *Reflections on Exile and other Essays*, 436–52. (Granta: London).

Saller, Richard P. 1998. 'American classical historiography'. In Anthony Molho and Gordon S. Wood (eds.), *Imagined Histories: American Historians Interpret the Past*, 222–37. (Princeton University Press: Princeton, NJ).

  2013. 'The young Moses Finley and the disciplines of economics'. In William V. Harris (ed.), 49–60. *Moses Finley and Politics* (Brill: Leiden).

Salway, Peter. 1981. *Roman Britain* (Clarendon Press: Oxford).

Sands, Percy C. 1908. *The Client Princes of the Roman Empire under the Republic* (Cambridge University Press: Cambridge).

Sauvy, Alfred. 1986. 'Document: trois mondes, une planète', *Vingtième Siècle. Revue d'histoire* 12: 81–83.

Scheidel, Walter, Ian Morris, and Richard P. Saller. 2007. 'Introduction'. In Walter Scheidel, Ian Morris and Richard P. Saller (eds.), *The Cambridge Economic History of the Greco-Roman World*, 1–12. (Cambridge University Press: Cambridge).

Schiesaro, Alessandro, and Thomas N. Habinek (eds.). 1998. *The Roman Cultural Revolution* (Cambridge University Press: Cambridge).

Schwartz, Seth R. 2013. 'Finkelstein the Orientalist'. In William V. Harris (ed.), *Moses Finley and Politics*, 31–48. (Brill: Leiden).
Scott, Sarah, and Jane Webster. 2003. *Roman Imperialism and Provincial Art* (Cambridge University Press: Cambridge).
Senghor, Léopold S. 1945. *Chants d'ombre* (Seuil: Paris).
  1948. *Hosties noires* (Seuil: Paris).
  1970. 'Négritude: a humanism of the twentieth century'. In Wilfred Cartey and Martin Kilson (eds.), *The Africa Reader: Independent Africa*, 179–83. (Random House: New York).
Shaw, Brent D. 1980. 'Archaeology and knowledge: the history of the African provinces of the Roman Empire', *Florilegium*, 2: 28–60.
  1982. 'Social science and ancient history: Keith Hopkins in partibus infidelium', *Helios*, 9: 17–57.
Sherwin-White, A. N. 1980. 'Rome the aggressor?', *The Journal of Roman Studies*, 70: 177–81.
Smouts, Marie-Claude. 2007. *La situation postcoloniale: les postcolonial studies dans le débat français* (Presses de Sciences Po: Paris).
Spivak, Gayatri Chakravorty. 1985. 'Subaltern studies: deconstructing historiography.' in Ranajit Guha (ed.), *Subaltern Studies IV: Writings on South Asian History and Society*, 330–63. (Oxford University Press: Delhi).
  1988. 'Can the subaltern speak?' in Cary Nelson and Lawrence Grossberg (eds.), *Marxism and the Interpretation of Culture*, 271–313. (University of Illinois Press: Urbana).
  1993. *Outside in the Teaching Machine* (Routledge: London).
Stahl, Hans-Peter (ed.). 1997. *Vergil's Aeneid: Augustan Epic and Political Context* (Duckworth: London).
Starr, Chester G. 1960. 'The history of the Roman Empire 1911–1960', *The Journal of Roman Studies*, 50: 149–60.
  1991. 'Ancient history in the twentieth century', *The Classical World*, 84: 177–85.
Stewart, Peter C. N. 1995. 'Inventing Britain: the Roman creation and adaptation of an image', *Britannia*, 26: 1–10.
Stiglitz, Joseph E. 2002. *Globalization and its Discontents* (Allen Lane: London).
Stobart, John C. 1912. *The Grandeur that Was Rome: A Survey of Roman Culture and Civilisation* (Sidgwick & Jackson: London).
Stray, Christopher. 1998. *Classics Transformed: Schools, Universities, and Society in England, 1830–1960* (Clarendon Press: Oxford).
  2010. '"Patriots and professors": a century of Roman studies, 1910–2010', *The Journal of Roman Studies*, 100: 1–31.
Syme, Ronald. 1939. *The Roman Revolution* (Clarendon Press: Oxford).
Taplin, Oliver (ed.). 2000. *Literature in the Roman World* (Oxford University Press: Oxford).
Taylor, Lily Ross. 1949. *Party Politics in the Age of Caesar* (University of California Press: Berkeley).
Terrenato, Nicola. 1998. 'The Romanization of Italy: global acculturation or cultural *bricolage*?', *Theoretical Roman Archaeology Journal* 1997 : 20–27.

Thébert, Yvon. 1978. 'Romanisation et déromanisation en Afrique: histoire décolonisée ou histoire inversée?', *Annales. Histoire, Sciences Sociales*, 33: 64–82.

Thompson, E. P. 1963. *The Making of the English Working Class* (Gollancz: London).

Tiffin, Helen. 1988. 'Post-colonialism, post-modernism and the rehabilitation of post-colonial history', *Journal of Commonwealth literature*, 23: 169–81.

Tomlin, Roger. 1988. 'Tabellae Sulis: Roman inscribed tablets of tin and lead from the sacred springs at Bath'. In Roger Tomlin and Barry Cunliffe (eds.), *The Temple of Sulis Minerva at Bath Vol.2, The Finds from the Sacred Spring*, 59–269. (Oxford University Committee for Archaeology: Oxford).

   2002. 'Writing to the gods in Britain'. In Alison E. Cooley and Andrew Burnet (eds.), *Becoming Roman, Writing Latin?: Literacy and Epigraphy in the Roman West*, 165–79. (Journal of Roman Archaeology: Portsmouth, RI).

Trouillot, Terence. 2017. 'What is "Black Dada"? Artist Adam Pendleton lays out his disruptive theory in a new book: what began as "a collage in book format" is now officially on book stands.' In Artnet News. Available at https://news.artnet.com/art-world/adam-pendletons-black-dada-reader-1103051#:~:text=So%20what%20is%20Black%20Dada,juxtapositions%20do%20have%20a%20point.

Umachandran, Mathura. 2019. 'More than a common tongue: dividing race and classics across the Atlantic.' *Eidolon*. Available at https://eidolon.pub/more-than-a-common-tongue-cfd7edeb6368.

Vance, Norman. 1997. *The Victorians and Ancient Rome* (Blackwell: Oxford).

Vasunia, Phiroze. 2013. *The Classics and Colonial India* (Oxford University Press: Oxford).

Vergès, Françoise. 1999. 'Colonizing citizenship', *Radical Philosophy* 95: 3–7.

   2005. 'L'Outre-Mer, une survivance de l'utopie coloniale républicaine?' In Pascal Blanchard, Nicolas Bancel and Sandrine Lemaire (eds.), *La fracture coloniale: la société française au prisme de l'héritage colonial*, 67–74. (Découverte: Paris).

Vernant, Jean-Pierre. 1965. *Mythe et pensée chez les Grecs: études de psychologie historique* (F. Maspero: Paris).

Versluys, Miguel J. 2014. 'Understanding objects in motion: an archaeological dialogue on Romanization', *Archaeological Dialogues*, 21: 1–20.

Veyne, Paul. 1971. *Comment on écrit l'histoire: essai d'épistémologie* (Editions du Seuil: Paris).

   1975. 'Y a-t-il eu un impérialisme romain?', *Mélanges de l'École française de Rome. Antiquité*, 87: 793–855.

Wallace-Hadrill, Andrew. 1993. *Augustan Rome* (Bristol Classical Press Duckworth: Bristol).

   2008. *Rome's Cultural Revolution* (Cambridge University Press: Cambridge).

Watts, Dorothy. 2007. 'Roman Britain', *The Classical Review*, 57: 494–6.

Webster, Jane. 1995a. '"Interpretatio": Roman word power and the Celtic gods', *Britannia*, 26: 153–61.

1995b. 'Translation and subjection: interpretatio and the Celtic gods'. In J. D. Hill and C. G. Cumberpatch (eds.), *Different Iron Ages: Studies on the Iron Age in Temperate Europe*, 170–83. (B.A.R.: Oxford).

1996. 'Roman imperialism and the "post imperial age"'. In Jane Webster and Nicholas Cooper (eds.), *Roman Imperialism: Post-colonial Perspectives*, 1–17. (School of Archaeological Studies, University of Leicester: Leicester).

1997. 'A negotiated syncretism: readings on the development of Romano-Celtic religion'. In David J. Mattingly and Susan Alcock (eds.), *Dialogues in Roman Imperialism: Power, Discourse, and Discrepant Experience in the Roman Empire*, 165–84. (Journal of Roman Archaeology: Portsmouth, RI).

2001. 'Creolizing the Roman provinces', *American Journal of Archaeology*, 105: 209–25.

Webster, Jane, and Nicholas Cooper (eds.). 1996. *Roman Imperialism: Post-colonial Perspectives* (School of Archaeological Studies, University of Leicester: Leicester).

Wells, Peter S. 1999. *The Barbarians Speak: How the Conquered Peoples shaped Roman Europe* (Princeton University Press: Princeton, N.J.; Oxford).

Werner, Michael, and Bénédicte Zimmermann. 2003. 'Penser l'histoire croisée: entre empirie et réflexivité', *Annales. Histoire, Sciences Sociales*, 58e année: 7–36.

Whittaker, C. R. 1994. *Frontiers of the Roman Empire: A Social and Economic Study* (Johns Hopkins University Press: Baltimore).

Wiedemann, Thomas E. J. 1986. 'Between men and beasts: barbarians in Ammianus Marcellinus'. In I. S. Moxon, J. D. Smart and A. J. Woodman (eds.), *Past Perspectives: Studies in Greek and Roman Historical Writing*, 189–201. (Cambridge University Press: Cambridge).

Williamson, John. 1990. 'What Washington means by policy reform'. In John Williamson (ed.), *Latin American Adjustment: How Much Has Happened?* 7–20. (Institute for International Economics: Washington, D.C.).

Wilson, R. J. A. 1992. 'Reviewed work: The Romanization of Britain. An Essay in Archaeological Interpretation by M. Millett', *The Journal of Roman Studies*, 82: 290–93.

Wiseman, T. P. 1971. *New Men in the Roman Senate, 139 B.C.–A.D. 14* (Oxford University Press: London).

Woolf, Greg. 1991. 'Reviewed work: The Romanization of Britain: An Essay in Archaeological Interpretation by M. Millet', *Britannia*, 22: 341–42.

1992. 'The unity and diversity of Romanisation', *Journal of Roman Archaeology*, 5: 349–52.

1996. 'Monumental writing and the expansion of Roman society in the Early Empire', *Journal of Roman Studies*, 86: 22–39.

1997. 'Beyond Romans and natives', *World Archaeology*, 28: 339–50.

1998. *Becoming Roman: The Origins of Provincial Civilization in Gaul* (Cambridge University Press: Cambridge).

2014. 'Romanization 2.0 and its alternatives', *Archaeological Dialogues*, 21: 45–50.
Yee, Jennifer. 2009. 'French theory and the exotic'. In Charles Forsdick and David Murphy (eds.), *Postcolonial Thought in the French-speaking World*, 185–94. (Liverpool University Press: Liverpool).
Yentsch, Anne E. 2003. *A Chesapeake Family and their Slaves: A Study in Historical Archaeology* (Cambridge University Press: Cambridge).
Young, Robert. 1990. *White Mythologies: Writing History and the West* (Routledge: London).
Zanker, Paul. 1988. *The Power of Amages in the age of Augustus* (University of Michigan Press: Ann Arbor).
Zuckerberg, Donna. 2015. 'About *EIDOLON*'. *Eidolon*. Available at https://eidolon.pub/introducing-eidolon-3488e1bc6f2f.
2018. 'How the alt-right is weaponizing the classics'. Available at https://gen.medium.com/how-the-alt-right-is-weaponizing-the-classics-d4c1c8dfcb73.

Index

#MeToo, 199

1931 Exposition coloniale, 75, 77
2019 Society for Classical Studies conference, 200

acculturation, 132–3, 159–64, 174
adaptation, 129, 162, 177, 193
Afrocentrism, 85
alterity, 59–60, 62, 64, 89, 105, 109, 113, 115, 157–8
Altertumswissenschaft, 26
ambiguity, 159–65, 179
ambivalence, 5, 69–71, 139, 154, 159–62, 164–6, 177, 191, 193
American imperialism, 17, 107–8, 114
American optimism, 15, 42–6
American pragmatism, 42, 46
amphorae, 144
Anderson, Benedict, 4
Ando, Clifford, 135–7, 139
Anglo-centrism, 184
Annales school, 11, 48, 49, 50, 81, 87, 88, 109, 136–7, 148
anti-colonialism, 68, 69, 72, 74–8, 92, 149–50, 163
antiquarianism, 83, 86
Arab Spring, 198
Arminius, 92
assimilation, 22–4, 40, 75
Augustan revolution, 176

barbarian, 29, 35, 40, 94, 114, 123–5, 130–2, 145, 149, 184
Bath Gorgon, 38
Bato the Daesitiatian, 92
Beard, Mary, 85, 201
Becoming Roman, 133–5, 139, 175–6, 178, 190, 198
bellum iustum, 110
Bénabou, Marcel, 149–50, 195
Bernal, Martin, 85–6
Bhabha, Homi K., 4–8, 69–72, 139, 154, 157, 159, 161–2, 164–6, 174, 192, 199, 203–5
Black Athena. *See* Bernal, Martin

Black Dada, 166
Black Lives Matter, 5, 199
Bloch, Marc, 48
Boudicca, 35, 92
Bradley, Mark, 123, 156
Braudel, Fernand, 48, 136
British imperialism, 15–25, 32–4, 40, 49, 114, 180
British India, 22, 27
British museum, 123, 156

Campanian ware, 144
Catullus, 19
Césaire, Aimé, 162
citoyenneté paradoxale, 76
civilizing ethos, 141–4, 172, 176
Classical Association, 18, 204
Claudian conquest, 121, 124, 129–31
cliometrics revolution, 11, 87, 88, 97, 104, 116
Cold War, 81, 85, 107, 133, 151–2, 153, 191
collective amnesia, 77, 80, 150
Collingwood, Robin G., 15, 26, 29, 31, 34, 35–40, 118, 160
colonial dialectics, 70–1, 134, 139–40, 154, 161–5, 176
Colston statue, 199
Columbia group, 96, 98
counterculture, 161–5, 175, 178
COVID-19, 199
creolization, 157, 158–66, 179, 191, 192
critical history, 17, 25–9, 39
Cromer, Earl of, 17–23
cultural authority, 5–8, 29, 200–2
cultural difference, 5–6, 204
cultural diversity, 4–5, 79, 204
cultural relativism, 5, 75
curse tablets. *See defixiones*

decolonization, 2, 15–16, 52, 65–8, 81, 117, 118, 133, 191
defixiones, 189
Dench, Emma, 198

225

Index

Derrida, Jacques, 9, 147
deviant readings, 177
diffusion model, 11
discrepant experiences, 157, 175, 179–80, 184
discursive knowledge, 57–9, 60, 64, 141–2
double consciousness, 159, 165–6
Du Bois, W. E. B., 158–9, 165–6
Durkheim, Émile, 81
Dyson, Stephen L., 90–6, 128, 133, 149, 157, 163, 191, 198

Early Adopter, 11, 12, 89–91, 95, 96, 100, 103, 106, 109, 116, 149–50, 154, 165, 167, 191–3, 195, 198
Eidolon (online journal), 201
empiricist history, 62, 83, 86, 120–2, 128–9, 203–5
emulation, 70, 125, 131–2, 138–9, 143–4, 157, 160, 164, 176–8
epidemic curve, 11, 120, 122, 195
epigraphic habit, 144, 188
epistemological boundary/periphery, 60, 115, 135, 158, 161–3, 170, 173–6, 178, 179, 180, 183, 188, 192–3
epistemological shift, 89–91, 95–6, 99–100, 103–6, 109, 112, 114–17, 122, 132, 150, 154, 156–8, 165–75, 180–5, 191–6, 203
epistemology, 26, 36–9, 42, 50, 95, 105–6, 112, 115, 119–22, 134, 136, 148, 155, 161, 167, 168–9, 171, 183–8, 190–6, 200, 204–5
    colonial/imperial, 12, 53, 89, 95, 115–16, 126, 128–9, 132, 143, 145, 149–50, 158–9, 163–5, 174, 180, 197
    Eurocentric. *See* Eurocentrism
    postcolonial, 89
    Romano-centric. *See* Romano-centrism
    Western, 61–5, 89, 158
Epona, 162–3, 192–3
ethnocentrism, 60, 143
EU migrant crisis, 198
Eurocentrism, 59–80, 85–6, 94–5, 126, 129, 135, 149–50, 158, 168, 171–4, 178–80, 185, 191
European colonization, 1, 7, 51–2
exemplary history, 17, 27–9, 39
exoticism, 74, 75, 80

Facebook-Cambridge Analytica data misuse, 199
factoid, 122
Fanon, Frantz, 60, 65–72, 92–3, 95, 143, 153, 157, 162, 163, 191
Febvre, Lucien, 48
field survey, 122–5
Finley, Moses I., 83–5, 89–90, 95–106, 108–9, 113–16, 122, 126, 137, 154, 157, 191
First World War, 26, 35, 37, 110
Foucault, Michel, 9, 29, 36, 56–62, 65, 91, 94, 99, 112–14, 137–46, 147, 191, 194
Fracture coloniale, 73, 76, 78

francophonie, 76, 79
Frank, Tenney, 41–6
Frankfurt School, 85, 96
Frere, Sheppard, 88, 118
Freud, Sigmund, 164
Friedman, Thomas L., 151–3, 191–2
frontier studies, 28

gentlemen scholars, 17–21, 24, 27–9, 86
George the Poet, 3
Gibbon, Edward, 18
Gilley, Bruce, 1, 197
Gladwell, Malcom, 10–12, 89, 118, 167
globalization, 63, 79, 151–4, 157, 166–80, 186–7, 191–3
gloria, 110
Gramsci, Antonio, 63, 157
gravitas, 142
Great Depression, 15, 81

Harris, William V., 88, 106–17, 122, 126–7, 137, 154, 157, 183, 191
Haselgrove, Colin C., 129, 160
Haverfield, Francis J., 2, 25–40, 88, 118, 119, 123, 125, 126, 134, 160–1
Hegel, 29, 56, 60
heritage memory, 50, 77, 149
Herskovits-Frazier debate, 159–60
Hingley, Richard, 19, 25, 31–3, 37, 155–8, 166–81, 184, 185, 186, 191, 192, 198
historical intervention, 6–8, 203–5
historical memory, 5–6
historiography
    Eurocentric. *See* Eurocentrism
    Romano-centric. *See* Romano-centrism
Holland, Tom, 182, 190
Holleaux, Maurice, 49–50
homogeneous empty time, 4
Hopkins, Keith, 104–5
humanism, 60, 69, 143, 146, 168, 172
humanitas, 142–3, 145, 146, 172
hybridity, 71–2, 156, 159–66, 191, 193

imagined community, 4–6, 203
imperial possession, 180–91
Innovator, 90, 95, 99, 115, 149, 165, 167, 191
intellectual engagé, 147
interpretatio, 188
ius fetiale, 110

Julius Civilis, 92
Jullian, Camille, 26, 49–50

Kant, Immanuel, 29
Kipling, Joseph Rudyard, 180
Kolko, Gabriel, 107
Kuhn, Thomas S., 10–11

Lacan, Jacques, 9
Laroui, Abdallah, 149–50
laus, 110
Lexus and the Olive Tree, 151–2, 191
liberté pour l'histoire, 73
linear progress, 5–6, 21, 35, 204
Literae Humaniores, 26
longue durée, 48–50, 72, 78, 136
LPRIA [Late pre-Roman Iron Age]
  archaeology, 123–5, 131
  Britain, 128–32
Lucas, Sir Charles P., 17–24

MacMullen, Ramsay, 91
marginalization, 82–3, 86, 146–8, 155
Marxism, 11, 50, 60, 68, 69, 81–9, 97–9, 107, 109, 113, 116, 147, 148, 155–6
material culture, 52, 141, 160, 162–4
Mattingly, David J., 155–8, 197–8
McCarthyism, 85, 96
mémoire patrimoniale. *See* heritage memory
mentalité. *See* mentality
mentality, 121, 137
  ancient, 100–3
  imperial, 52
  Roman, 108–17, 143
Meroë head, 156
Millett, Martin, 117–35, 137–8, 154, 157, 160, 166, 181, 185, 191, 193
mirror study, 20
Mommsen, Theodor, 2, 26, 30, 48, 49–50
monotheism, 22
mores, 142
multiculturalism, 4, 73, 79, 80, 86, 147, 155
myths of belonging, 5–8, 12, 204–5

native revolts, 90–5
negotiation, 117, 120, 125, 132–3, 137, 163, 174–6, 179, 203
Negritude, 74
Nehalennia, 139
neo-colonialism, 63–4, 68, 90, 153–4, 192
neo-liberalism, 152–4, 192
Nora, Pierre, 77

orientalism, 2, 51, 60–2, 64, 70, 71, 141, 155, 156
originary Past, 6, 8, 14, 199, 201
Other, 60–76, 89–106, 112, 114–16, 122, 141–4, 157–8, 161–5, 170–93

paideia, 142
paradigm shift, 10
parallel discourse, 25, 27, 29, 35, 42, 44, 46, 49–50, 91, 95, 100, 103–4, 105–6, 107–9, 112–15, 116, 203

past-present, 4
Pax Britannica, 25, 184
Pax Romana, 25
Peralta, Dan-el Padilla, 200–1
philology, 83, 90, 96, 98, 141
pietas, 145
Pliny the Elder, 141
Pliny the Younger, 19
Polanyi, Karl, 96, 98–100, 103
Polybius, 111
polytheism, 22
positivism, 25–6, 29, 31, 36, 48–50, 120–2, 128–9, 147–8, 167, 183
postclassicisms, 202
postcolonialism, 1–3, 7, 10–14, 16, 39, 50, 91, 92, 95, 153–96, 197–205
  à la française, 80
  in the discourse on Romanization, 117–18, 122–35, 143, 149–50
  theories, 51–6, 59–60, 62–72
postmodernism, 116, 133, 147, 166–75, 179–80
poststructuralism, 9, 11, 56, 59–60, 62–5, 68, 72, 80, 87–9, 91, 92, 95, 99, 100, 103–6, 109, 112–17, 122, 143, 149, 158, 167, 169, 171, 173, 180, 183, 191–4, 203
power asymmetry, 132, 162, 179, 186–92
power network, 58, 91, 94–5, 137–40, 144–6
Power of Context, 118–19
power-knowledge, 60, 64, 71–2, 80, 95, 134
Procopius, 184
professional academics, 15–32, 39, 48, 82, 86, 147
professionalization, 17, 26–7, 30, 47, 82, 118, 146–8
projective past, 6–8, 203–5
prosopographical studies, 28
psychoanalysis, 70, 164

Queen Victoria, 16

Red Scare. *See* McCarthyism
régime of truth, 58–9, 70, 140–2, 176, 178, 179, 191, 202
  colonialist/imperialist, 31, 39, 113, 184
  Eurocentric, 60, 70, 172
  historical knowledge, 29, 36, 114, 121
  Romano-centric, 146, 172
religio, 145
republicanism, 74–80, 195
resistance, 5, 38, 45, 72, 94–5, 138–9, 143–4, 149, 160, 163, 164, 176–7, 193
  anti-Roman, 94, 156
  power and resistance, 58, 91
Richmond, Ian A., 88, 118, 182
right to narrate, 4–8, 205
Roman Africa, 149–50

Roman Centurion's Song, 180
Roman economy, 101–4, 108–9, 115
　primitivist-modernist, 103
Roman Gaul, 134–40, 145, 149
Roman imperialism
　aggressive, 106–16, 122, 183
　defensive, 21, 44, 49, 89, 106–16, 128
　military despotism, 21, 24
Romanising, 2, 30
romanitas, 129, 131, 132, 145, 188
Romanization, 2–3, 8–14, 51–6, 158, 198, 202–5
　imperial age, 15–17, 19, 22, 40, 45–7
　postcolonial turn, 88–96, 105, 115
　revisionist, 133–46, 158–93
　tipping point, 116–33
Romano-British
　archaeology, 30–2, 123
　culture, 38–9, 129–33, 161–6, 184–90
　scholarship, 31–2, 35, 50, 90, 117–25, 134–7, 168, 182, 183–5, 193
Romano-centrism, 91–5, 125–35, 141–2, 149–50, 158, 161–3, 169–91
Römische Geschichte, 2, 30
Rushdie, Salman, 7

Said, Edward W., 2, 8–9, 12–14, 51, 60–2, 70, 71, 140–2, 143, 145–6, 154, 155, 157, 162, 186–8, 190, 191
Saller, Richard P., 41, 43–4, 84, 85, 97, 104–5, 107
Salway, Peter, 118
Samian ware. *See terra sigillata*
Second World War, 81, 88, 110
Self, 55, 60–75, 89–95, 101–5, 109, 112, 114–16, 141–3, 157–8, 163–5, 191
self-governing colonies, 22
Senghor, Léopold S., 162
Sherwin-White, A. N., 111–12
social epidemics, 10–12
Spivak, Gayatri Chakravorty, 62–5, 157, 158, 163–4, 166, 174, 181, 191, 192
Stiglitz, Joseph E., 152–3
stigma of conquest, 33, 46, 92, 124
Strabo, 141
Stray, Christopher, 15, 16, 26, 29, 31
subaltern, 62–3, 69, 72, 95, 156–8, 163–5, 170, 173, 176, 179–81, 183, 187–96, 204
subaltern studies group, 63
subversion, 138, 162
Suetonius, 127–9

Syme, Sir Ronald, 28
syncretism, 38, 139, 143, 189
Syrian civil war, 198

teleology
　of European progress, 94
　of history, 56–7, 59, 68, 89, 98–100, 113, 116, 134, 169, 180
　of parallel discourse, 101–6, 109
　of Romanization, 95, 128, 130, 132, 144, 149, 157, 161–3
terra sigillata, 178–9, 192–3
Theoretical Roman Archaeology Conferences (TRAC), 155
Third Worldism, 63–4
Thompson, E. P., 82
Tiffin, Helen, 170
tipping point, 10–12
　in the discourse on Romanization, 118–20
totalization
　in history, 56–7, 59, 68, 89, 113, 116, 134, 169, 180
　of parallel discourse, 98–106, 109
　of Romano-centrism, 95, 121, 128, 132, 143, 149, 157, 161–3, 198, 203
travelling theory, 8–9
trickle-down, 131–2, 137, 152–3, 160–2
Trump, Donald, 198

University of Cambridge, 18, 82, 104
University of Oxford, 18, 25, 35, 82–3, 84
urbanitas, 144–5

Vasunia, Phiroze, 15–25, 29
Vercingetorix, 92
Veyne, Paul, 148, 195
Vietnam War, 90, 107–8, 153
　Vietnam Syndrome, 106–15, 183
Virgil, 177

Weber, Max, 81, 99
Webster, Jane, 53, 119, 155–66, 168, 174–5, 179, 181, 184, 185, 191, 192, 198, 203
Woolf, Greg, 122, 133–46, 154, 157, 168, 171, 175–6, 191

Young, Robert J. C., 59, 60, 64

Zonaras, 111
Zuckerberg, Donna, 201

Milton Keynes UK
Ingram Content Group UK Ltd.
UKHW021050031224
3319UKWH00076B/177